MAUPASSANT

Other Works by the same Author

Pierre Loti
(New York, Twayne, 1974)

Edouard Rod: A portrait of the Novelist and his Times
(The Hague, Mouton, 1975)

1   Maupassant, aged 31, at the Saint Romain fair, Rouen, in 1881

2   Maupassant, aged about 40

MAUPASSANT

MICHAEL G. LERNER

GEORGE BRAZILLER
NEW YORK

Published in the United States in 1975 by George Braziller, Inc.
Copyright © 1975 by Michael G. Lerner
Originally published in England by George Allen & Unwin Ltd.

International Standard Book Number: 0-8076-0803-3
Library of Congress Catalog Card Number: 75-10912
Printed in the United States of America
First Printing

For my mother Mrs Deborah Lerner

PREFACE

It is some years since a study of Maupassant in English has appeared, despite the continued interest in his works represented by the reprinting, television serialisation and film adaptation of many of them. Moreover, many of the books devoted to Maupassant are pre-War or in French. There seemed then to be a need for a new biographical study in English of Guy de Maupassant that would take into account a more up-to-date interpretation of his period's social and literary evolution and evaluate anew, in the light of this and all the fresh evidence available, the development of his career from being a pupil of the great Flaubert to becoming one of France's most famous writers, second only to Zola in his day. It is a story of spectacular success and rapid fame set against a private life of anguish and grief: a drama of triumph and tragedy that was reflected in the glittering sophistication and tormented decadence of the society of the period in which it took place. A knowledge of Maupassant's life is thus a colourful introduction to an appreciation of his works and the personal and social background in which they were written.

In preparing a biographical study of Maupassant one is, however, faced with two major problems. The first is the fact that the man himself never wished to have his private life discussed in public; during his lifetime he had few close friends and he did not often speak or write about himself; indeed, he twice told some of his more inquisitive correspondents that: 'All that I write belongs to the public and the critics and is open to discussion and people's curiosity, but I desire that nothing relating to my person and my private life should be divulged.' This secrecy of Maupassant and, after his death, of his family, as well as the usual tampering with and destruction of the evidence about him, particularly correspondence, by his friends and followers have led to the second problem of the biographer: the authenticity of much of the evidence available. Not only was Maupassant himself a great joker and boastful fabricator of tales about himself but after his death many of his friends and no doubt many more of his enemies added to these, intriguing memoirs were produced on him, and all sorts of sensational evidence was published about his private life. Now, much of this material is both unproven and inaccurate and is as dubious in value as it is suspect in origin. By being discriminating in using it in the present study it is hoped that, even if Maupassant's privacy has been transgressed against his wishes, a fairer and less monstrous portrait of him will emerge from these pages.

Finally, the author would like to record here his thanks to all those who have kindly contributed information or given him permission to use material and photographs in this book. A special debt of gratitude is due also to the publishers who made this work possible and the author's parents and friends, whose interest and encouragement contributed so much to its completion.

M. G. L.

CONTENTS

ILLUSTRATIONS

PART ONE

NORMANDY

CHAPTER 1

An Auspicious Arrival

The year was 1850. The nephew of the great Napoleon had just seized power in France and was preparing to restore some of her Revolutionary idealism and Imperial grandeur after decades of repression and stagnation. Victorian England under Palmerston, the Habsburgs under Francis-Joseph and the Russian Tsar Nicholas were viewing with relief the virtual restoration of peace and the *status quo* in Europe after the shattering series of liberal revolts of 1848 all over the continent including France, whence, after protests by intellectuals and a rising of the workers, King Louis-Philippe had fled into exile. These political upheavals and the uneasy peace that they produced also reflected to a large extent the social changes taking place within France as she became more industrial and urbanised, her population drifted from the land and small workshops to the towns with their factories and large commercial concerns, and the gulf between the complacent prosperity of the rising middle class and the wretchedness of the growing labour force increased.

The coming to power of Napoleon III or 'Napoleon the Little', as the poet Victor Hugo called him, brought with it the promise of order and prestige for the conservative middle classes in their pursuit of their business ambitions and of social reform and liberal aid to those in need. An era of industrial growth, grandiose city-building and scintillating social life in the capital as well as of adventurous schemes for expansion overseas had thus begun. In July 1850 the novelist Honoré de Balzac, who had depicted in his works the early commercialisation of France since the fall of the first Napoleon, had died; and with him there had passed away the image of an unspoilt rural France awakening to the advantages of town life. From now on the pace of France's industrialisation and urban development would quicken with the assistance of rail communications, scientific discovery and financial investment. It would not be long before Emile Zola would be describing in his epic novels the transformation society was undergoing at the hands of ambitious exploiters, speculators and self-indulgent tycoons in the second half of the nineteenth century.

Meanwhile, in the summer of 1850, in a rural part of the north-western province of Normandy unmoved by the recent political upheavals and as yet untouched by the developments of the towns, where the green fields and orchards were still being peacefully tended by the robust and hearty inhabitants of the old timbered farmhouses and cottages scattered among them, a private but not unimportant event was taking place at the imposing eighteenth-century Château de Miromesnil that lies some ten miles inland from the port and resort of Dieppe on the Channel coast. An ornate, dignified mansion in pink stone built for and named after its first owner, the Marquis de Miromesnil, a statesman in the decade before the 1789 Revolution, it dominates the avenue of beeches leading up to it and the expanse of cornfields surrounding it. It was at this august and historic site, according to the birth certificate issued at 6 p.m. on 5 August 1850 and witnessed by two inhabitants of the nearby village of Tourville-sur-Arques – Pierre Bimont a tobacco-merchant and Isidore Latonque a teacher – that Henri-René-Albert-Guy de Maupassant was born at 8 a.m. that day. According to a later statement of the child's mother, he entered life in the room just beneath the Château's imposing western turret. In a letter confirming that her son's birthplace had been at the Château, and describing the room in which he was born, Mme de Maupassant wrote in July 1894 to Henri Gadeau de Kerville that even the sun shone at Guy's birth to herald the glory he was to achieve:

'The apartment I was occupying then . . . was situated on the first floor as you turned right at the top of the staircase; it was in a rather narrow room with a large window facing south that looked on to a small park and a round adjoining room serving as a small bathroom that, as you have been told, my son was born . . . It was eight o'clock in the morning when Guy de Maupassant was born and the most brilliant summer sunshine seemed to bid welcome to him who was to die so young, but not without having achieved some glory.' [1]

Furthermore, if another statement is to be believed – this time from the writer himself – the doctor who delivered the baby, Dr Guiton, actually moulded the child's head by holding it firmly in his arm after the birth and squeezing it into the right shape.[2] Clearly, strenuous efforts were made both by the child's parents, who had recently rented the Château from its elderly keeper Mme de Marescot, and by the doctor to ensure that Guy's entry into this world was a propitious as possible.

Unfortunately, these efforts have not escaped the scrutiny of later critics who have pointed out that Guy's death certificate, issued in Paris, states he was born at Sotteville, some ten miles from the Château, and that, since there is no evidence of the Maupassants having actually rented the Château, it is more likely that the child was really born at his maternal grandmother's small, ungainly summer apartment in the Rue Sous-le-Bois at Fécamp on the coast thirty miles away, where Mme de Maupassant was staying shortly before the birth. It was rumoured locally that Guy arrived before he was due and before his parents had managed to move into their superior summer residence and that once he was born both mother and child were hustled into the Château and a false call for a midwife was sent out to maintain appearances. There is now no witness nor evidence to confirm or contradict these rumours. Simply judging by the known characters of the Maupassants, however, there can be little doubt that, wherever the child was actually born, they intended him to be delivered in aristocratic, even romantic, surroundings.

This is perhaps partly confirmed by Guy's christening held by special authority of the regional archbishop on 23 August 1850 in the small Renaissance chapel of the Château with its stone walls and beautiful stained-glass windows. It was attended by his parents, his maternal grandmother and paternal grandfather – the latter acting as godparents. Even this ceremony did not suffice, however, and a fuller baptism was given a year later on 17 August 1851. Such apparent snobbishness and attention to the conventions not only reflect a certain beneficent indulgence and a keen desire for an even better and higher social standing. They also reveal a romantic imagination that, as perhaps at Guy's birth, combined with social ambition to try to alter and shape reality just as the doctor is said to have moulded the newborn's skull. Both attempts were, alas, to prove tragically unsuccessful.

When Guy was born, his parents Gustave-François-Albert de Maupassant and Laure-Marie-Geneviève, née Le Poittevin, were both twenty-eight years old; they had been married in Rouen on 9 November 1846 and spent their honeymoon in Italy. On their return they had several temporary homes in Rouen and each year they would spend the summer by the sea at Dieppe or, some twenty miles further south, at the smaller resort of Etretat, renting an apartment or house nearby and visiting Laure's widowed mother at Fécamp, a fishing port just north of Etretat. Such arrangements were both pleasant during the warmer weather and also fashionable, since this coast was quite a favourite resort for elegant visitors from both sides of the Channel, particularly in 1851 when the London Exhibition was to open.

This leisurely life in picturesque surroundings suited Gustave de Maupassant, described on Guy's birth certificate as 'living on his private income', for he enjoyed being something of a dandy and man-about-town as well as an amateur painter. It was clearly his aristocratic tastes and dandyish manners as well as his artistic qualities that had first appealed to young Laure Le Poittevin. The further fact that he came from an upper-bourgeois, not to say noble, family and could use the aristocratic particle *de* in his surname – a matter settled by a Rouen tribunal, no doubt much to their satisfaction, just before their marriage – must have made him appear to her a very worthy prize indeed.

Not that the Le Poittevins were without significance in the Rouen area; the family had traditional, upper-bourgeois roots in the city's past and Laure's father, Paul Le Poittevin, prospered considerably as the owner of two important spinning mills – one at Rouen itself and the other nearby at St Léger du Bourg Denis. In 1815 he had married the extremely beautiful daughter of a Fécamp shipbuilder, Victoire-Marie Thurin, who bore him a son, Alfred, born in 1816, and two daughters, Laure, born on 18 September 1821, and Virginie in 1824. It is said that when Paul Le Poittevin first embarked on his career, he spent a night in a haunted house on an estate at Gonneville near Valognes and saw its ghost – a black sheep – who told him he and his family would prosper if he kept possession of the property; apparently, he did acquire it the very next day and the Le Poittevins did continue to flourish reasonably well!

The fact that the Le Poittevins were close friends of the Flauberts indicates perhaps the measure of their social standing in the city of Rouen, for Dr Achille-Cléophas Flaubert was not only a renowned surgeon but also head of the Hôtel-Dieu hospital there. Paul Le Poittevin's wife, Victoire-Marie, had moreover been a friend of Dr Flaubert's wife Caroline Fleuriot at school in Honfleur prior to her marriage in 1812 to the eminent young surgeon and when, later, both families began to have children Dr Flaubert and Paul Le Poittevin acted as godfather to each other's offspring. And, as might be expected, their children were in fact to spend much of their infancy and early years playing together: Alfred and Laure Le Poittevin, with their companions Gustave and Caroline Flaubert, would enjoy peeping with childish inquisitiveness through the garden railings of the Hôtel-Dieu hospital at the dissections and operations being carried out there. As they grew older they would listen to Alfred, who was five years older than the rest of them, telling them about English literature and classical history and philosophy or they would playfully act in the Flauberts' billiard-room some of young Gustave's earliest attempts at drama.

It was probably in this innocent, playful atmosphere, where

Laure fell under the literary spell of her elder brother and first imbibed his love of literature, particularly Shakespeare and the Classics, and where young, blond and blue-eyed Gustave fell in love with the dark, slim and delicate Alfred, who acted now as a brotherly spiritual leader for him in the realms of poetry and now as his older initiator into the mysteries of love and sex, that the literary seeds were sown in Laure, later to be passed on to her son. Not only did the intimacy and literary bent of this group of children bring out in her under Alfred's inspired guidance an intellectual awareness and poetic sensibility which might have been latently inherited (Paul Le Poittevin's grandmother, Madame Bérigny, had in fact been an eighteenth-century woman of letters of some repute among the *beaux-esprits* of her day), it also developed in her a sort of cult of literature and her brother, which her own frustrations in this direction and Alfred's early death in 1848, just two years after his marriage to Laura's sister-in-law, Louise de Maupassant, only served to intensify once her son was born in 1850. But if the Le Poittevin blood in Guy's veins might be seen to transmit some of his maternal family's literary and poetic sensibility to him, the de Maupassant branch of his ancestry with its interests in financial and military matters as well as court affairs could be said to have provided him not only with a certain dilettante interest in the arts and women but above all with a practical, often ambitiously active grasp of everyday, mercenary reality.

The Maupassants seem to have originated in Jeanne d'Arc country in the eastern province of Lorraine; there was a blacksmith at Aubréville near Verdun and a draper at Châlons bearing the name Maupassant in the late sixteenth century; by the mid-seventeenth century the family had risen in the world to the upper echelons of the bourgeoisie and virtually the nobility, for Claude Maupassant, an apothecary, took as his second wife in 1638 the daughter of a royal notary at Châlons, and Claude's son became an engineer at the siege of Candia in 1669, a cavalry officer in 1680, acquired the title of *sieur* or gentleman by his marriage with a noted Demoiselle Antoinette de Beaurepaire, and after her death married a daughter of a nobleman, Jeanne-Françoise-Senée-d'Arcolan, in 1725. By the late eighteenth century a Claude-Etienne Maupassant had become *procureur-général du roi* or governor-general in Corsica, a Marie-Anne-Adélaïde Maupassant had become the wife of the governor of Corsica as well as enjoying a short-lived affair with the libertine Duke de Lauzun; and a Jean-Baptiste Maupassant, one of the king's advisers, was created a nobleman by a diploma of the Austrian court of 3 May 1752 with a coat of arms of German origin.

Following the Revolution the *de* Maupassants seem to have drifted east towards Normandy; Louis de Maupassant, a royal treasurer at Versailles, settled after Louis XVIII's death on a farm at Chartres and married, first, a rich creole woman from Mauritius and, later, the widowed owner of the Château des Anthieux near Rouen. It was one of Louis's two brothers, a certain Maupassant de Valmont, a rent-collector in Paris, whose son, Pierre-Jules, born in 1795, was to become Guy's grandfather.

Born in Paris, Pierre-Jules worked as a tax inspector at Bernay until he moved in about 1840 to Rouen, where he opened a tobacco warehouse and later purchased a farm at Neuville-Champ-d'Oisel. It is claimed that his marriage to the blonde and rather plump daughter of a fellow tax-collector, Aglaé-Françoise-Joseph Pluchard, had had to be celebrated in secret on account of her family's disapproval, and that after a midnight wedding ceremony in a deserted village church at Pont Audemer the couple had got drenched in the rain trying to cross a ford on their way to their runaway honeymoon! Clearly, Pierre-Jules was quite a character, but one not devoid of business enterprise or literary and artistic interests despite the rustic portrait of him by Eugène Le Poittevin showing him relieving himself behind a haystack at the same time as he is trying to shoot at a hare running past. When he bought his property at Neuville, he quickly cleared part of the forest of Longboël on it so that he could grow crops and use the large house as a centre for local artists and writers including the Le Poittevins, the painter Hippolyte Bellangé, the tenor Achard and the artist Lavenu.

It was no doubt from his father that Gustave, born on 28 November 1821 at Bernay, inherited both an interest – even if not always a very successful one – in commerce and also his rather earthy sensuality. And it was largely due to the artistic gatherings Pierre-Jules held on his estate that Gustave became the talented water-colourist and the dandy he was. Moreover, it was probably at one of these gatherings that Gustave first saw and courted Laure Le Poittevin; for although the estate belonged to the Maupassants, it was a familiar haunt of the artistic Le Poittevins and later came to assume even greater significance for them since it was here that Alfred Le Poittevin died, his son Louis was born, and his widow, Gustave's sister Louise de Maupassant, lived when she remarried and Pierre-Jules returned to Rouen to spend there the last years of his life.

The ties between the Maupassants and the Le Poittevins were thus extremely close just as were those of the Le Poittevins and the Flauberts; but whereas the latter were founded on parental and childhood relations, the former had been cemented by the intermarriage of, first, Alfred Le Poittevin and Louise de Maupassant and then of Gustave de Maupassant and Laure Le Poittevin; the two young couples had even met on honeymoon in Italy. For Laure it must have seemed as if the tight intimacy and spellbound atmosphere of the children's group of the Hôtel-Dieu hospital had to some extent persisted in her marriage into her brother's in-laws, but unfortunately this was not to be.

The Maupassants spent some three years at Miromesnil after their son's birth, though Guy himself confessed on a visit to the Château much later in his life, in 1879, that he could remember nothing of his infancy there. When he was four years old the family moved to the less lordly mansion of Grainville-Ymanville near Le Havre, where in April 1856 Guy's younger brother Hervé was born. It is claimed that Guy used this residence for his description of the property of *Les Peuples* in his novel *Une Vie* and it has also been asserted that much of the detail of the young married couple's sexual experiences and disputes as well as the husband's unfaithfulness and his wife's false pregnancy in the novel derive from the Maupassants' actual life together during Guy's childhood.

The short tale, *Garçon, un bock!*, is usually quoted as evidence of the child's awareness of his parents' quarrelling and of the violent rows that were raging between them beneath the surface of their conventional home-life. Certainly, there must have been some fierce quarrels and there can be little doubt that young Guy was at least partially aware of his parents' disagreement and suffered from it emotionally. The reasons for their disputes are not hard to find: Gustave de Maupassant was used to an idle and pleasurable life long before his marriage and it is unlikely that any wife would have kept him for long from his Parisian mistresses and the coastal resorts' casinos. Moreover, Laure's emotional, neurotic temperament and rather possessive nature would hardly have made her the most flexible and understanding of wives in such circumstances. If the curly hair, seductive gaze, weak chin, sensuous lips and fancy clothes of Gustave in Bellangé's portrait of him in 1833 seem to indicate his dandyish weaknesses, the fixed stare and intelligently determined expression on Laure's dark, oval, not particularly pretty face in a full-length photograph of her might be taken not only as signs of a rather eccentric personality but also as giving some idea of the fiery resistance she would have mounted against her weak-willed husband.

Guy himself, though only nine years old, provides some evidence of his father's weakness when he writes to Laure from Paris, where he was staying with Gustave, to say that as a reward for doing well at school 'Madame X took me to the circus along with papa. It appears she also gives papa some kind of reward too but I don't know exactly what sort'. And there is also a story that on one occasion Guy managed to tease his father into tying his shoelaces for him before they went off to the theatre because he knew his father would not want to keep his lady-friend waiting there. Whatever truth there is in this tale, it is certain that by about 1860 Laure and Gustave were living separate lives with their sons staying now with their father in Paris, now with their mother on the coast: an enervating and confusing experience for any child, despite the greater variety of amusements and deeper understanding of life it might possibly have given at the time, and a contributory factor in the development of Maupassant's pessimistic views of love and marriage. However, though there was no legal divorce in France until 1884, Laure and Gustave drew up a formal contract of separation in 1863; in this Gustave was bound to support his family with an annual allowance of 1,600 francs – a fairly generous offer in those days – and both parents would still be responsible for their sons' upbringing. In reality, Gustave withdrew to the capital and saw his sons on occasional visits while Laure set up a home for them at Etretat and looked after their education.

The Maupassants had visited Etretat quite a lot before Laure settled there with her two sons; in fact, their names feature in a certain Mme Ledentu's register of bathers at the resort as early as June 1859 and some time before the separation contract. Etretat was in those days a small fishing village with a large beach and splendid cliffs. It was, however, in the process of being transformed into a fashionable resort with a casino, canvas beach-huts, paper-stands, and cafés. Moreover, many famous artists and celebrities as well as wealthy and retired bankers and politicians had begun renting summer cottages or building elegant villas in the vicinity now the village was growing into a resort. The writer Alphonse Karr and the composer Offenbach had summer residences constructed here overlooking the bay, and painters such as Monet and Courbet found the coastline sufficiently fascinating and the place not too noisy to come and work nearby. Young Guy de Maupassant recalled in fact in some newspaper articles published some fifteen years later how he had watched Courbet in 1869 painting a study of the sea called *La Vague* and seen Corot, now an old man with long white hair, working at his easel in the valley of Beaurepaire near Etretat in the summer of 1864. Guy's own description of Etretat in an article of 1880 published as 'The Devil's Cauldrons' in *Le Gaulois* shows how much the coastline and beach impressed him by the beauty of its shape and the naturalness of its landscape:

'The beach whose famous beauty has so often been illustrated by painters seems like some fairyland backcloth with its two superb arches through the cliffs called "The Gateways". It curves smoothly round like an amphitheatre with the casino situated at its centre; and the village, made up of a handful of variedly ornate and novel houses dotted about in all directions and facing different ways, appears as if it has been scattered there like the seeds of some heavenly sower and taken root where the seeds happened to fall. It has now grown right to the water's edge and closes one end of the delightful valley that extends its undulating terrain inland as far as can be seen and whose hillsides are spattered with cottages hiding under the trees in their gardens. All around there are numerous small valleys – unspoilt ravines covered in brambles and heather in all directions; and often, as you turn along a path up there, you catch sight through a deep cleft in the hills of the blue expanse of the sea glittering in the light with a veil of mist over its horizon.'

It was here at Etretat that Laure settled with her sons in an old, spacious but not particularly ornate house called *Les Verguies*, 'The Orchards'. Its owner was an elderly woman and its large weed-infested garden and its old-fashioned furnishings including much antique furniture, porcelain, chests and carpets and some dark blue wallpaper reflected perhaps its owner's staid taste and neglect. However, even if the interior was rather gloomy and the garden with its beeches and plane trees needed tidying – and Guy was to lend a hand in this as well as plant a yew tree which can still be seen – the house had at least one attraction for Laure, which might have influenced her choice of it for her home: it had a legendary ghost-story attached to it. According to this, the châtelaine of Etretat, the Lady Olive, was rescued by angels from pirates, who had surprised her and her maids on the beach, and she vowed to build a church nearby to show her gratitude; but the demon of *Les Verguies* kept removing the stones for the church from the site of the house and finally Lady Olive was obliged to build her church where the demon took the stones so that he would stop removing them; this she did and the church now stands some eighty yards from the house. Perhaps Laure hoped that this demon like the sheep's ghost her father had obeyed would similarly bring her some better luck in the raising of her family.

As has been already mentioned, Laure was a neurotically sensitive and highly emotional person, whose imagination had been kindled in her younger days by the literary and philosophical activities of the Hôtel-Dieu group and the examples of her brother Alfred and their friend Gustave Flaubert, who had devoted themselves to writing. It was natural then that, parted from her husband, she would lean more heavily on her sons and depend more on them emotionally, if not become rather possessive of them; and that, considering her own amateur interest in literature and the tragic premature death of Alfred, she would aspire to encouraging her children along the road to literary fame.

From the very first Laure took total charge of Guy; he was not handed over as a baby to a nurse to be weaned but cared for by his mother, apart from a few days when she was too unwell to provide for him. And for the next twelve years—with a few short breaks when he visited his father in Paris and attended school there for a couple of terms—he was brought up by Laure with a surfeit of maternal affection, pride and hope. There can be little doubt that young Guy had a fairly spoilt childhood. He was not only cared for by Laure and made a fuss of by his maternal grandmother at Fécamp and her old servant *mère* Josephe; his aunt, Laure's younger sister Virginie, who lived with her husband Georges d'Harnois de Blangues at the nearby Château de Bornambusc, would also invite Guy there to play with his small cousin Germer. With his mother he explored the coast and at least on one occasion they apparently both got drenched trying to climb the cliffs. He enjoyed the life by the sea and became ever more interested in boats – an interest he retained for the rest of his days. It is from this time, too, that he learnt much about Norman life from the local people – largely peasant lads and fishermen – with whom he came into contact and from whom he gradually picked up the regional *patois* and many a piece of gossip and local rumour. Furthermore, the sea air and the open-air life he enjoyed on the beach, on the clifftops, and in boats transformed the young lad's appearance; the delicate, girlish boy dressed in a skirt and with his hair neatly curled, seen in a photograph of him at the age of seven, soon becomes the sturdy-looking butcher-boy figure that appears in a portrait taken six years later and that he was always to remain.

His childhood was not without any instruction, however, even if it was largely without formal schooling. A local priest taught him the catechism, which he at this stage innocently and swiftly imbibed, and his mother read him Shakespeare – *Macbeth* and *A Midsummer Night's Dream* – and helped him arrange small dramatic performances at home with his friends; she clearly lost no time in initiating him into literature and perhaps hoped already to influence his choice of career in this field. The local priest Abbé Aubourg of Etretat also taught him French grammar, maths, and Latin for his first communion, though he was later to suggest that much of his time had been spent learning by heart the names on the graves in the nearby cemetery!

His first period of formal teaching seems to have taken place in 1859–60, when he stayed with his father at Passy in Paris and attended the Lycée Impérial Napoléon. The report sent to his father afterwards shows Guy to have been quite good at most of his subjects; his health is recorded as being good, his personality as very quiet, his work as conscientious, and his religious obser-vance as diligent. The general remarks at the end of the report state that Guy was 'an excellent student whose conscientiousness and effort deserve high praise and encouragement. He will gradually get used to the work here and we count on him making good progress'.

Unfortunately, he was soon back at Etretat and in 1863 he was sent to the Institution Ecclésiastique at Yvetot, a Catholic boarding-school not so very far from Etretat. He was to remain here until 1868. As in Paris, his work seems to have been good and diligently done, his conduct normal, and his personality is described as either 'always pleasant and agreeable' or 'polite and quiet'; the only weakness in his work is in science, and the only disturbing comment in the general remarks is a reference to his occasional absence because of illness. The verses he began writing at this time and Laure's allusion to these absences in a letter later to Flaubert seem to imply, however, that Guy was rather unhappy at Yvetot and not only took refuge in writing but also returned home every so often under a pretext of illness. As he mentions in his story *Une Surprise*, the religious discipline and routine of the school were obviously not to his liking; this can be seen in one poem in which he parodies his theology teacher on the torments of Hell and also in this extract from some verses contrasting his cousin's luck in getting married shortly with his own misery at Yvetot:

> *Mais dans le cloître solitaire,*
> *Où nous sommes ensevelis,*
> *Nous ne connaissons sur la terre*
> *Que soutanes et que surplis.*
> *Pauvres exilés que nous sommes,*
> *Il faut chanter des biens si doux*
> *Et du bonheur des autres hommes*
> *Ne jamais nous montrer jaloux.*[3]

Although it has been asserted by some critics that Maupassant at this stage was rebellious and virtually pagan in his agnosticism, there is little exact evidence to support this view and much, such as his school reports and his early correspondence, to deny it. It is perhaps true that, as Maupassant told his valet over twenty years later, he took part in a raid on the headmaster's pantry to destroy its provisions out of revenge for the horrible food and drink the pupils received there and that he was temporarily sent home for his part in the attempt, but it is still difficult to imagine young Guy in the leading role in it which he later gave himself. It is more likely that, as he later wrote in his tale *Après*, his days at Yvetot were lonely and frustrating after his spoilt, outdoor childhood at Etretat and this is why he had the time and concentration to compose the rather fine verses he sent with his letters to Laure at this time. Take the following lines which he enclosed in a letter to her of 2 May 1864, when he was only fourteen years old:

> *La vie est le sillon du vaisseau qui s'éloigne*
> *C'est l'éphémère fleur qui croît sur la montagne,*
> *C'est l'ombre de l'oiseau qui traverse l'éther,*
> *C'est le cri du marin englouti par la mer . . .*
> *La vie est un brouillard qui se change en lumière,*
> *C'est l'unique moment donné pour la prière.*[4]

Such a poem hardly shows Guy as a pagan or rebel; he seems in fact devout and reflective. He might have disliked the school's discipline and conditions, but he did not persuade his mother to take him away from it and seems to have written some fairly accomplished verse there despite his dislike of the place. Although some of the credit for Guy's early verse must go to the emphasis on versification and poetry exercises of the teaching at that time, much of it must have been due to his mother's eager encouragement of his reading and early efforts. It was not then surprising that when his grandmother, Mme Le Poittevin, died and Gustave Flaubert sent Laure in March 1866 a nostalgic letter of condolence, Guy's mother should have renewed contact with her former childhood friend, who conveyed his sympathy and told her 'to try to be brave for her children's sake', and tried to interest the now famous author of *Madame Bovary* and *Salammbô* in her sons, particularly Guy. Evoking her nostalgic memories of their childhood as a means of assuring herself of a favourable reception, she replied to him as follows:

'My youngest son (Hervé) is as yet only an honest peasant lad but the elder one (Guy) is already a serious young man. The poor boy has seen and understood quite a few things and he's almost too mature for his fifteen years. He'd remind you of his uncle Alfred whom he resembles in many ways and I am sure you would like him . . . I have just been obliged to withdraw him from the school at Yvetot where they have refused him a dispensation from the observance of Lent ordered by his doctors; it's either a strange way of understanding Christ's religion or I've got it all wrong! ... My son is not seriously ill but he is suffering from a nervous, weak condition that requires a tonic diet; in any case, he was not really very happy there : the austerity of their cloistered existence did not suit at all his delicate, impressionable temperament and the poor boy felt stifled behind those high walls that shut out any noise from outside. I think I will send him to the Lycée at Le Havre for eighteen months and then I'll go and live in Paris when he does there his philosophy and rhetoric courses.'

Flaubert did not reply to her letter on this occasion and Guy did not leave Yvetot immediately nor go on to Le Havre as his mother had planned. It was the discovery – possibly engineered by Guy himself to free himself from Yvetot – of his poem quoted above comparing his misery and his cousin's happiness on getting married that led to his expulsion and his being brought home by the school porter to an enraged Mme de Maupassant – not the 'irreligious and scandalous activities' he boasted of to Flaubert in October 1879. Guy spent much of the next few months at Etretat recovering from the wretchedness of the school food and enjoying the pleasures of the open air once more. His only complaint was, as he later told his cousin, Louis Le Poittevin, that he was rather lonely and would have liked to have had someone of his own age with whom he could share his boating, walks and reading.

It was during one of his stays at Etretat that Guy came into contact with the English poet Algernon Swinburne who was living with his friend G. E. J. Powell and a pet monkey called Nip in a remote cottage near Etretat. One day, Swinburne was out swimming when he got into difficulties and had to be rescued by local fishermen who heard his cries for help; Guy was in the boat of one of them, Théodule Vallin, and therefore witnessed the rescue. Swinburne's friend Powell, with whom Guy had occasionally chatted on the beach, heard of the handsome young lad's part in the rescue operations and invited him for lunch at his cottage, named the 'Chaumière Dolmancé' after the protagonist in one of the Marquis de Sade's works. Guy was later to describe his lunch with the thin, ghost-like poet who reminded him of a sensual, perverse Edgar Allan Poe, and the macabre and porno-graphic furnishings of the cottage in an article of 1882 entitled 'The Englishman of Etretat' that in 1891 became the preface to Gabriel Mourey's translation of Swinburne's *Poems and Ballads*.

Guy was impressionable, as his mother wrote to Flaubert, and he was fascinated both by the two poets' imaginatively colourful conversation, with its allusions to the Icelandic sagas which Powell had translated, and Victor Hugo whom Swinburne admired, and by the weird, nightmarish pictures, obscene photo-graphs of male nudes, and macabre objects he saw. Among these there was the famous hanged-man's hand with which he was presented by the poet and that he later used as the subject of one of his earliest horror stories, *La Main d'Ecorché*. The two poets clearly enjoyed the company of this fine, sturdy lad with his liking for poetry and literature and charming impressionability as much as Guy was captivated by their strange ways, and they invited him again to the cottage – this time, however, for a meal of roast monkey, the stench of which alone Guy was never to forget! Whether Guy saw more of the two English poets, as his remarks on their homosexuality and bestiality, which the writer Edmond de Goncourt recorded in his diary on 28 February 1875, might suggest, is not known, but clearly his contact with them must have encouraged him in his love of both the poetic and the fan-tastic, not to mention the perverse and the macabre, all of which play a large part in his later work.

In 1868, at the age of eighteen, Guy left Etretat for Rouen to continue his schooling. Rouen was, however, to be more than the furthering of his education; it was to witness in the next few years the maturing of the talents his mother had nurtured in him and the realisation of the literary ambitions she sought for her son.

CHAPTER 2

The Schoolboy Poet

At the time of young Maupassant's arrival in 1868 in Rouen, it was France's third largest city with some two hundred factories employing thousands of workers. It was also one of France's most historic cities since fourteen Norman dukes had died there, Joan of Arc had been burnt in its market-place, and it had been the birthplace of one of the greatest dramatists of France's seventeenth-century 'golden age', Pierre Corneille. To anyone arriving there from the country who looked down from the surrounding hills at the hundreds of belching chimneys and busy docks on the one side of the river and the myriad spires and antiquated buildings on the other, it must have seemed the epitome of the industrialisation of traditional, provincial life. For people living in the rural areas not so far away it represented the City with all the attractions and vices an industrialised population requires. If for the imaginative provincial heroine of Flaubert's novel of 1857, *Madame Bovary*, it represented the fulfilment of her dreams of ardent romance, it must have had no less an appeal for the eighteen-year-old Guy de Maupassant and his mother at Etretat. For Rouen was not only where Laure had spent most of her life but it was also where her memories of her childhood and youth were enshrined, particularly those associated with her brother, Alfred, and the 'little world' of the Hôtel-Dieu playroom. This cult of her brother's memory, together with her renewed contact with Flaubert, who lived not very far from Rouen at Croisset, probably encouraged her to send Guy to Rouen rather than Le Havre, as she had mentioned to Flaubert in March 1866. No doubt she hoped he would one day guide her eldest son into a literary career similar to her brother's. It was thus perhaps ambitiousness for her son as well as the good name of the long-established school that prompted Mme de Maupassant to enrol Guy at the Lycée Pierre Corneille in October 1868.

In the philosophy class at the Lycée Guy was fourth in the list of pupils recommended after the prizewinners in the examinations in French and Latin prose and translation, and gained his *baccalauréat* at Caen on 27 July 1869 with an examiner's comment of 'passable'. He was thus by no means a brilliant pupil. However, Guy's progress was greater in his extra-curricular activities than in his school ones as far as the literary career his mother had ordained for him was concerned. For while at Rouen young Guy came into contact with the 45-year-old poet Louis Bouilhet, who had become Gustave Flaubert's closest friend since Alfred Le Poittevin's death. Whether Laure de Maupassant, who was living in Rouen during her sons' education there, had pulled any strings with Flaubert or with his mother or niece Caroline to obtain this favour is not known. What is known is that she had sent Guy to visit the Flauberts in 1867 and herself called on them in Rouen in October 1868. Also that Guy procured a copy of Bouilhet's poems *Festons et Astragales*, learnt them virtually by heart, and presented himself very shyly at the house at 43 Rue Bihorel where since September 1867 the poet had lived quietly with his mistress Léonie and her illegitimate son. Later, in an article on Bouilhet in *Le Gaulois*, he described his arrival at the poet's door:

'He lived in the outskirts of Rouen in the rue Bihorel, one of those long provincial avenues that lead out from the city into the countryside. I pulled a rope beside a small door in a high wall and heard a bell tinkle in the distance. No one came to answer it for quite a while and I was about to go away when I heard footsteps from inside. The door opened and before me stood a large gentleman . . . He stared at me with surprise, expecting me to say something. However, in the few moments he had taken to unlock the door I had completely forgotten the fluent, flattering speech I had spent the past three days preparing for the occasion. I simply murmured my name. He had long known my family and so he gave me his hand and asked me to step inside.' [5]

This was not, however, the first time the young man had seen Bouilhet, for some years afterwards Maupassant mentioned in an article on the poet his first sighting of him:

'One day, as we were filing back to school after a walk, the prefect in charge – a highly respected chap, for once – suddenly motioned us to stop: then he greeted in a most humble and respectful manner a large man wearing a decoration, who had a long drooping moustache and walked along with his stomach well forward, his head well back and a pince-nez covering his eyes...' [6]

Despite the obvious resemblance to the Viking-like figure of Flaubert, Bouilhet was not related to the novelist. The two of them had known each other, but not very intimately, at school – Flaubert was just a year older than his friend. Bouilhet had studied medicine for a time under Dr Flaubert until in 1845 he abandoned the idea of following in his father's footsteps and gave up medicine in order to devote himself to more artistic pursuits. These included writing poetry, which Bouilhet had begun while on duty at night in the hospital wards. To support his poet's life he opened a cramming school for university entrants. This was a fairly miserable existence for someone who had been brilliant in Classics at school, was passionately interested in literature of all countries and periods, and had taught himself Chinese; his weekends with Flaubert at Croisset must have been a pleasant cultural relief. In 1857 he became librarian at Mantes outside Rouen and later, as he achieved some fame with his plays – *Madame de Montarcy* in 1856, *L'Oncle Million* in 1861, and *La Conjuration d'Amboise* in 1866 – and poems such as *Melaenis* of 1851 and *Festons et Astragales* of 1859, he was in 1867 offered the post of Chief Librarian at Rouen's Municipal Library. Although sometimes compared to Hugo, Bouilhet was not a great poet or dramatist but he was above all dedicated to Art and in this he was a twin spirit of Flaubert, for whom Art was virtually a religion and writing an agonised purgatory. Bouilhet was interested particularly in artistic form and, like his fellow believers in the Art for Art's Sake movement of the 1850s and 1860s, he attached the greatest importance to precision in the structure and wording of his work like a jeweller seeking to create the most beautiful combination of gems in a single setting. Bouilhet did not, of course, succeed very often in producing the perfect poem but he always maintained his ideals of one.

Flaubert, who sought Bouilhet's opinion on virtually everything he wrote and to whom the poet had dedicated his long poem *Melaenis* because the novelist had corrected it, described his friend's idealism in Art in his preface to the posthumous collection of verse *Dernières Chansons* of June 1870:

'His was an existence completely devoted to the Ideal and he was one of those rare devotees of literature for itself, one of the last fanatics of a religion that is dying out – if it is not already dead . . . He was intoxicated by the rhythm of verse and the cadence of prose, which must sound as good when it is read out loud as poetry. Sentences that are badly written do not stand up to this test; they affect one's breathing, alter one's heartbeat, and so lie outside our normal capabilities . . .'

Although some of Bouilhet's poems seem surprisingly casual and flow with a measured jauntiness that reflected his occasionally ebullient humour and *esprit gaulois* as well as his love of Aristophanes and Rabelais, the large majority of his work is serious and neo-Classical. Bouilhet was, according to Flaubert, as familiar with Latin as with French and knew the Classical authors thoroughly, particularly Homer's *Odyssey*. His subjects tend therefore to be Classical ones, as in the case of the Roman epic *Melaenis*, or historical ones as in his plays; and his favourite metre the solemn, formal Alexandrine. Most of the poems are of a melancholy mood and express Bouilhet's hard struggle to survive as a poet in a non-

poetic universe and his pessimistic reflections on the ephemeral
condition of human existence in the context of natural evolution
and death. An example of his melancholy thoughts on Man's fate
in the universe is the long poem *Les Fossiles*, dedicated to
Flaubert, in which he describes the evolution of the world and
Man's tragic role in it. In the following extract he depicts Man
breaking free at last from God and Nature to create his own
world and then suffering anguish at the helplessness he feels when
again confronted with his fate:

> *L'homme connut sa force, et, secouant ses chaînes,*
> *Poussa le cri joyeux des libertés humaines,*
> *Sous les débris du temple écrasa les pavois,*
> *Et, pesant dans sa main la couronne des rois,*
> *Sur la poudre du sol que son sang a trempée*
> *Il écrivit ses droits du bout de son épée,*
> *Et pour juger sa cause évoqua sans remords,*
> *Ainsi qu'un grand sénat, l'ombre des siècles morts.*
> *Il fut libre, il fut maître. O misère! ô démence!*
> *Cercle mystérieux qui toujours recommence!*
> *Voilà que, maintenant, vieillard au front pali,*
> *Dans la satiété de son œuvre accompli,*
> *Ployé sous le fardeau de ses six mille années,*
> *Il s'arrête, inquiet, au bord des destinées . . .*
> *Sa raison l'épouvante et sa croyance a fui!*
> *Sous le soleil qui baisse il marche sans appui,*
> *Et son âme débile où l'espérance est morte,*
> *Comme un vaisseau perdu, flotte au vent qui l'emporte!* [7]

There can be little doubt that much of the melancholy from
these sardonic reflections on Man rubbed off on his young visitor
in more serious moments just as the older man's bawdy humour
and fairly bawdy sex-life must have provided some fascinating
light relief for the shy youth awakening to sensual pleasure.
Maupassant was in fact to describe the mixture of irony and
humour he discovered in Bouilhet in an article of 21 August 1882
in *Le Gaulois*:

'Though shy in public, Louis Bouilhet showed in the privacy of his home an incomparable verve sustained with a great sense of humour of epic dimensions and yet full of finesse.

'His big, kindly eyes, infinitely kind and penetrating, would light up with a well-meaning yet sardonic sparkle. It was quite distinct this constant irony of his, always keen and yet paternal; it seemed to be the very foundation, the defensive lining of his artistic temperament. For this gentle, gracious and Cornelian poet – gentle by nature, gracious because of his refinement, and Cornelian in the doggedness of his literary education, admiration of others and will-power – had more than anyone else a mocking humour, a shrewd perceptiveness and a biting wit, that was, however, never cruel. His laugh was a joking one.'

Bouilhet's paternal kindness and humour must indeed have appealed to the largely fatherless 18-year-old away from home. Above all, however, it was Bouilhet's sense of artistic purpose and critical guidance that both influenced and encouraged Guy in his attempts at poetry at this time. His mother's cult of her brother and fostering of her son's literary talents had already made Guy receptive to Bouilhet's advice that continuous work and increased craftsmanship would lead gradually to individual perfection in one's art and his saying that a hundred lines could ensure a poet's reputation provided they were the nearest to perfection he could attain. How far Bouilhet actually influenced Guy's verses by his criticism is difficult to gauge. The young man was quite an accomplished writer of verse before going to Rouen, as has been seen. Moreover, it is by no means certain that Bouilhet saw Guy that often since at first he was busy with his plays, which were being staged in Paris at this time, and spent a large number of his weekends with Flaubert, who was completing *L'Education Sentimentale*; later on he was often ill. Maupassant himself later mentioned that he called on Bouilhet every week for about six months after he had first knocked on the poet's door and that he once or twice accompanied the poet to see Flaubert; their acquaintance was thus not a very long one compared with other

literary relationships and hardly familiar enough to have had a
profound influence on Guy. It is said in fact that Guy recited some
Alexandrines to Bouilhet on Saint-Charlemagne's Day, 28
January 1869, and that the poet scowled with disapproval,
remarking that the lines were too inflated but that he had, however, heard plenty worse!

Most of the verse Maupassant published later was composed
long after his contact with Bouilhet; one piece, however, that was
written in 1868 and lay hidden in the Book of Honour of the
Rouen Lycée until its author's death, was *Le Dieu Créateur*. It is
headed by a quotation, in which the early nineteenth-century
philosopher Jouffroy wonders whether Man might one day
become extinct like earlier species as Nature continued to evolve
towards a more perfect creation, and proceeds as follows:

> *Dieu, cet être inconnu dont nul n'a vu la face,*
> *Roi qui commande aux rois et règne dans l'espace,*
> *Las d'être toujours seul, lui dont l'infinité*
> *De l'univers sans bornes emplit l'immensité,*
> *Et d'embrasser toujours, seul, par sa plénitude*
> *De l'espace et des temps la sombre solitude,*
> *De rester toujours tel qu'il a toujours été,*
> *Solitaire et puissant durant l'éternité,*
> *Portant de sa grandeur la marque indélébile,*
> *D'être seul pour qui le temps soit immobile,*
> *Pour qui tout le passé reste sans souvenir*
> *Et qui n'attend rien de l'immense avenir;*
> *Qui de la nuit des temps perce l'ombre profonde;*
> *Pour qui tout soit égal, pour qui tout se confonde*
> *Dans l'éternel ennui d'un éternel présent,*
> *Solitaire et puissant et pourtant impuissant*
> *A changer son destin dont il n'est pas le maître,*
> *Le grand Dieu qui peut tout ne peut pas ne pas être!*
> *Et ce Dieu souverain, fatigué de son sort,*
> *Peut-être en sa grandeur a désiré la mort! . . .*
> *Enfin las de rester seul avec son ennui*
> *Des astres au front d'or il a peuplé la nuit;*
> *Dans l'espace flottait comme un chaos immonde;*

De la matière impure il a formé le monde . . .
Mais un jour, tout à coup, tout trembla sur la terre,
Sa globe n'était plus déserte et solitaire;
Le grand bois tressaillit car un être inconnu
Sur l'univers esclave a levé son bras nu.
Le monde tout entier a plié sous cet être;
Regardant la nature, il a dit: C'est pour moi.
Regardant le soleil, il a dit: C'est pour moi . . .
Seul, perdu dans l'espace, il se bâtit un monde.
Tout plia sous ses lois, le feu, la terre et l'onde.
Mais il marche toujours et depuis six mille ans,
Rien n'a pu ralentir ses progrès insolents,
Et souvent quand il parle, on a cru que la vie
Jaillissait du néant au gré de son envie . . .
L'homme n'est-il aussi qu'un ouvrage incomplet
Que l'ébauche et le plan d'un être plus parfait? . . .
Seigneur, Dieu tout puissant, quand je veux te comprendre,
Ta grandeur m'éblouit et vient me le défendre.
Quand ma raison s'élève à ton infinité
Dans le doute et la nuit je suis précipité,
Et je ne puis saisir, dans l'ombre qui m'enlace
Qu'un éclair passager qui brille et s'efface
Mais j'espère pourtant, car là-haut tu souris!
Car souvent quand un jour se lève triste et gris,
Quand on ne voit partout que de sombres images,
Un rayon de soleil glisse entre deux nuages
Qui nous montre là-bas un petit coin d'azur;
Quand l'homme doute et que tout lui paraît obscur,
Il a toujours à l'âme un rayon d'espérance;
Car il reste toujours, même dans la souffrance,
Au plus désespéré, par le temps le plus noir,
Un peu d'azur au ciel, au cœur un peu d'espoir.[8]

The poem is usually taken to show Maupassant's pessimism and irreverence towards God, largely because it is never quoted, if at all, at any length. Fuller consideration of the whole poem, particularly the end, proves that Maupassant is not being especially pessimistic or irreverent but is simply mystified by the processes of Nature and the Divinity and continues to have hope despite his ignorance of them. In tone and outlook the poem is reminiscent of the work of the stoic poet of the 1830s, Alfred de Vigny. Certainly the first four lines and several others are masterly in composition, but the rest are rather too repetitive and emphatic and often too complex in structure. It is interesting to see, however, the type of subject young Maupassant was treating, possibly as part of a school exercise; the seriousness of the poem's semiphilosophical theme is similar in its emphasis on evolution and Man's role in the universe both to his uncle Alfred Le Poittevin's philosophical epic *Une Promenade de Bélial,* and also of Louis Bouilhet's collection *Festons et Astragales,* from which *Les Fossiles,* written in 1854, was quoted above. This similarity of subject in *Les Fossiles* and *Le Dieu Créateur* is surely too close to be purely incidental and might be taken as a sign of Bouilhet's influence on Maupassant's writing at this time. Clearly, Guy had read an enormous amount and was an extremely studious, intellectually mature young man since the content and the form are so advanced and complex for someone of his age. Another poem, dated a year later, when Guy was approaching nineteen, shows a similar maturity of thought and outlook, although this time the metre and mood are not quite so solemn and heavy:

Voyez partir l'hirondelle
Elle fuit à tire d'aile
Mais revient toujours fidèle
A son nid
Sitôt que des hivers le grand froid est fini.

L'homme au gré de son envie,
Errant promène sa vie
Par le souvenir suivie
De ces lieux
Où sourit son enfance, où dorment ses aïeux.

Et puis, quand il sent que l'âge
A glacé son grand courage

Il les regrette et, plus sage,
Vient chercher
Un tranquille bonheur près de son vieux clocher.[9]

The theme is simple and rather sentimentally treated, but it again reveals the young Maupassant's moral concern with the human condition and Man's fate in the world – topics he had clearly absorbed from his reading of other poets and also no doubt from his contact with the serious-minded idealist of the Rue Bihorel. The fact that Maupassant later quotes some of Bouilhet's verses on the sublime dreamlike quality of ideal love in his stories *Mots d'Amour* (1882), *Découverte* (1884), *Lettre trouvée sur un Noyé* (1884), and *Les Sœurs Rondoli* (1885) shows perhaps that the schoolboy poet did indeed imbibe some of the older man's moral as well as his artistic idealism.

It is clear, too, that Guy was quite early on in his literary experimentation influenced also by the licentiousness of much of Bouilhet's verse. Guy must have enjoyed not only poems like *Les Fossiles* but also Rabelaisian pieces such as 'Cinq Doigts', 'Au Moineau de Mlle D', and 'L'Avocat Delattre', published in *Quatrains, Miettes et Rognures*. Signs of this influence on Guy, seen particularly in the erotic verse he wrote several years later, are visible in an unpublished poem called *Canards* describing the playfulness of the ducks on the river at dawn:

> *Le jour paraît. Le soleil dore*
> *Le brouillard fin qui flotte encore*
> *Ainsi qu'un voile au fil de l'eau.*
> *Debout à l'avant d'un bateau*
> *Le pêcheur guette, attend, balance*
> *D'un bras sur l'épervier qu'il lance,*
> *Et le filet s'élargissant*
> *Trace un grand cercle et puis descend*
> *Par tout le fond chercher sa proie.*
> *Les coqs jettent leurs chants de joie.*
> *Des mouches ronflent dans le vent.*
> *Soudain, l'un l'autre se suivant,*
> *La troupe des canards arrive*

En procession sur la rive,
Titubant comme des gens gris,
L'aile verte et la tête bleue,
Ils vont frétillant de la queue!
L'un saute à l'eau. L'autre le suit.
Chacun nage et chacune fuit,
Battant le fleuve de sa plume
Devant le gros canard qu'allume
Le gai soleil dans l'eau coulant.
Puis tous ensemble basculant
Devant le cul plongent la tête
Et l'on voit flotter la houpette
Des derrières pointus, îlots
Que balancent de légers flots.[10]

Guy's contact with Bouilhet not only served to develop and strengthen his own artistic outlook and discipline but also allowed the young man to see something of the great Flaubert himself on one of his few visits to Rouen inbetween bouts of work at his retreat at Croisset and trips to Paris for documentation and social engagements. Since the publicity of his trial in 1857 for offending public morality by his novel *Madame Bovary*, and the success of his historical novel *Salammbô* in 1862, Flaubert had been invited into the glittering upper-class *salons* of the capital and even to the colourful Imperial court of the Empress Eugénie. The 'Hermit of Croisset', as he was called, had now become something of a fashionable celebrity. This fact and the lack of communication between the Flauberts and the Maupassants in Guy's youth meant that he had had little contact with the famous novelist at this stage. Maupassant wrote later that 'I got to know Flaubert when I was much older . . . Circumstances keep kindred souls and families apart. I saw him therefore only twice or three times when I was a young man'. One such occasion, in October 1867, is described by Flaubert's mother when she wrote to her son's former school-friend Laure de Maupassant:

'I cannot tell you how much I enjoyed your son's visit. He is a charming boy and you may well be proud of him. He is a little like you and also like our poor dear Alfred. His clever, animated face is very attractive and his young friend said he was gifted in every way. Your old friend Gustave is delighted with him and asks me to congratulate you on having such a child.'

Another occasion, possibly some two years later, was while Guy was visiting Bouilhet in Rouen:

'One day (I was a pupil at the Rouen high-school at that time) – a Thursday I think it was – I went down to Rue Bihorel to show some verses to my famous friend Louis Bouilhet for his sharp scrutiny.

'When I entered the poet's study I saw through the clouds of cigar-smoke two tall, plump figures seated in the armchairs chatting as they smoked.

'Facing Louis Bouilhet there was Gustave Flaubert.

'I kept my verses in my pocket and sat down quietly in a corner listening to them. At about four o'clock Flaubert got up to leave. "Come with me to the end of the street. I'll walk to the ferry." When we reached the boulevard, where the annual Saint-Romain fair was being held, Bouilhet suddenly suggested: "What about going round some of the stalls?" And so they began walking round slowly side by side, towering above the rest of the crowd and amusing themselves like children, exchanging perceptive remarks on the people they came across as they did so.

'Just by looking at the people's faces they imagined their characters and made up conversations between the various husbands and wives. Bouilhet took the part of the man and Flaubert the woman, using the language of the Normandy peasants and the slow drawl and startled look of the local people of the region.

'When we came to the tent holding the pageant of St Anthony, Bouilhet said: "Let's go and hear the violinist in here." And so we went inside.' [11]

The tableau of St Antony's temptation in the desert they saw inside the tent had in fact been one of the sources of inspiration of Flaubert's work *La Tentation de Saint-Antoine*, a first draft of which Bouilhet and others had heavily criticised in 1849 and a third version of which Flaubert was still trying to write in the late 1860s. The visit to the fair described above might well have given renewed impetus to his efforts, for the revised novel was completed not long afterwards in 1872.

Guy also saw Flaubert at Croisset when he accompanied Bouilhet on one or two of his weekly visits, but at this stage their contact was limited and young Maupassant would simply have been rather over-awed by his illustrious senior companions even if entertained by the two bachelor artists' mixture of serious arguments on literary matters and bawdy humour about sex and prostitutes.

Since autumn 1868 Bouilhet had been ill with colds, coughs and influenza, and early in 1869 he suffered a complete nervous breakdown and was ordered to take a short holiday in Vichy to relax. For some time the poet had been very depressed and complained of being ill, but Flaubert had so far scoffed somewhat at what appeared to him to be Bouilhet's hypochondria. Now, however, Flaubert was alarmed and his concern for the closest friend he had had since Alfred Le Poittevin was justified not long after when news arrived of Bouilhet's death from albuminuria on 18 July.

For Flaubert it seemed as if the end had come and he wrote that there was no longer any purpose in him writing now that his dear and scrupulous Louis Bouilhet was gone. Although he had known him for only a few months, Maupassant too was very upset by his mentor's sudden death and was further saddened at the funeral on 20 July on seeing the coffin-bearers and the crowd of spectators trampling over the flowers the poet had so diligently nurtured in his garden. For Guy his first real contact with the secluded world of Art had passed away. He wrote in *Sur la Mort de Louis Bouilhet* shortly after the poet's death:

Il est mort, mon maître; il est mort, et pourquoi?
Lui si bon, lui si grand, si bienveillant pour moi.
..Oh! ces gens-là, grand Dieu, pourquoi veux-tu qu'ils meurent?
..Il ne reste plus rien mais rien qu'un pauvre corps,
Rien de lui. Même pas ce bienveillant sourire
Qui nous attirait tant et semblait toujours dire:
'Mon ami, je vous aime'. Et ce regard si beau,
Ce grand œil clair et doux si plein d'intelligence.
On sent qu'il doit souffrir une horrible souffrance
Pour demeurer ainsi fixe dans son tombeau.
Puisque rien ne périt dans la création,
Puisque tout est progrès et transformation,
Il n'a fait que laisser sa dépouille mortelle.
Mais son âme, mon Dieu, maintenant que fait-elle?
..Ah! si vous l'aviez vu sous ses poiriers en fleurs,
Quand son bras sur mon bras, jasant en vieux rimeur,
Il ouvrait sa belle âme aux longues causeries
Qui me laissaient après de longues rêveries,
Car il était si franc, si simple et naturel.
Pauvre Bouilhet! Lui mort! si bon, si paternel!
Lui qui m'apparaissait comme un autre Messie
Avec la clef du ciel où dort la Poésie.
Et puis le voilà mort et parti pour jamais
Vers ce monde éternel où le génie aspire.
Mais de là-haut, sans doute, il nous voit et peut lire
Ce que j'avais au cœur et combien je l'aimais.[12]

For the next decade Guy was to witness Flaubert's efforts to have
Bouilhet's works published or performed, and in February 1880
he was enlisted as a member of Flaubert's committee for the
erection of a monument to the poet. In fact, Bouilhet's memory
was to remain with Maupassant for the rest of his life. Paul
Bourget, the novelist, was to record that Maupassant knew many
of Bouilhet's poems by heart and recited *La Colombe* to him one
evening in 1877; and that as late as 1891, when Bouilhet's verse
was reprinted, Maupassant still had the greatest admiration for the
poet of his youth.[13] Certainly, Guy's articles on him in *Le Gaulois*
of 21 August and 7 September 1882 and 22 May 1883 testify to his

fondness for the kindly father-figure, who had become one of France's more significant, even if not most well-known, poets, despite the poverty and bad luck that had dogged his path, and who had been young Maupassant's first guide in the domain of the Artist.

CHAPTER 3

From Soldier to Bureaucrat

Having managed to pass his *baccalauréat* in July 1869, although it was held only ten days after Louis Bouilhet's death, Guy joined his father at 2 rue de Moncey in Paris in the following October to read law at the University. His life as a student was, however, neither a very exciting nor a very long one. He did not experience the bohemian existence for which university life in Paris is well known, but saw rather the more sophisticated aspects of Parisian social life alongside his father. He was more familiar with the *salon* and the opera than with either the garret or the café. His stay in the capital was in any case to be cut short by political events and his student days were to be suddenly curtailed by military circumstances.

As Zola's series of novels *Les Rougon-Macquart* was to show a decade or more later, the domestic economic policy of Napoleon III's Empire, which had begun a few years after Guy de Maupassant's birth and had helped to transform towns like Rouen into an industrialised city and Paris into a metropolis of wide avenues and parks and a sophisticated centre of high life, was not matched by equally successful social and foreign programmes. Industrial expansion and the growing self-indulgence of the newly rich middle classes, whose wealth derived from the rise in commerce and mechanisation, had to a large extent blinded France to the menacing forces on her borders and her military inadequacies. Furthermore, the social miseries of industrialisation and the censorship exercised on the press and writers under the Empire

had gained it the favour of neither the workers nor the intellectuals and there were few people in 1870 who wholeheartedly
wanted to defend the régime itself.

France under Napoleon III and Gramont was thus no match
for the 'blood and iron' policy of the Prussian Bismarck, who was
determined to unite Germany under Kaiser Wilhelm through
crafty diplomatic intrigue supported by the brute force of his
superbly organised army. His policy had already been successful
four years earlier against Austria; now only France stood in his
way. During much of the first half of 1870 France was caught in a
wrangling match with Prussia over the candidateship of a
Hohenzollern prince to the vacant throne of Spain. Eventually it
seemed that Bismarck and the Prussians were going to withdraw
their claim. When, however, the French Government insisted
that the claim be withdrawn permanently, the Prussians recognised in this further demand an opportunity to snub France and
a pretext to commence hostilities with her. The Prussians' reply in
the form of the telegram sent by Bismarck from Ems to the French
Government served to kindle the conflagration and on 15 July
1870 France declared war. Having enlisted a year early, with
other young men of his age, Maupassant took some aptitude tests
at the military headquarters in Paris at Vincennes and was posted
to the second division of the commissariat at Le Havre, from
where he was sent as a messenger to Rouen.

Hostilities began in earnest in the first weeks of August 1870
and the news of some victories spurred on the French armies
against their invaders from the East. Soon, however, reports that
Alsace had fallen to the Prussian foe and that the main French
army was cut off at Metz reached the capital. On 2 September the
French suffered a crushing defeat at Sedan – an event later
immortalised in Zola's novel *La Débâcle* – and by October Metz
fell to the Germans. Still the French continued to hope and to
believe all was not lost since Paris had not been taken. By
December the Germans were approaching Rouen and, while
Flaubert was hurriedly burying the manuscript of his novel *La
Tentation de Saint-Antoine* in his garden at Croisset and retreating

with his elderly mother to Rouen itself, Maupassant was acting as courier with the retreating army withdrawing east from there towards Paris. It is at this time that Guy sent news of himself to Laure at Etretat:

'I have told the driver of the Le Havre coach to give you news of me, dear mama, but fearing he might not be able to, I am writing to you myself. I have fled with our army in retreat; I was very nearly captured. I went from the vanguard to the rear of the column to carry an order from the officer-in-charge to the general. I have done 15 leagues on foot. After having walked and run all the previous night to carry messages, I slept on the stone floor of an ice-cold cellar. If I hadn't such sturdy legs, I'd have been taken prisoner. I am getting along fine . . .'

This affectionate, reassuring note was followed a month or so later by a longer letter from Paris, where the exhausted army had retreated only to be faced with the further horror of a prolonged siege. Clearly, Guy still hoped France would be victorious and his youthful zeal contrasts with his father's more conventional concern for his son's safety:

'I will write you a few more lines today, dear mama, because in two days' time all communications between Paris and the rest of France will be cut. The Prussians are advancing on us by forced marches. As for the outcome of the War, there's no longer any doubt: the Prussians have lost and they know it; their only hope is to take Paris in one swoop but we're ready for that.

'As for me, I am not yet sleeping at the commissariat at Vincennes and I am in no great hurry to have a bed there. I prefer to be in Paris itself for the duration of the siege rather than in the old fort where we are housed at Vincennes which will be destroyed by the Prussians' cannons. My father is desperately anxious about the situation and insists on me entering the military quarters here – and he keeps giving me the weirdest advice for avoiding any mishaps. If I were to pay attention to him, I would go and ask to become superintendent of the main sewer so as not to be hit by any bombs . . .'

Guy's youthful optimism was to receive a shock when, after weeks of suffering and starvation, Paris surrendered on 28 January 1871. By then, however, Guy had left the capital and was away on leave at Etretat and he continued to be there and on duty as an orderly at Le Havre until well after the peace treaty had been ratified. The Third Republic was about to replace the Second Empire and the bloody Commune rising of the working people of Paris was suppressed in March that year.

While Maupassant's views of the Commune rising are rather uncertain and he seems, from articles written later for *Le Gaulois*, to have sympathised with and criticised both sides in the civil strife between Parisian workers and the Government, his impressions of the war he actually witnessed are much more distinct and vivid. It is natural that the personal experiences of the war Guy went through should have made such a deep impression on so sensitive a character. Furthermore, he was young and full of a desire for meaningful action, particularly when it involved the protection of both France and, above all, his family. A certain amount of youthful idealism as well as a protective attitude towards his mother and brother no doubt played their part in making him so active and also so receptive to the events taking place around him. Although many of the stories he published a decade or more after the period they describe are tinged with a more violent anti-bourgeois feeling than Guy experienced at the time of the war, three impressions of the scenes he witnessed in 1870 stand out very clearly: the sad demoralised state of the French army, the cowardly complacency of the middle classes, and the humbler but keener patriotism of the peasant and the lower classes. No one can fail to recall the harrowing description of the shreds of France's army entering Rouen which opens *Boule de Suif* nor the satirical remarks in *Un Coup d'Etat* about the incompetent shopkeepers who have suddenly turned into soldiers and leaders of men:

'Bonnet-makers were made colonels doing the job of generals; revolvers and daggers hung from around large, pacifist waistlines wearing red belts; small shopkeepers and the like who had suddenly been transformed into warriors for the occasion were put in command of battalions of rough-and-ready volunteers and swore like troopers so as to appear as martial as possible.

'The mere fact that they were carrying arms and handling guns excited these men, who had up until now only worked a pair of scales, and caused them, quite unjustifiably, to be feared by anyone coming across them. They executed innocent souls to show off they could shoot; and while patrolling through countryside still free of a single Prussian soldier, they shot at stray dogs, cows quietly munching in the fields, and sick horses grazing in the meadows.

'Each man saw himself called upon to play out a great military role . . .'

The pusillanimity and complacency of the bourgeois classes, who were more concerned with the smooth running of their businesses than defending their country, was brought home to Maupassant after the war was lost, when he witnessed the German occupation of Etretat and complained about it to the town's mayor – an incident he described in late 1870 to his uncle Charles Cordhomme:

'A Prussian officer came and walked through Etretat in full uniform. The local population rioted at the outrage. Then, several shopkeepers and I went off to speak to the mayor about it . . . He told us in an insolent manner that the French people were noisy louts and cowards and that since the Prussians had beaten us we had no cause to complain . . .'

In contrast to the bourgeois who disliked the war and submitted to the invaders for selfish, material reasons, the peasants of Normandy are depicted as naïve but sincere patriots; indeed, the honest and rosy-cheeked prostitute Boule de Suif almost becomes a tragic symbol of France betrayed by the shopkeeper classes and handed over by these to the country's Prussian invaders. The Jewish prostitute in *Mademoiselle Fifi* who defies the German officers, the old man in *Le Père Milon* who avenges his father's and his son's death by killing Prussians, the peasant woman in *La Mère Sauvage* who burns alive some German soldiers staying in her barn, and Monsieur Dubuis in *Un Duel* who kills a Prussian officer in his train compartment are all examples of the poorer people's patriotic resistance against the enemy. Their efforts are justified in Maupassant's eyes by not only the occupation of France by the Prussians but by the atrocities the invaders commit: for example, the destruction of the château's interior in *Mademoiselle Fifi* and the brutal shooting of the two naïve fishermen for not giving the required password in *Deux Amis*. Criticism of the French army and hatred of the Prussian occupiers remained with Maupassant as they did in the minds of most Frenchmen for many years to come after the German troops had left and the war indemnity had been paid and it was partly for this reason that *Boule de Suif* was to be such an instant success a decade later.

Although the war was over by the end of January 1871, Guy was not out of uniform until the end of September and not discharged from the army until November. The process took so long because the imminent introduction of a new law had forced him to find a long-term replacement or face being in uniform for another seven years. Nor was this his only problem at this time: there was also the question of his various periods of leave to be settled to the satisfaction of a scrupulous military bureaucracy. In both these situations Guy was obliged to seek the aid of his father, who fortunately managed to discover for his son both a replacement and the necessary documentation justifying Guy's leave permits.

Where Gustave de Maupassant could not so easily help his son was when he needed money. The Maupassant family finances had declined soon after Pierre-Jules' retirement and Gustave's expensive living had hardly helped in their recovery. The family finances were in fact to become so encumbered with debts that by 1874, when Pierre-Jules was dying, Gustave was afraid to visit him for fear of being required to settle the outstanding sums and Guy was sent along to represent him at the funeral. Before then, however, Gustave had had to find himself a living as a broker's agent with the firm of Stolz in order to continue to support his wife and son in Etretat and himself and Guy in Paris. As is shown by an angry letter from Guy to his mother of November 1872 complaining of how little pocket-money he was receiving from his father, even this measure was not satisfactory for Guy and this must have been one of the main reasons for his applying for a job a few months earlier.

There is no evidence of his consulting Flaubert on the chances of a literary career, as has been suggested in the past, nor of the novelist's negative reply at this stage. It was simply that, having been made more independent and resourceful by his experiences in the war and finding himself in the capital with the possibility of completing his studies and participating in its social life and literary activity, Guy wanted to stand on his own feet and for this he needed money. Hence his letter to Admiral Pothau of 7 January 1972 applying for a post in the naval administration. However, this letter received a negative reply eleven days later. Once more Gustave de Maupassant was to be of service to his son. On 19 February Gustave wrote to the Admiral mentioning the names of his acquaintances Admiral Saisset and MM. Faure, de l'Arbre and de Pardieu and the next day Guy himself sent in a fresh application from Etretat as follows:

'I have the honour of asking from Your Excellency a favour which would be of great value to me: that of being attached to the Ministry of the Navy ... The great favour I am writing to ask of Your Excellency would be all the more precious to me since it would allow me to continue here in Paris my studies in law which were abruptly curtailed by the War, without them of course preventing me from accomplishing the task assigned me with zeal and efficiency ...' [14]

The supplicant tone of the letter and Gustave's good connections in high places must have swayed the Admiral in his decision: on 20 March Vice-Admiral Krantz, head of the naval administration, informed Saisset that Maupassant could work in the offices of the Administration Centrale, but while awaiting a definite posting he could possibly replace someone in the library. Thus it was that Guy began work as a clerk in the library of the Ministry of the Navy in March 1872. Efforts continued to be made, nevertheless, to have Guy established in the Central Administration, as the following letter of 16 May 1872 from an official named Fournichon to Admiral Saisset clearly shows:

'Monsieur Guy de Maupassant concerning whom you have received the attached letter is in fact an excellent employee with whom we are most satisfied. He has been placed in the clerical section of the internal administration, where they are prepared, when a vacancy arises among the supernumerary staff, to let him join as one of them and count in his period of supernumerary employment the time he has spent as an applicant.

'I have informed M. Cordier of the interest you have in this young man. I will also speak about him to M. de l'Arbre so that he might be seconded to the Central Administration, which is what he indeed deserves.' [15]

In the following October he was moved to the Ministry's Department for the Colonies, where, thanks once more to Saisset's efforts, he was appointed on 1 February 1873 with a salary of 125 francs a month plus an annual bonus of 150 francs – an adequate but not very high salary for those days, which was slightly increased a year later when he was made permanent. Indeed, Maupassant was to complain later in an article in *Le Gaulois* of 4 January 1882 about the low wages of the clerical workers in Government service who 'cannot complain or revolt but must remain bound and gagged in their respectable penury'. Guy continued, however, to receive a pension of 600 francs a year from his father until 1878 – when he was 28! – and he would not in fact have been too badly off financially, had he been more economical.

Guy was to remain in the Colonial Office until 1877, when, after promotion, he entered for a while the Bureau des Approvisionments and the Bureau des Equipages, the Supplies Office and Personnel Division respectively, before joining the Ministry of Education in 1878, with the help of a recommendation from Flaubert. The young civil servant worked well and his superiors actually had cause to praise 'his intelligence, his enthusiasm and his perfect conduct' in one of their annual reports. An idea of Maupassant's experiences as a clerk can be gained from his brief insights into the everyday life of a civil servant in the Naval Ministry's bureaucracy in his short stories *En Famille* and *Le Parapluie* as well as in *L'Héritage* of 1884 and *Les Dimanches d'un Bourgeois de Paris* of 1880. The first of these reveals both the dull routine of the dozens of offices leading off from the long corridors of the Ministry and the avid jostling for promotion within the staff; *Les Dimanches d'un Bourgeois de Paris* describes how a middle-aged clerk of not very great intelligence fails despite all his plodding and because of his lack of sufficient obsequiousness to gain promotion, and eventually discovers a compensating pleasure in the excursions he makes out of Paris at the weekends to improve his health. Like his Monsieur Patissot, Guy also needed recreation and sought an escape from the sedentary routine of his clerical post. If the pleasure he had derived from walking and boating ever since his childhood in Etretat could provide for his physical needs, the love of literature nurtured in him over the years was to serve those of his imaginative sensibility. His new life in Paris was soon in fact to satisfy both these desires.

PART TWO

PARIS

CHAPTER 1

Down on the River

Although France had suffered a crushing defeat in 1870 and her society had been shocked by the events of the Commune rising, she soon managed to pay off her war indemnity to Germany and continued to expand economically and politically under the Third Republic as she had under the Second Empire. Only the shock of her defeat remained and with other factors gave rise to a pessimism that clashed with the prosperity and sophistication of society.

Maupassant was young, sensitive and idealistic enough to have been one of those deeply shocked and depressed by what he saw during the war and by its outcome. His scepticism had become more profound and he was thus receptive to the even more cynical views of life he was to absorb from Flaubert and the 'Naturalists' in a few years' time. Moreover, at the beginning of his career as a civil servant in the Ministry of the Navy Guy's life seems to have been not only rather monotonous and intellectually restricted but also a lonely one. Occasionally, it is true, he could call on Flaubert or on some of the friends from his Rouen schooldays who now lived in the capital; or he might infrequently visit some acquaintances of his father with whom he shared an apartment at 2 rue de Moncey until in 1876, when he moved into a small flat not far away at 17 rue Clauzel quite close to Places Pigalle and Clichy. But in general his social life in Paris prior to his closer association with Flaubert and his circle does not seem to have been a very busy one. This combination of a monotonous job among mediocre people of largely philistine tastes – a matter he never ceased complaining about later to his literary acquaintances – and of a lonely out-of-hours existence restricted by his meagre earnings seems in fact to have affected the already sensitive, downcast youth quite seriously and given rise to bouts of nervous depression.

On 24 September 1873 he wrote to his mother shortly after spending his annual fortnight's leave at Etretat with her:

'You see I am not slow in writing to you; but I just could not wait any longer before doing so. I feel so lost, so isolated, and so demoralised that I am obliged to come and ask you to send me a few pages I can read. I fear the winter which is approaching, I am all alone and my long, lonely evenings are sometimes quite terrible. I often feel so utterly depressed at particular moments when I find myself alone at my table with the lamp burning in front of me that I do not know to whom to turn for help. I often used to tell myself in such moments during last winter that you must also be experiencing such depressing feelings during the long, cold evenings in December and January. I have resumed my monotonous life here for yet another three months. Léon Fontaine cannot dine with me tonight because he is already dining out; that's a nuisance because we might have been able to have chatted together. . . . I would dearly love to be able to go back a fortnight in time; it's such a short leave; one barely has time to see each other and have a chat; and once it's over, one asks oneself: "How's that come about? I had just about arrived, I had hardly spoken with anyone."'

This same impression of loneliness and depression following the long-awaited fortnight with his mother at Etretat is evoked by his letter to her of 3 September two years later; once more a sense of emotional isolation as well as loneliness is conveyed by the fear expressed of the approaching winter just as it is again implied that the annual fortnight's leave at Etretat in particular is filled with summer warmth and affection:

'It's over once more, dear mama, how short it is! I wait eleven long months for that fortnight which is my sole pleasure in the whole year, and it passes so quickly, so very quickly, that I ask myself today how it is that the fifteen days are over. Is it really possible that I have been to Etretat and spent a fortnight there? It seems as if I have never left the office and I am still looking forward to this leave . . . which alas is over this morning. What has made my leaving even more sad this time is that I feel so afraid for you in that total isolation you are going to find yourself in this winter; I foresee those long evenings you are going to spend by yourself, alone with your dreams of those who are far from you, distressing dreams that will leave you ill and depressed; and very often I too will be alone in my room working during those long winter evenings and I will be imagining you sitting there on your low chair staring into the fire as one does when thinking of elsewhere. Furthermore, despite the terrible heat here and the blue sky, I can already feel the winter in the air. I have taken a look at the Tuileries gardens: the trees have lost their leaves and suddenly I felt there a sense of the ice and snow to come; I thought of the lamps being lit at three in the afternoon, of the rain beating on the windows, of the terrible cold, and all that going on for months and months . . .

'I am wrong to write all this to you as it occurs to me. You are already inclined to look on the dark side without my depressing you further with my sorrows. But it's difficult to laugh when you do not feel like it and I can assure you I do not feel like it at all . . .

'Today seems absolutely endless, far longer than the fortnight I have spent at Etretat.'

Guy relied heavily on his mother not only emotionally but also intellectually; for it was she who was encouraging at this time his first literary efforts and his closer association with Flaubert. Trying to write poems and short stories after a day in the office was, however, no easy matter and Guy soon began to suffer mentally as well as physically from the strain of remaining sufficiently conscientious by day and exerting his talents as a writer by night. The irritations of working under men with little talent and philistine taste and having to spend his time and energy doing monotonous, uninteresting paper-work were almost as hard to bear as the frustrations of his strenuous efforts to be able to concentrate and write during the evening. Writing at the end of a day's work by candlelight in a very small room with only limited heating could not have been very pleasant. It is then not really surprising that at times Guy nearly gave way under the strain, as he explains to Flaubert in July 1878:

'Add to what I have already said that my post at the Ministry is sending me mad, that I cannot work, that my mind is vacant and worn-out by the adding-up that I do from morn till night, that I become only too aware at certain moments of the futility of everything, the unconscious wickedness of Creation, the void that is my future (whatever it may be), and that I feel coming over me an utter indifference for everything and a desire to remain quietly in a corner without any hopes or irritations.

'I live completely alone because other people annoy me and I get annoyed with myself when I cannot work. I find my thoughts mediocre and monotonous and my mind is so incapacitated that I cannot even express them. I am, however, making fewer errors in my adding-up so I cannot be all that stupid . . .'

Guy had always been a quiet, reflective, highly sensitive child despite his apparent robustness and energy and it was not long, therefore, before his nervous, emotional temperament began to break under the combined pressures of his work and his writing; this with the effect of other ailments was to contribute to the undermining of his health. Moreover, the depressing gloom of his letters to his mother and the pessimism of his letter above to Flaubert hint even at this stage at the cynicism and irony of the later writer.

Both Maupassant's boring, sedentary job and his solitary disposition attracted him to boating as a recreation and a means of peaceful escape. The physical satisfaction he obtained from strenuous action was also no doubt a contributory factor to his choice. He had always been keen on boats ever since he first went out in them at Etretat and asked his mother to help him acquire one while at school at Yvetot. It is then natural that he should resume this hobby of his youth as a leisure activity when he later wanted to shake off the dust of his office and take some exercise in rural surroundings that resembled the maritime ones he liked at Etretat but were nearer to Paris. These were on a loop of the Seine some six to eight miles north-west of the capital at Sartrouville, Chatou, Bougival, Bezons and Argenteuil – riverside haunts further and further downstream that were to be increasingly frequented by leisure and pleasure seekers from the ever more industrialised urban areas of the capital and to be depicted as such by the Impressionist painters in search of outdoor scenes of everyday life. It was initially here at Argenteuil that Guy rented a room in a little white house, *Le Petit Matelot*, surrounded by plane trees, not far from the water's edge, which he shared with Léon Fontaine, a friend from his Rouen days who now also worked in Paris. The latter was to describe this accommodation in an interview he gave in *Le Temps* on 7 December 1897:

'When evening came we went back to a riverside inn. The food was mediocre and the beds terrible, but when you are twenty, gaiety and pleasure compensate for everything else and no dinner can be dull with such seasonings.'

As the years passed, Maupassant not only acquired from builders in Rouen and Argenteuil more boats than the *Etretat* and the *Feuille de Rose* he began with – the *Bon Cosaque* named in the Russian writer Turgenev's honour and *Le Frère Jean* probably named after Rabelais' famous friar—but also gathered around him quite a large band of friends. Among these were the aforementioned Léon Fontaine; Robert Pinchon, the son of a master at the Rouen Lycée and later himself head of that city's Library; Albert de Joinville; and probably Henri de Brainne. To stress the adventurous *camaraderie* of the youthful band, they were known among themselves, however, as Petit-Bleu, La Toque, Hadji and Tomahawk, respectively, and Maupassant himself went under the nickname of Joseph Prunier. Not quite all of them were strong rowers or keen boatsmen – Pinchon and Fontaine were both fairly frail sorts – but they all enjoyed the social life of the landing stages and the riverside even if they could not emulate Maupassant's enthusiasm for boating itself nor possess his apparent muscular strength for it.

Often Guy would spend a night or two during the week as well as his weekends at his riverside homes – at first near Argenteuil and later at the Fournaises' inn at Bougival and at the *Poulain* at Bezons – so that he could go sailing in the evening after work and get in some rowing at dawn before taking the train to Paris. He liked these early morning sprees when he rose with the sun, cleaned his skiff, and enjoyed the unusual pleasure of being alone amid awakening Nature and gliding past the frogs and birds on the river still bathed in mist. He enjoyed boating in the peace of the night too and told his mother in a letter of 29 July 1875 of similar evening excursions:

'I row, I swim, I take another swim, and I do some more rowing. The rats and the frogs are so used to seeing me pass by at all hours of the night with my lantern at the front of the boat that they come out to greet me. I handle my large craft like anyone else would handle a skiff and the rowers among my friends who stay at Bougival (seven miles from Bezons) are absolutely staggered when I arrive there around midnight for a glass of rum.'

Such solitary moments appealed to the shy, idealistic artist in him just as his more boisterous activities with his band of young friends satisfied a desire for the company of an audience and having fun, which had evolved during his childhood from the close relationship he had had with his highly imaginative, admiring mother. As a youngster he had terrified his grandmother with the spiders he collected. At a slightly later date he had shocked a rather prim matronly Englishwoman on the beach at Etretat by disguising himself as a young lady and telling her that 'he' was being attended by not only two maids but also a couple of dragoons!

3 Madame Laure de Maupassant

4 Monsieur Gustave de Maupassant

5 Hervé de Maupassant

6　Louis Bouilhet

7　Gustave Flaubert by Nadar

8　Emile Zola

Now he liked to entertain his boating companions with similar pranks and, above all, by telling them about such adventures.

Dressed in white linen trousers, a striped, sleeveless jersey that left his muscular arms bare and clung tight to his sturdy corpulent frame, and wearing a fisherman's straw hat, Maupassant loved recounting tales to his friends, some merely entertaining and parodying the Establishment, others of spicier material, as they glided along the river or sat drinking with some female company at the landing stages. It is said that he founded with his boating companions a 'Society of Crepitus', inspired by Flaubert's references to this mythical god in his novel *La Tentation de Saint-Antoine* which he had just completed; that this all-male group indulged in grandiose orgies – such as that playfully described in Rabelaisian style in one of Guy's letters to Léon Fontaine of 28 August 1873; and instituted a series of initiation tests which in one case caused the death soon after of an initiate who was unfortunately frailer than he appeared.

However, despite Maupassant's grandiose descriptions in his correspondence of the orgiastic atmosphere of their banquets at the riverside – which he calls Aspergopolis – and his sick-humorous letter informing Fontaine of the supposed initiate's death at his office desk, it seems extremely unlikely that the adventures of Guy or his companions were as magnificent or as brutal as he liked to boast they were. Young and temporarily free from the pressures of work, Guy enjoyed playing pranks and boasting to and teasing his friends on the river; he liked to frighten the sedate middle-class citizens he was obliged to tolerate at work and provide some fun for his friends; for example, he once held an alarm clock so suspiciously in the train to Paris as to appear like an anarchist bomber; on other occasions he delighted in amazing his friends by writing phrases such as 'Have I caused some scandals!' in a letter to Fontaine in September 1873. Both Flaubert and Bouilhet had had great fun in making jokes about the primness and fears of the conventional middle classes and the Establishment. They had enjoyed displaying a certain verbal virility by telling spicy stories and there can be little doubt that some of their humour had been absorbed by their receptive young visitor.

That is not to say that Guy merely exaggerated and boasted of the fun he and his band had between Argenteuil and Sartrouville. Both Maupassant himself and some of his companions were later to recall with nostalgia in their writing the wonderful time they had experienced there rowing, drinking, and having fun together with their female acquaintances. One of these was in fact to be the subject of Maupassant's most famous tale of his life on the river, *Mouche*, in which he looked back at the good times he had shared with his five friends and their female companion on the Seine:

'What a gay life I had with my companions! There were five of us, a band of youths now transformed into serious adults. As we were all fairly poor, we had found for ourselves a meeting place in a ghastly pub in Argenteuil that was so terrible that our accommodation consisted of only a single room-cum-dormitory, where I spent the most exciting evenings of my life. We only cared about having fun and rowing, since all but one of us adored this sport. I remember we had such strange adventures, such unusual pranks, invented by these five scoundrels, that no one would believe them now. No one leads such a life any more, even on the Seine, for the imaginative and rebellious spirit which fired us is extinguished in the people of today.'

Similar descriptions of the Seine and its various landing places can be found in a large number of Maupassant's stories including *Yvette, La Femme de Paul, Deux Amis, Sur l'Eau, Souvenir* and *Une Partie de Campagne*; and his impressions of the Grenouillère landing-stage in particular can be compared with the actual painting of it by Renoir and Monet in 1868–9. He writes of it in *Yvette* as follows:

'A constant babble of human voices in the distance, a monotonous rumbling sound indicated they were approaching the haunt of the boating people.

'Suddenly they came upon it. An enormous boat topped with a roof and moored to the river-bank. On it a mass of men and women were sitting drinking or on their feet shouting, singing, dancing, or making capers to the out-of-tune groans of a piano as resonant as a cauldron.

'Tall girls with masses of reddish hair and rouged lips, three-quarters tipsy, moved among the rest displaying the double temptations of their bodies, their buttocks and their breasts, with a seductive look in their eyes and many an obscenity on their lips. Others danced crazily with semi-naked fellows clad in linen trousers and cotton vests and sporting coloured jockey-caps . . .

'From time to time a swimmer standing on the roof dived into the water splashing the people sitting drinking nearby who shouted vociferously at him. Meanwhile a whole fleet of boats glided past on the river. Long, narrow skiffs slid by, propelled by the naked arms of the rowers whose flexed muscles could be seen under their tanned skin. The women on the boats, dressed in blue or red flannel and protected from the fierce sun by a parasol of also a red or blue hue spread over them, sat face down in their seat at the back of the boats as if they were floating over the water in this motionless, dreamy posture.'

In contrast to the dark mood of Guy's days in Paris the atmosphere here was clearly a lively, frivolous, even sensual one and Guy was as energetic and jocular on the river as he was deflated and depressed at work. It seems that Guy devoted some of his energies to sex as well as boating for he contracted some form of syphilis. He who was to write in jest among some verses commenting on the scenes of life on the river painted on the wall of a restaurant at Chatou: '*Garde à la caresse | Des filles qu'on trouve en chemin*' ('Beware of the embraces of girls you find on the wayside') obviously did not heed his own advice nor that of Flaubert in his letters of 25 October 1876 and 15 July 1878. It is unlikely that these were his first sexual encounters – these had probably been in Rouen or with the prostitutes of the Rue Clauzel area in

Paris – but it was here on the river, by Guy's own confession, that he contracted venereal disease.

Because of the pressures of his nervous condition and possibly the strain of the exercise he took to escape from them, the disease he had caught caused him to suffer pains in his stomach and heart. Some of these could, however, have been the early symptoms of a glandular disease that Guy may have inherited from his mother who seems to have been suffering at this time from the nervous effects of hyperthyroidism in the form of a nascent exophthalmic goitre. This seems to have caused her to be subject to moments of great vitality and deep depression and to bouts of pain and debility similar to her son's; similar too were the eye troubles which Guy was to have later and from which Flaubert reported Laure to be suffering in a letter to the Princess Mathilde of 30 October 1878:

'I saw a harrowing sight at Etretat: that of an old childhood friend (Mme de Maupassant) so suffering from her nerves that she can no longer stand the light and is obliged to live in darkness. The light from a lamp makes her cry out. It's really terrible.'

By March 1876 Guy's doctors prescribed him doses of potassium iodide, arsenic, and tincture of colchinum and ordered him to stop smoking and rest. In August 1877, on the orders of Dr Ladreit de la Charrière, he spent a month at Louèche, a spa in Switzerland, to relax and in particular to try to stop more of his hair falling away – a condition that had made Flaubert refer to him jovially as 'Guy the Bald' in a letter of January that year; and in the autumn of 1879 he toured Brittany and the Channel Islands both as a holiday and in order to improve his health. In 1878, after further consultations with eminent specialists like Potain, Love and Abadie, he was asked to take a rather expensive course of steam baths and other medicines to cure what was diagnosed as being a rheumatic rather than a nervous or venereal condition.

Maupassant's doctors, like most of their profession at this time, were, despite the epidemic prevalence of syphilis, still fairly ignorant of the infection's side-effects. In Guy's case diagnosis was even more difficult because of the nervous and glandular complications of his condition. Nevertheless, Guy himself seems to have had no doubt about one of his complaints and wrote to Pinchon in March 1877 with his usual flamboyant humour that he had caught 'the real pox, the pox that Francis I died from' and in consequence felt more defiant of the bourgeois than ever. Despite this jesting diagnosis of Maupassant himself, he continued to consult his doctors and they in their uncertainty carried on prescribing various medicines and baths. None of the treatments had any success; nor did Maupassant relax his physical or his literary efforts. Moreover, apart from his losing some of his hair including his beard which he burnt off by accident, no one really knew how ill he was. He continued to look robust and tanned, and his pains and their often unpleasant treatment were suffered in private. As the pressures of work and writing increased, however, even his healthy appearance and sporting reputation could no longer hide the miseries this poet suffered in his particular garret.

CHAPTER 2

At Home with the Master

If Saturdays were Maupassant's sacrosanct days for escaping to
the river and rowing, his Sunday afternoons were devoted to the
other equally divine activity of his life: literature. For it was then
that the young disciple visited the Master, Flaubert, at his three-
room apartment at 4 Rue Murillo near the Parc Monceau and,
after autumn 1875, at his rooms at 240 Rue du Faubourg Saint
Honoré, near Avenue Hoch, where his niece Caroline and her
husband Ernest Commanville lived. After 1876, having lost many
of his close friends and given over most of his assets to release the
Commanvilles from financial embarrassment, Flaubert only
occasionally visited the capital, so as to apply himself more easily
to the writing of his last works, *Trois Contes* and *Bouvard et
Pécuchet*, in his retreat at Croisset. The years from the end of the
Franco-Prussian war until 1876, however, witnessed the flower-
ing of the unique friendship between the great novelist and the
budding writer that had been germinating almost since before
Guy was even born.

It had its seeds in the close ties that had existed between Laure's
family, the Le Poittevins, and the Flauberts in Rouen and that had
manifested themselves in the intimacy of the Hôtel-Dieu playroom, where Gustave Flaubert and Alfred Le Poittevin had fallen
in love both with literature and each other and Laure and Gustave's sister Caroline had looked up to their brothers' idealistic
partnership with awe and adoration. The early death of Caroline
and the sudden passing of Alfred when he was only thirty-two
years of age shattered this dream-world; Gustave had lost not
only a sister he loved but above all the intimate twin-soul with

whom he had shared his affections, his ideals and his dreams; Laure saw all her hopes for her brother's fame and fortune in literature suddenly founder and only some manuscripts of poems remained out of all the great ideals they had cherished together as children.

It was natural then that, given her own literary inclinations and imaginative personality, Laure should try to stimulate those same inclinations in her son in an emotional effort to replace her brother; nothing would surely be dearer to her than to rear a child who would achieve her ambitions for Alfred. The fact that Guy grew up tall, corpulent and sturdy with gingerish-brown hair and was quite unlike the small, frail, dark-haired Alfred did not deter her; and she never tired of telling her son about the brother she had adored and of instilling into him the idealism of the Hôtel-Dieu playroom.

Her plans for Guy began to succeed when he showed a liking for poetry. Louis Bouilhet was to help in furthering her literary aspirations for her son by taking the lad under his wing and making him known to Flaubert. With Bouilhet's death it was natural that Guy's need for both another father-figure and another teacher would satisfy Flaubert's emotional one for companionship and literary idealism, particularly as Guy was so closely associated with the memory of Alfred and the last years of Bouilhet. In short, Laure's desire to reincarnate Alfred in Guy and thereby realise the ambitions she cherished for her brother in their youth coincided with Flaubert's increasing nostalgia for the past and his frustrated efforts to conserve it in the literary idealism and neo-homosexual relationships that reminded him of it. Hence, while Guy's letters to his Master tend to be taken up with the favours the ambitious younger man sought from his famous elder, Laure and Flaubert's correspondence dwells on their memories of the past with Laure using them to encourage her former childhood friend to help turn Guy into Alfred's successor and with Flaubert recalling them to stress to her the almost paternal fondness of his emotional and literary relationship with Guy. For Maupassant's two guardians at this time his literary career was, then, to a large extent the product of a prolonged childhood dream they had both first experienced long ago and wished, each in their own way, to retain forever.

It is perhaps appropriate that the first letter Laure wrote to Flaubert in January 1872, not long after Guy had paid one of his first calls on the novelist, should be inspired by her enthusiastic support of Flaubert's philippic to the Rouen city council for refusing to allow the construction of a memorial to Bouilhet; her sympathy for Flaubert's cause on behalf of their common friend Bouilhet led her to express nostalgic gratitude too for his sympathetic treatment of Guy in Paris, which was her 'cause':

'Guy is still here at my side and it is together that we read that so eloquently indignant and mocking letter of yours. It provided us with some comforting moments in our isolation where we have few distractions especially of this calibre . . . Moreover we have taken up the habit of speaking of our friends in the evening by the fireside and your name is always coming up, as is only right. Guy has been telling me of his last visit to you in Paris and has passed on to me his impressions of hearing you read the last poems of poor Louis Bouilhet. He assures me you asked his advice on them now and then and he felt very proud and grown-up because of it. I too thank you for what you are doing for him and for what you mean to the boy. I feel I am not alone in remembering the past and those happy days when our two families were virtually one. When I look back and recall those things that are no more, there is a strange shifting of perspective in my eyes. The past comes close to me, so that I feel I can touch it, and the present seems to become pale and fade away. Nothing can make one forget those happy days of our childhood and youth . . .'

Laure continued to remind Flaubert of their common past in other letters such as that of 10 October 1873 in which she agreed to Flaubert's suggestion that they meet and have a long chat on what has happened to them since their childhood:

'I too am often thinking of those that are now dead and I feel their memory becomes more alive, more real and palpable, as one advances in age. The future still offers me hope, however, in my two dear boys; yet the bonds that link us to the people and things of years gone-by are terribly strong. They make us keep turning round to look back. Do you think the dead can no longer love us?... You are right, we really should meet, we have so much to talk about ...'

Although Laure continued to dwell on the past and Flaubert still desired that they meet, her bad health and his hard labours on his novels and financial problems prevented them seeing each other as often as they would have liked. Flaubert visited Etretat in October 1878 and 1879 and Laure accompanied Guy to Croisset on one occasion. Laure's sentimental evocation of the past and vague promise of a meeting did, however, touch upon a sensitive and vulnerable spot in Flaubert's emotional constitution and caused him to promise to do all he could for her son in memory of the past and Alfred Le Poittevin. As the following letter of 30 October 1872 shows, the fact that he was about to complete a novel he had originally discussed with Alfred was probably yet another factor in his willingness to comply with Laure's aspirations for her son:

'Your son has reason to like me for I feel a real affection for him. He is pleasant, well-read, and charming, and then he is your son, the nephew of my poor Alfred.

'The next work I will have printed is going to have at the front the name of your brother, for in my mind *La Tentation de Saint-Antoine* has always been dedicated 'To Alfred Le Poittevin'. I spoke to him about the work some six months before he died. I have now finished with this work that I have laboured over intermittently for some twenty-five years! And since HE is not here, I would have loved to have read my manuscript to you, my dear Laure ...'

And later that year, on 2 December, he again mentions to Laure the trinity of personal factors that inspire him to take care of Guy:

'Write to your son then and tell him to call on me next Sunday. You surely know I will do all I possibly can for your dear Guy because of you, because of Alfred and because he is a charming fellow I like a great deal.'

So delighted was Flaubert to have a chance to aid this young 'reincarnation' of Alfred that he began to treat him and see him as his former companion; he wrote to Laure in February 1873:

'Despite the difference in our ages I look upon him as 'a companion' especially as he reminds me so much of my dear Alfred! I have given myself occasionally quite a fright because of this, particularly at moments when Guy looks down to read out some poems. What a man he was, dear Alfred! He has remained without comparison in my memory. Not a day passes when I do not think of him . . .

That same month Laure sought Flaubert's advice on whether Guy had Alfred's talents as well as a 'similar' appearance; after stressing once more how much Guy enjoyed his Sundays with Flaubert, how much she appreciated such kindness to her son and after mentioning again the Alfred-Guy resemblance, she asked him to let her know:

'. . . if Guy has read you some of his poems and if you feel there is something other than mere facility in them.

'You know how much confidence I have in you; I will believe what you believe and will follow your advice. If you say "yes", we will encourage the lad in this career which he prefers; but if you say "no", we will send him out to make wigs . . . or something like that . . . Speak frankly then to your old friend . . .'

Flaubert the literary idealist was not prepared to give Laure the wholly affirmative answer she really sought; on the other hand, his own particular attachment to her son would have prevented him from giving her a negative opinion. He merely replied that he did not have enough evidence to judge Guy's capabilities, but that the lad, though not as conscientious as he might be, should be encouraged in his literary pursuits:

'... You must encourage your son in his love of poetry because it is a noble passion, because literature can be a great consolation in many misfortunes, and because he may perhaps have talent: who knows? Until now he has not produced enough to allow me to give his horoscope as a poet; anyway, who is allowed to decide another man's future?

'I think our young man is a bit of an idler and only mediocre in his application to literary work. I should like to see him undertake some broader and longer work, even if it were terrible. What he has shown me is as good as anything published by the Parnassian school of poets ... With time he will gain originality, an individual manner of observing and feeling things (for that is everything); as far as the results of his writing and his success as a writer is concerned, what do these things matter! The main thing in this life is to maintain one's soul on some higher level, far away from the slime of the bourgeois and their democratic society. The worship of Art gives one pride. One never has enough of it. That is my moral.

And so Guy continued to visit the great worshipper of pure Art and fanatic for perfect, individual style; and the Master in turn continued to guide Laure's son and Alfred's nephew in the ideal world of Art.

Although Flaubert did read through and correct much of his young visitor's verse and, later, his drama and short stories, his influence on Guy was in effect little more than a prolongation of that already exerted by Bouilhet, as Maupassant himself implies in the preface to his novel *Pierre et Jean* of 1888. Both were Romantics at heart by their love of the exotic, historical, and mystical and by their basic idealism. Like Bouilhet, Flaubert worshipped Art for itself and believed that the conventions and taste of contemporary middle-class society and the introduction of democratic innovations into it were anathema to the sanctity of Art and the considerations of the literary artist. Though essentially conservative in outlook and bourgeois in his style of life, he hated all that was bourgeois and conformist in taste; and though an idealist at heart was deeply pessimistic, even nihilistic, in his disillusioned thoughts on human weaknesses and life's mystery and futility. Indeed it is the failure of virtually all human ideals that lies at the centre of most of his works, whether in a contemporary setting such as in *Madame Bovary* (1857) and *L'Education Sentimentale* (1869) or against an historical background as in *Salammbô* (1862) and *La Tentation de Saint-Antoine* (1872); and that gives rise to the mockery, sometimes harsh but often humorous, of humanity with which he describes his characters' vain hopes and futile actions. He therefore led a fairly hermitic existence at Croisset, devoted to creating an art-form in his writing that was impersonally and objectively realistic in content and the most individually apt and original in expression. His was a life given over to not only vast research both in historical documents and contemporary affairs for the realistic depiction of his novel's locations and characters but above all to finding the most perfect and individual expression to convey his particular view of and insight into what he was describing.

It was by stressing the originality of the literary artist's point of view and individuality of expressing it that Flaubert supplemented what Louis Bouilhet had already taught Guy by his example of the poet's devotion to Art for its own sake and regardless of society and his desire for the most perfect form. Flaubert impressed on Maupassant that the writer had to be conscientious in his documentation, selective and discriminating in his objective use of it, and patient in evolving just the right mode and words of expression. Had he not taken detailed notes of Rouen Cathedral for his depiction of Emma Bovary's rendez-vous there with her lover and read so much about arsenic poisoning that he tasted it in his mouth as he described her desperate suicide? Had he not also visited Tunisia and read through piles of erudite ancient works to describe with accuracy Salammbô's romance with the leader of the mercenaries in revolt in Punic Carthage, and the religious and philosophical temptations of Saint Anthony in the desert? And did he not take years both to accumulate this documentation and also to sift through it and find the precise form and expression for what he was writing, as happened in the case of *La Tentation de Saint-Antoine* and *L'Education Sentimentale* which he revised over quite a long period? It was these aspects of Flaubert the literary artist that Maupassant stressed in his preface to the volume of letters from Flaubert to George Sand, published in 1884. Here, he described both Flaubert's appearance and his manner when he was about to write:

'Writing was for him, therefore, a fearful experience full of agony, fear of possible disasters, and fatigue. He would go and sit at his desk with both a fear of and a keenness for this task that he loved and yet found so tormenting. He would remain sitting there for hours, intent on the formidable task before him like some patient, scrupulous giant set on constructing a pyramid with children's building-bricks.

'Reclining in his oak chair with the high back, his head tucked between his sturdy shoulders, he would keep glancing at his sheet of paper with those blue eyes of his, whose pupils, like tiny black dots, never ceased stirring. A light silk skull-cap, like those worn by priests, crowned the top of his head, and from under it long strands of hair, curling at their tips, trailed over his neck. He wore a vast dressing-gown in brown cloth which completely enveloped him; and his red face, divided by a broad drooping moustache turning grey at its ends, became swollen with the sudden rush of blood into it. His gaze sped along the lines he had already written from under his dark, shadowy eyelashes, sifting through the words, turning the various phrases round, taking a look at the lay-out of the words strung together, attentive to the precise effect they would have like a hunter preparing to lie in wait. Then he would begin to write, slowly, continually stopping and beginning again, crossing something out, adding something, filling up the margins, writing words across the page, covering twenty pages with ink all to complete one page of actual text, and groaning like some-one laboriously sawing wood under the strain of his thoughts and effort.'

No one could fail to be impressed by Flaubert's self-torturing efforts – '*les affres*' or agonies as he himself called them – to exercise to the full and for the most perfect and original effect his choice and mode of expression – the famous '*gueuloir*'. Clearly Maupassant was. Did he not write to another of the young visitors to the Rue Murillo, Gustave Toudouze,[16] on 20 January 1878: 'Your book gave me the greatest pleasure, the only true pleasure, that coming from the style, for which I have and will always have, I hope, my most violent and deepest affection (if I become famous, I hope you will not publish this letter which could considerably harm my relations with women!)'? And did not the realistic objectivity and selectiveness of his approach and his style in his work later prove his admiration of his master?

However, he could not emulate the hermitic devotion and vast documentation of the older man for his work; to begin with, he had neither the time nor the money to do so. Secondly, he had no wish to live outside society and everyday reality, for which he criticised Flaubert in his 1884 preface. When he later began to write, he was probably following Turgenev rather than Flaubert in basing his tales on actual incidents and not on documentary evidence. Flaubert, for his part, was quite aware of young Guy's pursuits and distractions on the river, as his letter to Laure showed in its comments on the lad's 'idleness'. He knew that his would-be disciple's fidelity to literature might not be as constant or scholarly as his own, Bouilhet's or Alfred's. Indeed, when Maupassant complained to Flaubert about the monotony of his life and its pleasures, the latter replied in a letter of 15 August 1878 by reminding his pupil of the ideals of Art and the discipline and objectivity necessary to the writer:

'In short, my dear friend, you seem to be terribly fed-up and your depression pains me because you could use your time more enjoyably. My dear boy, you must understand you need to work more than at present. I begin to suspect you are a bit of a shirker. Far too many women, much too much rowing, and all that exercise! Oh, yes! A civilised man does not need all that locomotion, as our friends the doctors tell us. You were born to write verse, so get on and write some! "Everything else is futile" – beginning with your desire for pleasure and your concern for your health – get that in your head! Besides, your health will be all right if you follow your vocation. This I know from philosophical conviction or a profound understanding of individual hygiene.

'You live and work in a hell-hole, I know, and you have all my sympathy in this regard. But from 5 in the evening until 10 in the morning your time can be devoted to the muse who is still the best mistress. So raise that head of yours, old chap! What's the point of submerging yourself in your depression? You must stand and face yourself like a brave man; that's the way to become one. And let's have more pride in yourself, for heaven's sake! What you lack are principles. For an artist, there's only really one: sacrifice everything to Art. Life must be seen by him as just the means, nothing more, and the first person to be got out of the way is himself.'

Flaubert continued to afford Guy, nevertheless, all the help he could by his advice and his example. More effective in practical terms were, however, the introductions that he could give his young friend into the worlds of both literature and the press. Flaubert's example and advice might, like Bouilhet's before him, encourage Guy in his literary efforts but it would be the Master's virtual patronage of him that would bring him into contact not only with other famous writers but, more important, with editors and publishers.

Maupassant wrote, in the 1884 preface to the Flaubert-George Sand correspondence already mentioned, a fascinating account of a typical Sunday afternoon gathering at Flaubert's. It was here that the young man met some of the older writer's more senior and famous acquaintances such as the Russian novelist Turgenev; Daudet, the Provençal author of the sentimental childhood story *Le Petit Chose* and the humorous epic *Tartarin dans les Alpes*; Goncourt, the refined, aristocratic art historian and one of the first objective painters of low-life in the novel; and Taine, the philosopher on whose precepts of social conditioning such objective realism was based. He also became acquainted with younger men such as the poet Catulle Mendès, the publisher Charpentier, and the group of writers who were shortly to gather around a young, vigorous journalist and novelist from the south, Emile Zola, and call themselves 'Naturalists' after the type of physical realism inherited from Goncourt and Taine that they championed. These last three – Mendès, Charpentier and Zola – were to help Guy further along the road to literary fame under Flaubert's tutelage. Maupassant described the scene in the Rue Murillo as follows:

'Flaubert used to entertain on Sundays from one o'clock until seven in a very simple bachelor apartment on the fifth floor. Its walls were bare and the furnishings extremely modest for he hated the idea of artistic bibelots. As soon as the doorbell announced the arrival of the first visitor he would throw over his work-desk, on which sheets with lots of writing on them lay scattered about, a light red silk cloth that served to contain and conceal these tools of his trade that were as sacred to him as the church vessels would be to a priest. Then, since his housekeeper was out most Sundays, he would go and open the door himself.

'The first to arrive was often Ivan Turgenev whom he hugged like a brother. Taller even than Flaubert, the Russian writer cherished an unusual and deep affection for the French novelist ... Turgenev would sit back in an armchair and speak slowly in a quiet voice that sounded a little weak and hesitant but which gave to what he said an infinite charm and interest. Flaubert would listen to him with a religious awe, staring at the large, white-haired figure of his friend with the vivacious gaze of his big blue eyes, and would reply in his resonant voice that boomed out like a clarion call from beneath his thick Gallic warrior's moustache. Their conversation rarely touched on current affairs and hardly ever departed from matters of literature or literary history. Often Turgenev came along with some works of foreign writers and would translate fluently the poems of Goethe, Pushkin or Swinburne. Lots of other people would gradually arrive. For example, there would be M. Hippolyte Taine with his face hidden behind his spectacles and a timid look about him, bringing with him some historic documents or unknown historic facts as well as the peculiar atmosphere and flavour of his research in the archives and a whole new perspective of the past seen through his philosopher's eye . . .

'Then there was Alphonse Daudet who conveyed in his personality the whole atmosphere of Paris, of a Paris that was lively, vivacious, active and gay. He could conjure up in a few words extremely comic portraits of people and applied to everyone and everything his particular mixture of irony and charm from the south of France . . . His fine-featured, handsome head was covered with jet-black hair which fell down over his shoulders and mingled with his curly beard. His eyes, long and narrow and barely open, had a gaze as black as ink and occasionally a certain vagueness in them due to his short-sightedness. His voice almost sang when he spoke; his gestures were quick; his manner full of movement; in fact, he had all the traits of a native of the south.

'Emile Zola arrived in his turn, panting after ascending five flights of stairs and always accompanied by his faithful follower Paul Alexis. He would sit himself down in an armchair and by glancing at the faces of those present would try to gauge the mood, tone and direction of the conversation. Seated a little on one side with one leg beneath him and holding the ankle of the other in his hand, he would say little and listen attentively . . . He was of medium height and rather plump and had a straightforward, tenacious look about him. His head was like those seen in Italian Renaissance paintings . . . the whole of the lower half of his plump but forceful face was covered in a dark beard cut close to the skin. His eyes, dark and myopic, were penetrating in their scrutiny and often seemed to smile in an ironic way . . .

'There was also the publisher Charpentier. Had it not been for some grey hairs among his long, black locks, he could have been taken for a youth. He was a slim, handsome young man with a slightly pointed chin tinged with blue where he had closely shaved his thick beard. He had just a moustache. He laughed easily in a young man's sceptical way and listened and promised everything to each writer who grabbed him and forced him into a corner to seek so many favours of him. Here too was the charming poet Catulle Mendès, whose pale, delicate face like that of a sensual and seductive Christ was surrounded by the blond aura of his fine hair and beard. An incomparable speaker and a refined, subtle artist who could appreciate the most fleeting nuances in literature, he was particularly liked by Flaubert for the charm of his conversation and the delicacy of his sensibility. Here too came his brother-in-law Emile Bergerat and also José-Maria de Heredia, the famous sonneteer who will be one of the most perfect poets of our age. In too came Huysmans, Hennique, Céard, and many others such as Léon Cladel and Gustave Toudouze.

'Finally, nearly always the last to arrive, there was a fairly tall, slim man whose serious expression, though he did often smile, bore the mark of rank and nobility. He had long hair of a greyish colour as if it had faded, a moustache of a more distinctly white shade, and strange eyes with extraordinarily large pupils. He had a gentlemanly appearance and the refined and finical air of one of ancient aristocratic lineage. He was, one felt, a society man and of the highest society at that. His name was Edmond de Goncourt. He would come in holding in one hand the packet of special tobacco he always carried with him and offering his other hand to his friends.

'The small lounge soon became full and groups of people would pass into the dining-room. It was then that Gustave Flaubert was to be seen. With sweeping gestures with which he seemed to take flight he dashed in a single stride across the apartment from one visitor to another, his long dressing-gown floating after him in his excited bounds like the brown sails of a fishing boat . . . amusing his guests by his impassioned tirades, charming them by his affability, and often astounding them by his prodigious erudition . . .

'Then it would be time for his friends to leave one after the other. He would accompany them to the hallway, where he would chat alone with each for a while, vigorously shaking him by the hand and patting him on the back with a hearty and affectionate laugh.'

No young would-be poet or writer could have had a better initiation into the Parisian literary world of the 1870s; nor a more profitable one. For Catulle Mendès, in his capacity as editor of Henri Roujon's paper *La République des Lettres*, was persuaded by Flaubert to accept two of Maupassant's poems as well as a flattering article on the Master of Croisset for its March, September and October 1876 issues; Charpentier later published Maupassant's work after Flaubert had intervened on his disciple's behalf with the influential Mme Charpentier, whose *salon* he frequented (Flaubert had switched from Michel Lévy *frères*, the publishers of his earlier novels, to Charpentier for the publication of Bouilhet's posthumous verse and his own later works). Zola and his group were to provide Maupassant with the impetus, support and *camaraderie* he needed to make his literary début and stand on his own two feet when Flaubert was no longer there to help him.

Flaubert's aid to Guy extended, moreover, beyond the confines of the Rue Murillo's Sunday gatherings. He wrote in 1876, for example, to a close acquaintance of his old friends the Lapierres, Edgar Raoul-Duval, who was editor of *La Nation*, to see if Guy could be taken on as a literary critic:

'Are all your posts on *La Nation* filled? Have you got a theatre reporter? If not, I would like to offer you a disciple of mine I wholeheartedly recommend: M. Guy de Maupassant, a young poet full of wit and talent . . .'

When Raoul-Duval seemed interested, Guy went to see him with the following letter of introduction dated 1 October 1876:

'Regarding your proposal, allow me to introduce to you my friend *Guy de Maupassant*, of whom M. Lapierre has spoken to you.

'See if you can get him onto the staff of your paper as a literary critic (for reviews of books and theatre shows).

'At the moment there is a dearth of such people in the press. There's a lot to be done in this field.

'The young man I am recommending to you is certainly a poet and I believe a great literary future lies ahead of him. Do give him a chance and see what he can do.'

Although *La Nation* already had a literary critic, Raoul-Duval did manage to insert Maupassant's two articles on Balzac's correspondence and Sainte-Beuve's volume on sixteenth-century literature in the November 1876 and January 1877 issues of the paper. And even if Guy's attachment to *La Nation* was short-lived – they would not publish any further material by him because of the protests of their permanent critic – the incident does show Flaubert's confident and generous promotion of his young visitor. This same assurance and willingness were seen, too, in Flaubert's introduction of the young man to many of the upper-class friends he had made in various sophisticated *salons*, largely following the success of his novel *Salammbô* in 1862. It was through Flaubert that Guy was invited to the *salon* of Mme Brainne and the even more refined and elitist one at 18 rue de Berri or outside Paris at Saint-Gratien of the Princess Mathilde, niece of the first Napoleon, whom the critic Sainte-Beuve called '*Notre Dame de Arts*' because of her lavish entertaining of such literary figures as Gautier, Mérimée, Renan, Goncourt and Taine. It was from Flaubert's contacts in the theatrical world, where he had tried and continued trying to stage his own and Bouilhet's plays, that Guy became acquainted with the actresses Suzanne Lagier, Apollonie Sabatier and Mme Pasca. It was again through

Flaubert's intervention with his friends in high places that Maupassant managed to change his job in 1878.

In August and September 1878 Guy complained to Flaubert about his work at the Naval Ministry: his seven hours in the office prevented him from writing after work because he was so exhausted; and his supervisor was unfavourably disposed towards him and made sure he had no time in office hours to do any writing:

'My boss, no doubt for the sole purpose of being disagreeable to me, has given me the most frightful duty of all those in the office, a job a stupid elderly employee used to do extremely well: it's the preparation of the annual budget and the settlement accounts for the ports: nothing but loads and loads of figures. Furthermore, my desk is close to that of my boss, so it's quite impossible for me to do any of my own work even when I have an hour's break. And that's precisely what he is trying to ensure.'

It is hard to say whether life at the Ministry was quite as bad as Maupassant made out to Flaubert – after all, many other young writers such as Céard, Huysmans and Mirbeau were also or had been civil servants – or whether he painted it in this light so that the celebrated novelist might be coaxed into feeling compassion for his young disciple who was being prevented from writing and take suitable action. Guy did often complain to other people about his job and the dull bureaucrats he was obliged to come in contact with during it; but it would seem that, knowing the pension he received from his father was soon going to lapse, he deliberately heaped up his complaints in his letters to Flaubert in order to force his mentor's hand into seeking promotion for him. Already in February 1878 he had sought to apply, with Flaubert's help, for a vacant librarian's post at the Ecole des Beaux-Arts, but the novelist had been too slow in taking action and Guy had commented sourly to his mother: 'As soon as it's a practical matter, my dear Master has no idea how to handle it.' This unfruitful experience taught Guy that he needed to put more pressure on Flaubert if he was to succeed in future applications.

Apart from continually complaining about his job to Flaubert, Guy therefore urged his mother to contact the novelist and put her emotional kind of pressure on her old schoolfriend; she willingly complied and wrote to him in early 1878:

'Since you call Guy your adopted son, you will forgive me, my dear Gustave, if I want therefore to talk to you about the boy. The fondness for him which you openly declared to him in my presence so touched me that I have taken your declaration quite literally and presumed it now imposes some sort of paternal responsibility on you. I know in fact that you are aware how things are with Guy and that my poor clerk at the Ministry has told you his grievances. You have as always acted excellently in consoling and encouraging him and now he hopes that, thanks to your kind words on his behalf, the time is near when he will be able to leave his prison and say goodbye to that kind official who guards its door.

'If you can, my dear old friend, do something for Guy's future and find him an appropriate position, you will be a thousand times blessed and a thousandfold thanked. But there is no need for me to insist on it with you for I know in advance that both my son and I his mother can count on your support. Had I not been so far away from Paris . . . I would have claimed a small place at your fireside and we would have sat there for a long while chatting together like childhood friends who are delighted to see each other again and still bear affection for each other despite the many years of separation . . .'

Laure's letter – partly ambitious and partly nostalgic – had, as on similar occasions in the past, the desired effect. Moved by Laure's plea as well as by his disciple's complaints, and possibly also touched by references in Guy's later letters to Laure's poor state of health, Flaubert promised to mention the matter to his former fellow law-student and now the Minister of Education, Agénor Bardoux, whom he saw quite often. Apparently, there was a secretarial post that would soon be vacant in the Ministry of Education and the Arts. With his artist's lack of concern for the worldly pursuit of money, Flaubert had forgotten, much to the ambitious Guy's annoyance, to ask about the pay of the proposed posting. He therefore saw Bardoux again to obtain more precise details and gave him a sample of Guy's work. Maupassant thus expected to see himself tranferred before long.

However, although Bardoux discussed a likely posting for Guy with Flaubert in September and again promised to Flaubert's niece Caroline in November 1878 that Guy would definitely be taken on by the Ministry of Education and had only to wait to be summoned by the minister or his chief of staff, Xavier Charmes, nothing happened for several more weeks. This was largely because Bardoux was trying to find an alternative post for the person Maupassant was replacing – also the son of a friend – and on account of the uncertain political situation of Dufaure's government. Furthermore, Guy's boss would not allow him any more time to call on Charmes to remind him of Bardoux's promise, and resented the young man's desire to leave the Naval Ministry. When in December Bardoux proposed that Guy be only loaned to his Ministry while still being considered part of the Naval Ministry's administration, Guy's boss was extremely annoyed and insisted that he stated whether he intended to resign or not. Fearing that he might find himself without a job Guy did not resign but returned to Charmes, who promised he would find him a definite posting, should Bardoux not offer one beforehand. Eventually, after Maupassant had seen Charmes and Bardoux again to discuss the awkwardness of his position and urged them to act, he was moved to the secretariat of the Minister of Education, Religion and the Arts in late December 1878 with an annual salary of just over 3,000 francs – a substantial rise on his previous pay of some 2,000 francs. Pleased and yet still ambitious, he wrote to Flaubert on 26 December:

'I have not yet seen the minister but I often see M. Charmes who has done me many great favours and may still do me some more. I have a position and I need now to establish myself firmly in it and advance quickly while I can ...

'I am treated with great consideration. The principals behave towards me with deference and the clerical supervisors with awe. The rest remain at a distance. My colleagues assume various poses. They find me, I think, too plain and simple. I still find certain things farcical, absolutely farcical, and others that are really sad and pathetic; in short, everyone and everything is as daft and stupid here as everywhere else . . .'

Maupassant was to remain in the Ministry of Education, first under Bardoux and, then, after February 1879 when Dufaure retired, under Jules Ferry, for the next two years – until, in fact, he could support himself by his pen.

While at the Ministry of Education, Religion and the Arts Maupassant did manage to repay Flaubert for his support of him not only by obtaining the marble needed for the monument to Bouilhet, which the novelist was still trying to have built, but also by helping to gain a State pension for his mentor. Early in 1879 the Princess Mathilde and some of Flaubert's other friends such as Taine, Turgenev, Mme Adam, Goncourt, and Zola thought that they could perhaps obtain the Librarianship of the Mazarine Library in Paris for the great writer, whom they knew to be in financial difficulties as a result of his help to his niece and her nearly bankrupt husband. The current occupant of the Librarianship, de Sacy, was said to be dying, and since the post was in the gift of the Ministry of Education, Religion and the Arts, and Flaubert and his friends had influential contacts in the government such as the ministers Bardoux and Gambetta, they thought it would be easy to gain it for him. Foreseeing Flaubert's possible embarrassment, his friends had not kept him informed of all the details and he was obliged to rely in part on Maupassant for news of what was going on in Paris while he was recovering from a fracture at Croisset. He wrote to Guy on 21 February 1879:

'The uncertainty of the position I find myself in with regard to the library matter irritates me terribly. You who are in the minister's secretariat, could you find out from Charmes what's happening?

I only ask to know what's going on. It's my good friend Turge-nev's fault. I should in any case hate to become an official . . . I should like to know, nevertheless, what it's all about so as not to wonder about it any more . . .'

Maupassant informed Flaubert of what was going on and at the latter's suggestion had a meeting with the rival candidate for the post, Frédéric Baudry, after Baudry was elected to the Librarian-ship on 17 February. Not only had Baudry been destined for Sacy's job by the government before Flaubert's name had been mentioned, but the novelist's friends had failed to put his case forcibly enough to Gambetta and had simply relied on Bardoux who had gone from office before the election was made. The whole matter of Flaubert's finances might have remained there, had the newspaper *Le Figaro* not published an article mentioning them in the context of the recently awarded Librarianship at the Mazarine. Flaubert was hurt at this public exposure of his embar-rassing situation and his friends quickly sought to compensate for their failure by obtaining for him a State pension under the title of a supernumerary librarianship at the Mazarine without any duties attached to it. At first, Flaubert disliked the idea and con-sidered the pension as charity. It was left to Maupassant, with whom he had confidentially discussed his material interests and financial position in mid-February 1879, to persuade him that acceptance of a pension from the State was not a humiliation but an honour; Guy wrote to him in March:

'I have just spoken to M. Charmes and we both agree on this. Everyone, I mean everyone, sees the offer of a State pension by the Ministry to a man of letters as a token of esteem. All the kings in the past have granted them to their great men. Why should our government not do the same thing? And why should something hitherto considered as an honour seem to you so painful and humiliating?' [17]

Flaubert accepted Maupassant's reasoning and consented to the pension offered by the new Minister of Education and the Arts, Jules Ferry. The sum of 3,000 francs a year which Ferry granted in July and Flaubert began to draw on in October was not enormous but it went a long way towards releasing Flaubert from anxiety over his finances for the short remainder of his life.

Apart from running odd errands for books, periodicals or news in Paris, the Mazarine Library pension was the one practical favour that Maupassant was able to render to Flaubert in return for all those he had received. To a young man who had barely written anything and needed Flaubert's advice on how to address his reply to the Princess Mathilde's invitation to Saint-Gratien in May 1879, such favours necessarily meant a great deal. Without them he might not have changed his government post. And, more important, without them he would not have had the opportunities and means he subsequently exploited to become the writer his mother and his patron so ardently desired him to be.

CHAPTER 3

The Obscene Idealist

If the first six or seven years of the 1870s saw the development of the friendship between Maupassant and Flaubert, the last years of the decade witnessed the young man's early attempts at writing and his closer contact with the people he had met through Flaubert. This was the period when the idealistic poet and the jocular sporting-man in Maupassant were both reflected in what he produced. The taciturn, melancholy figure with the ruddy face and simple ways of a countryman who had little conversation apart from his praise of Flaubert and his hatred of his colleagues at work and who – as Henri Roujon recorded in the *Grande Revue* in February 1904 – declared he was in no hurry to write and was still learning the art of writing and literary form, was also – as Paul Alexis described him in *Le Journal* on 31 January 1893 – the enthusiastic purveyor of dirty jokes and the author of several obscene works. The admirer of Bouilhet's desire for perfect artistic form and the convert to Flaubert's religion of literary expression took a delight in the sensual and pornographic that made the 'Hermit of Croisset' refer to him in his correspondence as 'Guy the obscene' and 'my young pornographer' and the followers of Zola acclaim him for the audacity of his realism.

The presence of these two elements within the one person is not of course unusual; they were particularly present in the relations between Flaubert and both Alfred Le Poittevin and Louis Bouilhet, as is revealed by their correspondence as well as their writings. It is as if the rebellious and voyeuristic aspects of pornography provided a sort of vulgar relief from the chaste sublimity of their intellectual and artistic idealism; at the same time, its pessimistic, dehumanised view of sexual relationships was a measure of their disillusionment with life. It represented their alienation as artists from the vulgar taste of the world around them which they despised and often revolted against in their work by showing up the less respectable or attractive side of middle-class life and 'shocking the bourgeois' out of their complacent conventionality. Their mutual enjoyment of obscenity gave them, moreover, a sense of power in the intimacy they shared as both men and artists – men who were shy and ascetic by nature in their contact with women, and artists who withdrew to their ivory-towers to mock at life and society from the outside.

There can be little doubt that the young, taciturn poet who often found life lonely and monotonous and preferred his visits to the rue Bihorel and rue Murillo to either school or office enjoyed the obscene and sensual for similar reasons, and profited greatly from the two older men's company in this respect. He obviously relished Bouilhet's erotic verses which owed so much to Catullus, Martial and Rabelais, and the two men's gossip about the local brothels they occasionally frequented. His own youthful libido, which was made all the keener by a certain basic timidity with women and the excessive energy and nervosity of his medical condition (Goncourt was to record in his diary on 9 April 1893 and 11 March 1894 how Guy had once amazed the Russian Boborykine by his sexual athleticism and stamina with a couple of girls from the Folies Bergère), and his sporting life on the river merely served to provide further stimuli to this side of his outlook.

Just as Bouilhet and Flaubert's attitude to writing was to become the foundation of Maupassant's own literary ideals, so the poet's cynical views of life and the novelist's working on his epic deriding the whole of bourgeois life, *Bouvard et Pécuchet*, which he read over with Guy, who provided him with botanical information and with details of the coastal typography from Antifer to Etretat, inspired Maupassant in his revolt against his own existence and the bourgeois. This can be seen in his early verse and in the *Bouvard et Pécuchet* type of mockery of the inadequate, unsuccessful bourgeois in his stories *Dimanches d'un Bourgeois de Paris*. As he became more involved in his writing, so his reaction to the world about him took a more distinct literary form. Besides revolting against conventional taste by showing off his body and muscles on the river and telling dirty jokes to a riotous company at the landing-stages, he could now find relief from his depressions and frustrations and gain a sense of power and intimacy with other writers by pornography. That is not to say that all Maupassant's early writings can be called obscene. When he first began to write, the idealistic and the sensual were kept apart and treated as separate entities, but gradually, with his greater desire for objective realism, the sexual, the sensual and the risqué came more and more to the foreground in his work. Moreover, Maupassant enjoyed his reputation as a sensualist in the *salons* and literary gatherings he frequented and soon saw that this image of himself could be used to further his fame and fortune as a writer.

Before he made his name as a sensual writer, however, Maupassant composed a couple of tales that reflected his liking for the fantastic, horrific and macabre which had already been seen in his accounts of his visits to the English inhabitants of the Chaumière Dolmancé at Etretat. He had written to his mother on 30 October 1874 asking for subjects he could use for stories he might find time to write in the office, and it could well be that she suggested the idea of the horror tale *Le Docteur Héraclius Gloss*, which he mentions to her in a letter of 6 October 1875. The subject of the other story, *La Main d'Ecorché*, was proposed by Maupassant's friend Léon Fontaine, who asked him to write something for his cousin's provincial newssheet, *L'Almanach Lorrain de Pont à Mousson*, where it appeared under Guy's pseudonym Joseph Prunier in 1875. *La Main d'Ecorché* tells how a young man is apparently attacked by the spirit of the hand of an executed criminal which he displays to friends in his apartment, and later becomes insane owing to the incident. *Le Docteur Héraclius Gloss*, for its part, describes an eccentric professor's discovery of an ancient manuscript, which, when deciphered, informs him of the theory of metempsychosis. This so obsesses him that he at one stage believes his pet monkey is his reincarnated double from a previous existence; he is later driven mad by his research into the identity of his earlier incarnation. Long before his novel *Le Horla* and his own tragic fate, these two stories as well as the tale *En Canot* and the poem *Terreur*, also of the mid-1870s, reveal Maupassant's sceptical fears about life and his sensitivity to the supernatural; this was no doubt fostered by his rural concern with superstition and his reading of Poe (translated by Baudelaire in 1856), Hoffmann and Barbey d'Aurevilly, as well as by his family's belief in ghosts and spirits and the rumours he heard of his uncle Alfred's hallucinations. *Le Docteur Héraclius Gloss* reflects, however, not only Maupassant's own insecurity but his interest in the idea of reincarnation and doubles – matters also largely derived from his reading of the authors just mentioned. Maupassant did quite often claim later in life, however, that he had seen his double and was, it is said, curiously fascinated by staring at himself in a mirror or at his reflection on water. His gripping account of Dr Gloss's coming face to face with his double in the shape of his monkey might then have already been more than mere fantasy for him:

'Without making a sound the Doctor reached his study door and went in. Now Heraclius was without doubt a courageous man. He was not afraid of spectres or ghosts; but however fearless a man may be, there exist certain terrors which, like cannon-balls, will pierce the most indomitable courage. The Doctor stood transfixed, livid, horror-stricken, his face haggard and his hair on end, his teeth chattering and his whole body quivering from head to foot in a dreadful way, before the incomprehensible sight which confronted him.

'His lamp was alight on his table and before the fire, with his back turned to the door by which he himself had entered, he saw ... Dr Heraclius Gloss studiously perusing his manuscript. There was no possible doubt. It was certainly himself ... The Doctor realised that if this other self of his were to turn round ... he who was shaking in his skin at that very moment would fall shrivelled before this reproduction of himself. Then . . . the candlestick which he was carrying fell to the floor with a crash that made him jump in terror. His other self turned round sharply and the petrified Doctor recognised – his monkey.' [18]

Apart from these two horror stories, which reveal in the young Maupassant the same taste for mystery, the macabre and the visionary as had appealed to the Romantics of the 1830s and 1840s and still enthralled Flaubert, he also began some of the stories which were later included in *Les Dimanches d'un Bourgeois de Paris* serialised in *Le Gaulois* in 1880 and in the volume *La Maison Tellier* of 1881. These were probably among the subjects suggested by his mother and included *Coco, Coco Frais!*, the story of a man who superstitiously believes that a vendor selling liquorice water brings good luck and leaves part of his will to one; and *Le Donneur d'Eau Bénite*, the tale of a father who becomes a giver of holy water at a church in order to find his son who has been kidnapped by itinerant acrobats; also a chilling account of a misty night spent on the river first called *En Canot* and later renamed *Sur L'Eau*. The first two appeared in *La Mosaïque* in 1866 and the last one in the *Bulletin Français* in March that year. Already the realism drawn from contemporary life and some of the subjects Maupassant used later with great success – bourgeois habits and beliefs, a peasant's private tragedy, life on the river – were present; and so too were his qualities as a simple, yet intriguing and often spine-chilling, narrator.

Maupassant also wrote some plays at this time. Like his early horror stories, they show the Romantic poet in him and reveal the influence of Flaubert and Bouilhet by his interest in the past and history and his love of verse. He had always been keen on drama. Just as in his childhood his mother had helped him and his schoolfriends arrange the production of some playlets at his home in Etretat, so he continued in the mid-1870s to put on and participate in amateur performances of plays with his cousin Louis Le Poittevin and some of their mutual friends.

It was natural then that when Guy began to write and try to become known, he should experiment with drama. His first work in this genre was a one-act comedy of some 300 lines in verse entitled *Une Répétition* which he began in early October 1875. The rehearsal of the title is that of a love scene for a pastoral play-let to be performed in a *salon*; Mme Destournelles tries to get her young partner René to act naturally but he cannot because he is too gauche and his role too stylised. When she eventually tells him to confess his love as if he did love her – which he does – he acts with real passion and astounds Mme Destournelles' husband by the naturalness of his acting! Unfortunately the piece was considered too refined for the Vaudeville theatre to which it had been submitted by his friend Raymond Deslandes and was simply published later in 1879 by Stock in their playlet series 'Saynètes et Monologues'.

Maupassant was not deterred, however, and encouraged by Flaubert's love of history – seen in his completion of *Trois Contes* at this time – and his own liking for the work of Hugo, he began in November 1876 to write in verse an historical drama in three acts set in fourteenth-century Brittany called *La Trahison de la Comtesse de Rhune*. He finished this in early 1877 and altered it considerably during the rest of that year before submitting it to Flaubert and Zola in January 1878. The action of the play takes place in 1341 in the fortress of the Count of Rhune, who has departed to help Charles de Blois of France against the English. The Countess of Rhune loves the English general Sir Gautier Romas, and pretends to her household that her husband has been killed so as to surrender the fortress and herself to Romas when he arrives. Unfortunately, the Count returns and discovers the Countess's plot to kill him with the aid of an innocent young admirer Valderose, to whom she falsely promises herself in return for the deed. He falters, however, in carrying it out and when her treachery to both the Count and Valderose is revealed, the Countess kills herself. Although the plot is melodramatic and quite complex, the 170 lines of verse are impressive and occasionally reminiscent of Corneille. Nevertheless, neither the publisher Perrin nor the actress Sarah Bernhardt to whom Flaubert and Zola had recommended it, were attracted to it. In March 1878, Guy wrote to his mother that he had heard nothing from the Théâtre Français, where he had submitted the play, and he felt sure it was going to be rejected. On 23 April, in a letter to Robert Pinchon, the playwright from Rouen who was his closest comrade apart from Fontaine in his literary as well as his boating adventures, he cursed the theatre and declared he would not write for it again.

But this decision did not last long. By September 1878 Maupassant was correcting – again with Flaubert's help – another verse comedy called *Histoire du Vieux Temps*. This was not so grandiose as his previous effort and would therefore be less demanding and expensive to perform. The producer Ballande had promised Pinchon, whose *Mort de Molière* he had staged for the second centenary of Molière's death in 1873, that he would produce a play by Maupassant at one of the matinée performances he had introduced at his newly opened Troisième Théâtre Français, provided it could be put on without any expense or fees. It was thus there that *Histoire de Vieux Temps*, dedicated to Flaubert's niece, had its *première* at a matinée performance on 19 February 1879. A week later Guy wrote to Flaubert, whose fracture had kept him at Croisset, and who was annoyed with his niece for not representing him at the theatre, that the play had been more successful than he had even hoped. It had been well received by both the newspaper critics and most of the literary celebrities such as the poet Banville, Daudet and Zola, whom Flaubert had advised him to invite for the play's publicity. The play concerns the meeting of an elderly count and an aged countess, who in their youth had fallen in love in a Brittany village during the Terror and only now renew their acquaintance and realise each other's identity. This simple plot was admirably suited by its few characters and lack of scenery to being performed in small theatres and private homes.

Flaubert was particularly keen to see the play performed at the Princess Mathilde's august *salon* in the rue de Berri, with his actress friend Mme Pasca in the role of the countess. He suggested this to the Princess, who promised him in March 1879 she would arrange a performance as soon as he was well enough to return to Paris. She wrote to Maupassant on 15 May that she was seeking Mme Pasca's services that very day and hoped he 'would be pleased to come so as to be present at the performance and above all so as to produce it'.[19] Unfortunately Mme Pasca was too upset by the break in her romance with her lover Ricard to perform. Moreover, both Flaubert and Maupassant were often absent from Paris during the rest of the summer. Thus, although Maupassant dined at the Princess Mathilde's on 20 May, it was not until 10 October that Maupassant again proposed to put on the play at the Princess's, when he wrote to congratulate Mme Pasca on her part in the summer production of the play at the casino in Etretat. Flaubert continued, however, to be absent from Paris while he slaved away at his novel *Bouvard et Pécuchet* at Croisset and it is possible that neither *Histoire du Vieux Temps* nor Maupassant's first dramatic work *Une Répétition*, which the novelist recommended to the Princess in February 1880 after its publication, was actually performed in the aristocratic *salon* with the crimson furnishings and Buonaparte busts.

One play, which contrasted with the idealistic passions in medieval, pastoral, and *salon* settings of his other drama, that was staged, was an obscene farce called *A La Feuille de Rose, Maison Turque*, composed by Maupassant and Robert Pinchon to provide some fun for themselves and their friends. Guy announced the staging of this 'absolutely obscene play' to his mother in March 1875, and told Flaubert's friend Edmond Laporte the following month: 'The solemnity is finally arranged for Monday 19 April. Only men above twenty and women previously deflowered will be allowed in.' Flaubert supervised one of the rehearsals, and there is an amusing account of the tall, corpulent novelist panting up to the painter Leloir's studio on the fifth floor where they took place, shedding his clothes the higher he climbed so that he eventually arrived in his top-hat and shirt-sleeves![20] Despite the steep climb up the stairs Flaubert still exhorted his friend Turgenev, who suffered from gout, to come along and wrote to him the day before the performance: 'Come just the same. I have seen one of the rehearsals. It's really superb. You will enjoy it immensely.'[21] Unfortunately, Turgenev, like many of Maupassant's friends, did not attend this first performance, which was held in the same lofty studio on the Quai Voltaire belonging to Maurice Leloir who had painted the scenery for the piece; Turgenev had gout and Zola, Goncourt, Daudet and many others were still fairly unknown to Maupassant.

A second staging of the farce was therefore arranged and Maupassant wrote to Zola to encourage him to come: 'Remember it is for you, Daudet and Edmond de Goncourt that we have arranged this repeat performance.' The second performance of the farce was given on 15 May 1877 in Georges Becker's studio at 26 rue de la Fleurus, although the rehearsals were again held in Leloir's apartment since Maupassant's one was too small. Flaubert, Turgenev, Goncourt, Zola, and many minor writers and artists attended; Maupassant's father came along and some six or seven women including the actresses Suzanne Lagier and Mme Valtesse were there too. It is claimed that the grave and illustrious Princess Mathilde had also wanted to come along and Flaubert had had to dissuade her from doing so, but this detail seems to have its origins in jest rather than in fact.

The farce is set in the Turkish-styled *salon* of a Paris brothel, reminiscent of that visited by Flaubert's Frédéric Moreau at the end of *L'Education Sentimentale*. It is here that a highly respectable but dim bourgeois mayor and his wife from the provinces arrive, believing it to be a hotel, and where several other curious types come in search of amusement and pleasure. The seduction of the mayor of the significantly named city of Conville by the brothel's inhabitants Raphaële and Fatima and the tricks played on his naïve wife provide plenty of satirical fun and mockery of bourgeois respectability. For example, when the mayor, who has explained his status as that of a pacha to his two apparently Turkish female seducers, is threatened by the brothel's pimp Miché with the severe penalties of Turkish law if he creates too much fuss as he catches sight of his wife with another visitor. Or the scene where the two prostitutes have a dialogue completely at cross purposes with the innocent mayor's wife who takes their expressions literally and does not realise they relate to prostitution and lovemaking positions:

Raphaële: Oh, it's the first time you've been inside a 'house'.
Mme Beauflanquet: A ... Turkish one, yes, Madam.
R: And yet you've knocked about a bit.
Mme B: Oh yes, Madam.
R: You must have tried all sorts of positions, I suppose?
Mme B: Oh no, Monsieur Beauflanquet has never changed his.
R: Who's Beauflanquet? Don't know the ponce.
Mme B: Ponce? That must be a Turkish title.
R: So you know the lotus-flower?
Mme B: Lotus-flower? (aside) why, that must be a Turkish form of jam! (aloud) No, I have never tried it.
Fatima: Fancy, she hasn't heard of the lotus-flower! What then does she know?
R: Perhaps you know what the foetus is like?
Mme B: Why, of course.
R: And you have heard of the mare?
Mme B: Yes!
R: And you know what the cruciform, the crab, sixty-nine, the missionary and the wheelbarrow are ...?
Mme B: Yes, I know all these things. (Aside) What strange questions these Turkish women ask one! And yet I was once told harem women were terribly ignorant ...
R: I quite like this little lady ... Do you like your pussy being caressed?
Mme B: Oh, I love cats ...[22]

Other more obscene fun is provided by: the brothel's scavenger who uses sordid slang and stutters with words like *vider, pitié, cabinets, occupé,* and *désemmerder* while he washes the contraceptives; by the other visitors to the house such as the English-

man who thinks it is a waxworks and has sex with a motionless
Raphaële; a penniless soldier who has to be content with a sample
of Raphaële's urine because he cannot pay for her other services;
a hunchback who needs special treatment; and an impotent man
from Marseilles who is stimulated in his lovemaking efforts by the
brothel's servant-boy, suitably named Cock, who makes a giant
phallus – said to be the stuffed one of the pimp's grandfather! –
erect to a gigantic size! The whole obscene farce ends with the
troupe – Maupassant played Raphaële, Léon Fontaine Mme Beauflanquet, Pinchon most of the visitors, and Maurice Leloir the
servant-boy – dancing in wild abandon round the giant erect
phallus.

Clearly, the play has little dramatic value, but it is interesting
as an example of Maupassant's schoolboyish delight in the
satirical and the obscene. The audience's reaction varied: Flaubert
could not stop laughing and enjoyed the outrageous youthful
liveliness of the whole enterprise; Turgenev was said to be
shocked by the starkness of the simulated female nudity of the
cast; the fairly promiscuous Suzanne Lagier, strangely enough,
apparently left before the end, slamming the door behind her in
protest; and the ageing Edmond de Goncourt wrote rather
sulkily in his diary on 31 May 1877:

'It is a sorry sight, these young man disguised as women with
large, gaping vaginas painted on their tights. You cannot help but
feel a certain kind of repulsion for these play-actors fondling
each other and going through the motions of lovemaking with
each other . . .'

Maupassant himself was so pleased with the farce that he named
one of his boats *Feuille de Rose* after it and so further promoted
his reputation as the obscene Don Juan he liked to appear.

Another example of his pornographic interests is the verse he –
like Bouilhet before him – contributed to the clandestine publication *Le Nouveau Parnasse Satyrique* which was printed in 1881 in
Brussels to avoid censorship in France. While composing his

more serious verse which was published in a collected edition in 1880, Maupassant had also written poems of a more vulgar kind such as *Ma Source, Salut, grosse Putain,* and *La Femme à Barbe.* Despite the cruder, more obscene realism of these works, they owe as little to reality as his other verse. Many aspects of them correspond to the stereotyped pornographic poem and Maupassant's imaginative interest in the perverse and macabre. *Ma Source* is devoted to describing the poet kissing his mistress's private parts:

> *Elle est fermée et l'on y boit*
> *En écartant un peu la mousse*
> *Avec la lèvre, avec le doigt.*
> *Nulle soif ne semble plus douce.*
>
> *Senteur divine! Et ma moustache,*
> *Ainsi qu'un souffle d'encensoir*
> *Jette à mon cerveau jusqu'au soir*
> *Ce fumet où mon cœur s'attache!*

Salut, grosse putain again concentrates on the physical merits of a prostitute's body and the pleasures of fornication:

> *Salut, grosse putain, dont les larges gargouilles*
> *Ont fait éjaculer trois générations!*
> *Et dont la vieille main tripota plus de couilles*
> *Qu'il n'est d'étoiles d'or aux constellations!*
>
> *J'aime tes gros tétons, ton gros cul, ton gros ventre!*
> *Ton nombril au milieu, noir et creux comme un antre*
> *Où s'emmagasina la poussière du temps.*
> *Ta peau moite et gonflée, et qu'on dirait une outre*
> *Que des troupeaux de vits injectèrent de foutre*
> *Dont la viscosité suinte à travers tes flancs!*

It is to be noted not only how vulgar in approach Maupassant is in such a poem but also how impersonal and contemptuous his attitude is towards the woman involved; she is not shown as being human in any way but merely an instrument for the poet's sexual appetite and he mocks at her continued service over many years.

The third poem in the *Nouveau Parnasse Satyrique*, *La Femme à Barbe*, was probably written in late 1875 or early 1876, since Maupassant mentions it in a letter of 11 March 1876 to Robert Pinchon saying it has brought him into closer contact with Suzanne Lagier, who had declared her passionate admiration of him and his work. Guy henceforth visited her quite often and in November 1880 acted as go-between in her libel case against the paper *Le Voltaire*. The poem she liked so much describes its author's meeting with a handsome bearded youth who turned out to be a girl and the curious lovemaking that subsequently took place between them:

> *Elle y vint, elle était habillée en jeune homme!*
> *Un frisson singulier me courut sur la peau;*
> *La fille était fort laide et cet homme assez beau . . .*
>
> *A peine fûmes nous arrivées dans ma chambre,*
> *Elle ouvrit ma culotte et caressa mon membre,*
> *Puis se déshabilla très vite. Deux boutons*
> *D'une chair noire et sèche indiquaient ses tétons.*
>
> *Elle était jaune, maigre, efflanquée et très haute.*
> *Sa carcasse montrait les creux de chaque côté.*
> *Pas de seins, pas de ventre – un homme – avec un trou.*
> *Quand j'aperçus cela je me dressai debout.*
>
> *Mais elle m'étreignit sur sa poitrine nue,*
> *Elle me terrassa d'une force inconnue . . .*
> *Sa grande barbe noire ombrageait sa poitrine;*
> *Son masque grimaçait d'une étrange façon;*
> *Et je crus que j'étais baisé par un garçon!*

Here lovemaking is not merely vulgar and impersonal copulation but also perverse and more than a little macabre with the references to the thinness of her body and the grimacing of her face. It is as if an element of the horror story has crept in here and the poet's mistress has been suddenly turned into a skeleton-like figure of Death and the Devil. The horrific and the obscene, the grotesque and sadistic, were, of course, closely related in Maupassant's imagination; they both in fact represent the dehumanising pessimism and the related insecurity into which his idealism sank, when he was overcome by his depressing view of life and the gloom of his immediate circumstances. It was then that he gave vent to his fears and frustrations through the fantasy world of his imagination.

In the more serious poems published as *Des Vers* by Charpentier on 25 April 1880 there is both a Romantic love of the historic and macabre and a crude realism; the idealism and pessimism of Maupassant's outlook and other early work are juxtaposed and his sensuality is mixed in with his moral themes from myth and legend. Most of the verse included in this volume was written between 1872 and 1878, and many poems had been published separately in various newspapers and periodicals, to which Flaubert usually gave his disciple access; *La Dernière Escapade*, and *Au Bord de l'Eau* had, for example, first appeared in Mendès' *République des Lettres* in 1876. It had been Flaubert too who had persuaded Charpentier to publish the collected poems together with *Histoire du Vieux Temps* and who, at Maupassant's impatient and repeated requests, kept on prodding the publisher to hasten the appearance of the work. Indeed, on one occasion Flaubert wrote forceful letters on the matter to both Charpentier and his wife, who exercised great power over her husband, but only to discover that the publisher was kept to his bed by influenza and that Mme Charpentier was similarly installed and about to give birth! The volume's dedication to Flaubert was thus more than justified when it eventually appeared in view of his promotion of its contents for over two years.

The mood of the poet of *Des Vers* is one of disillusioned idealism; Romantic ideals in love are destroyed by a cruel and crudely sensual reality. In *Fin d'Amour* the end of a romance is described; the girl still remains full of hope for their love's continuance, but the lad insists that their romance is over and love is but ephemeral; and in *Dernière Escapade* two lovers, now elderly, return to the place of their first passion, but only to die from the cold and their vain efforts to rekindle their desires. A similar theme is embodied in *Un Coup de Soleil* where a lover flies off ecstatically to heaven with his loved-one in his arms only to discover she has died in his embrace; and in *Vénus Rustique*, where the human incarnation of the goddess of Beauty and Love is slain by her ugly, coarse suitor, the Devil, in the guise of a solitary shepherd. Since love does not last and brings disillusionment and anguish – a feeling anticipated by the poet in *Découverte* as he gazes at a young blonde girl he likes – the only real pleasure to be had is the carnal, physical one; all the rest is really idealistic dreaming, that leads to disenchantment and is unsatisfying in this life on earth.

This point is forcefully made in *Une Conquête*: the poet sees an attractive girl among a boating party on the river and idealistically falls in love with her, seeing her as his gentle, beautiful goddess; unfortunately, when he overcomes his timidity and makes her acquaintance, he is disillusioned to find she is an ordinary prostitute; despite his deception, however, he makes her his mistress simply because the physical woman rather than the ideal he sought in his dreams is the only one available. Maupassant expands on this theme in *Désirs*; he would like to have lots of short affairs with different mistresses so that his idealistic hopes might never be totally crushed by the inevitable disillusionment resulting from each affair:

> *Je voudrais que pour moi nulle ne restât sage,*
> *Choisir l'une aujourd'hui, prendre l'autre demain;*
> *Car j'aimerais cueillir l'amour sur mon passage,*
> *Comme on cueille des fruits en étendant la main.*
>
> *Puis, sans un trouble au cœur, sans un regret mordant,*
> *Partir d'un pied léger vers une autre chimère.*
> *– Il faut dans ces fruits-là ne mettre que la dent:*
> *On trouverait au fond une saveur amère.*[23]

It is the celebration of these brief moments of great physical pleasure such as that of Venus and her suitors in *Vénus Rustique*, of the lad and his mistress, a laundry-girl, in *Au Bord de l'Eau*, and of the lovers caressing in the moonlight silhouetted against a wall in *Le Mur* that give the volume its more pornographic slant. And it was this element that caused Maupassant quite a lot of trouble when he tried to get particular poems into print.

Maupassant already knew when he was writing *Vénus Rustique* that it might not be suitable for publication in the press, but he carried on with it trying not to be 'too carnal', as he wrote to his mother on 21 March 1878. By the beginning of the following month he had nearly finished it and told Laure: 'As far as my *Vénus Rustique* is concerned, I am very pleased with it; I have got, I think, the effect I wanted, but by God it's strong, very strong stuff. All right for a newspaper, not for a magazine.' On 23 April he was so pleased with the poem, which he was on the point of completing, that he confessed to Pinchon: 'I've virtually finished my *Venus* and I'd love to screw her!' When in November 1879 Guy submitted the poem to Flaubert, he too praised it highly, no doubt enjoying the 'carnal' element in it, and forwarded it with an accompanying letter to Mme Juliette Adam, friend of the Goncourt and Daudet and editor of the recently founded *Nouvelle Revue*. Given the following lines in the poem about Venus's fate on earth and Mme Adam's necessary concern for middle-class taste particularly in the early days of her review, it is not surprising that she returned Maupassant's manuscript to him in early December:

> *Mais un corps tout à coup s'abattit sur son corps;*
> *Des lèvres qui brûlaient tombèrent sur sa bouche;*
> *Et, dans l'épais gazon, moelleux comme une couche,*
> *Deux bras d'homme crispés lièrent ses efforts.*
> *Un autre le tenait couché sous son genou . . .*
> *Puis soudain un nouveau choc étendit cet homme*
> *Tout du long sur le sol, comme un bœuf qu'on assomme.*
> *Mais lui-même roula, la face martelée*
> *Par un poing furieux. A travers les halliers*

On entendait venir des pas multipliés.
Alors ce fut dans l'ombre une opaque mêlée,
Un tas d'hommes en rut luttant, comme des cerfs
Lorsque la blonde biche a fait bramer les mâles.[24]

Refused by Mme Adam, the poem appeared in *Le Gaulois* newspaper.

The other poem which caused Maupassant quite a lot of trouble was *Au Bord de l'Eau*. This piece, about a young man's passion for a girl washing clothes by a stream and the death that the couple suffer from too much lovemaking, was commended by Flaubert and passed on by him to Catulle Mendès the poet and editor of the *République des Lettres*, where it appeared on 20 March 1876. Even at this time Maupassant realised that his poem was fairly 'strong stuff' as he mentioned to Pinchon in March 1876, and feared that, though Mendès had read the poem to one of the literary gatherings at his home and his fellow poets had praised it, the other editors of the *République des Lettres* might have rejected it on moral grounds. This time, however, the references in the piece to the 'roundness of the girl's rump and the curves of her breasts' and the description of the lover's caressing of her breasts, the erotic swaying of these as she did her washing, and the avid kissing of the couple, were allowed after some omissions and the poem's theme of mortal, passionate fornication was passed over.

When, however, Maupassant submitted the same poem to the *Revue Moderne et Naturaliste* of Harry Alis, where it appeared in full in the 1 November 1879 issue, he was charged with 'an outrage against decency and public morality' and in January 1880 ordered to appear before a magistrate. The reason for this was that the local magistrature and notables at Etampes, where the review was printed, were seeking an opportunity to suppress Alis and his paper. Enterprising and adventurous, Alis, whose real name was Hippolyte Percher, had launched the *Revue* in December 1878 to promote realist literature and bring about 'the destruction of the conventional in the arts and literature'. He had also taken over another paper owned by his patron Auguste Allien, *L'Abeille*, with a similar revolutionary purpose. From being a news-sheet of local and largely legal matters *L'Abeille* became a vehicle for contemporary literature and criticism of the Church and the bourgeois. It was to get their own back on the stinging comments of *L'Abeille* that the authorities at Etampes tried to find fault and bring charges against the *Revue*.

Maupassant's poem provided a perfect opportunity for this. However, when Alis explained that *Au Bord de l'Eau*, re-titled *Une Fille* in the *Revue*, had already appeared years earlier in the *République des Lettres*, the local magistrate said no more. They might have stifled the whole matter, had not Alis and his friend Aurélien Scholl used the issue of the poem to start a campaign against the magistrate's charges and censorship in general by their articles in the newspaper *L'Evénement* in February 1880. Scholl even quoted in his article of 19 February a letter Maupassant had sent him mentioning that it was *Au Bord de l'Eau* which Flaubert had shown the Minister of the Arts, Bardoux, to obtain him his new posting and saying how surprised he was now to find himself being prosecuted for a poem that had earned him his job at the Ministry! This same point was to be made by Flaubert in a letter to his disciple, which he sent on 16 February to the newspaper *Gaulois* where it appeared five days later. The Etampes magistrates had been goaded into taking further action against Alis and Maupassant, and Guy had begun to fear for his job; it was this that had made him write to Flaubert, who had himself faced a similar charge in 1857 with *Madame Bovary*. Once more Guy was obliged to exploit his filial relationship with Flaubert in order to extricate himself from an awkward situation. His letter of early February 1880 was accordingly both flattering and forceful in its mixture of sentiment and calculation:

'I would need a letter from you to me that was fairly lengthy, reassuring, paternal and philosophical with high ideas on the moral value of censorship trials that relate you to other top writers when you are condemned or occasionally allow you to be decorated when you are acquitted. What is needed is your opinion of my poem *Au Bord de l'Eau* from the literary and also the moral point of view (the morality of an artist is Beauty) and a show of your affection for me. My lawyer, a friend of mine, has given me this advice, which I think is excellent . . . Your exceptional, unique status as a man of genius prosecuted for a masterpiece in the past, acquitted after a struggle, then glorified and eventually classed as an impeccable artist and accepted as such by all schools of literature would be so influential that my lawyer thinks the whole matter would be immediately suppressed after your letter had appeared. The letter must appear at once so that it looks like a message of consolation sent by the Master to his Disciple . . . Please excuse me once again, my dear Master, for imposing such a heavy burden on you, but what can I do? I am alone in defending myself with my very livelihood threatened, without any support from my family or my relations and unable to offer vast sums of money to a well-known lawyer. I stand by my poem and will not abandon it: literature comes before everything else . . .'

It was this fear for his disciple's job that prompted Flaubert to stop his writing on his novel and compose a four-page letter for Guy and several others to well-placed friends. At the same time he advised Guy to go and see certain influential people to gain their support, and urged his friend Raoul-Duval, who had published Maupassant's articles in *La Nation*, to persuade the magistrates to halt legal proceedings against the young poet. Flaubert's letter published in *Le Gaulois* by Raoul-Duval stressed that the poem had already appeared once in Paris with impunity and been favourably considered by Bardoux and that 'what is Beautiful is moral' in Art. It provoked a wave of criticism of the magistrates' action in the press and together with the other steps he had taken succeeded in rescuing his young disciple.

Despite the publicity Maupassant gained from such a situation, *Des Vers* would have normally attracted little attention when they eventually appeared; but that very same month, just a week earlier, his story *Boule de Suif* had been published with others by Zola and his circle and instantly acclaimed as a gem of its kind; *Des Vers* benefited from such acclaim and received favourable notices in the press. Nevertheless, it was not as a Romantic poet and dramatist, at times morally idealistic and at others outrageously crude, but as a 'Naturalist' short-story writer that Maupassant was to achieve fame in April 1880. The disciple of Flaubert was, in consequence, to become known as a follower of Zola; and visits to Croisset were soon to be replaced by others to Médan.

CHAPTER 4

Under the Wing of 'Naturalism'

In April 1875 Maupassant received a novel called *La Faute de l'Abbé Mouret* from a young man ten years his senior whom he had met at Flaubert's the previous year. The name of the author was Emile Zola – a name that for the next twenty years or more was to dominate French literature and that at the turn of the century was to become a household word in the controversy of the Dreyfus case. Though himself steeped in the flamboyance and emotional extravagance of the Romantics, which can be seen in the great historical and exotic novels and poetry of Hugo, the adventurous melodramas of Musset, and the neo-mystical outpourings of Nerval and Lamartine's verse, Zola sought to break away from such highly imaginative literature and, following the trend towards everyday realism in the works of Balzac, Duranty, Flaubert and the Goncourt, to write about the contemporary world. What Balzac had done in describing the evolving commercial society of the 1830s and 1840s, Zola wanted to do for the more industrialised and speculative world of the 1860s and 1870s. Moreover, whereas Balzac had largely depicted members of the rising middle class in the commercial struggle for survival that took place in individual apartments and offices, Zola was intent also on showing the life and sufferings of the working class and their massive exploitation by business and industry.

A start in this direction had already been made by the Goncourt brothers, who, as the authors of several historical monographs and as art critics, were fascinated by the aesthetic features and sociological value of aspects of working-class life and produced in 1865 a novel entitled *Germinie Lacerteux* on the disastrous private life of a maid who takes to prostitution and drink. To obtain maximum veracity in their account the Goncourt had like Flaubert documented themselves on the locations and habits of the characters they were describing. They had gone with their notebooks to low dance-halls, prisons and hospitals and acquired details of the lives and slang of workers and prostitutes. To convey the real-life scenes of their novels with greater sensitivity and immediacy they had, like the Impressionist painters, made on-the-spot sketches of sites for their novels' action. And with the detached curiosity of the art critic and social historian they had studied the facts about Germinie Lacerteux's nymphomania and alcoholism from numerous medical treatises.

Zola similarly relied on documentation taken *in situ* and on medical books for the series of novels that were going to make up his *Social and Natural History of the Rougon-Macquart Family under the Second Empire*, which he launched in 1871. As the title suggests, this was to be the history of the descendants of Adélaïde Fouque's marriages to a gardener named Rougon and a smuggler called Macquart. It tells of their exploits in Paris during the years prior to the 1870 War, and of the taint which many of them inherited from the marriage of this hysterical, cataleptic ancestor with Macquart. This initial theoretical emphasis on heredity and genealogical and environmental factors in Zola's novels derived from his reading of the philosopher Hippolyte Taine as well as a host of treatises on physiology and psychological abnormalities. These works fired Zola's imagination with the idea that by basing his series of novels on an exact genealogical foundation and tracing his characters' lives with the accuracy afforded by medical theories and details of their environment, the novelist could emulate the scientist in his experiments. As well as providing a picture of life in Paris, particularly that of the proletariat, such as the Impressionist painters Manet, Degas, and Pissaro were already producing in their art, Zola also saw himself as a literary scientist whose work would describe both the hereditary and physiological mechanics and the environmental conditions governing human behaviour.

Before embarking on his *Rougon-Macquart* series, Zola had already tried out his pseudo-scientific method in two separate novels, *Thérèse Raquin* of 1867 and *Madeleine Férat* of 1868. In the preface to the first of them he had declared himself to be as detached and accurate in motivating his characters' sexual desires and consequent criminal deeds as the surgeon treating his patient. Moral and spiritual considerations were no longer taken into account; only the depiction of physical phenomena and the diagnosis of the physiological mattered; the novel's accuracy and detachment in dealing with these would turn it into an apparatus capable of making experimental investigations into social conditions.

Zola saw himself as bringing science to literature in an age that had witnessed the coming of the industrial revolution and the railways and a consequent interest in scientific theory and experimentation. And using 'science' as his tool and weapon, he continued that virtual tradition among later nineteenth-century writers of 'shocking' the philistine and stolidly conventional bourgeois by showing them aspects of low life they had not read about before with a new pseudo-scientific accuracy and forcefulness. This was the very essence of what came to be termed 'Naturalism'. Although the scientific theories of Zola were soon lost amid the epic descriptive qualities of his works, his emphasis on science as well as on sexual instincts and corrupting environments ensured that 'Naturalism' appealed to the younger generation of writers of the 1870s, including Maupassant. It was both novel and modern and in its concern with the social phenomena and problems of city life reflected to some extent the fascination the newly industrialised city and its working population had for Zola and the young writers and artists of the day. For most of them came, like Maupassant, from the provinces and countryside and were still only partly integrated into urban life.

It was natural, anyway, that the young author of *A La Feuille de Rose* and *Vénus Rustique* should be attracted to Zola's novels, for in them he found a constant and stimulating sensuality and lustiness that responded to his own libido and delight in pornography. In *Thérèse Raquin* the adulterous lovers act like wild beasts in their ravenous lust for each other, motivated by the hitherto suppressed sexual instincts within them; in *La Curée* the success in Paris of one of the Rougon-Macquarts, Aristide Saccard, and the corrupting influence of the wealth he gains from his speculations are reflected in the increasing nudity and perverse sexuality of his wife Renée, epitomised by her making love with her effeminate stepson Maxime in the seething hothouse; in *Le Ventre de Paris* the Central Markets of Paris become a symbol of sexual as well as commercial activity by Zola's sensuous descriptions of both the piles of goods and the people buying them; and in *La Faute de l'Abbé Mouret* a sort of Adam and Eve idyll is evoked when a young priest, suffering from amnesia, is sent into the country to recover and falls in love with his host's innocent daughter Albine in the lush walled garden of Le Paradou – a theme which allows Zola to uphold the pagan rites of Nature and the countryside in contrast to the bonds of Christianity by his descriptions of the young lovers' fornication and the orgies taking place within Nature itself. Little wonder that when Maupassant received a complimentary copy of this work in 1875 he replied to Zola:

'I have just finished reading your book and, if my opinion is of value, I can assure you that I found it quite beautiful and extraordinarily powerful; I am terribly enthusiastic about it and few works have made such a forceful impression on me. I notice, moreover, with real pleasure that the press which has so far been hostile towards you have now at last been obliged to give up and admire you.

'As for my personal views, I felt a strange sensation right through the book; at the same time as I imagined what you were describing, I could also breathe it in; a sort of strong, persistent odour came up from each page; you make the reader feel so forcefully the earth, the trees, the fermentation and the germinating

going on and you thrust him into such a vast orgy of copulation that he is overwhelmed; and I must admit that when I had
finished reading the book and had breathed in one after the other
"the pungent aromas of a woman bathed in the sweat of sleep . . .
of this parched countryside lying sprawled out in the sun like
some passionate yet sterile female", the Eve of Paradou "who
smelt like the scent of a thousand flowers", the perfumes of the
garden itself – "a nuptial haven filled with creatures in each
other's arms" – and even the *magnificent* Father Archangias who
"stank like an old goat always thirsting for more", I realised that
your book had absolutely intoxicated me and also got me really
excited!'

But it was not *La Faute de l'Abbé Mouret* that brought fame
and success to Zola and created a group of followers around him.
Such popularity or, better, notoriety came a year later, in late 1876
and early 1877, when his novel solely devoted to the working
class, *L'Assommoir*, was published first in serial-form and then in
hardback. Even while it was being serialised complaints were
made that Zola's depiction of the working class was too vulgar
and severe and he was obliged to take the novel from the liberal
paper *Le Bien Public*, which banned further publication of it, to
the more literary-minded *République des Lettres* of his friend
Catulle Mendès, where the last instalments of the work appeared.
When, however, the hardback version of the novel came out
without any of the cuts which had been imposed by the newspaper editors for fear of shocking their readers, there were
protests from all sides that the novel was vile and pornographic
and an insult to the proletariat.

Virtually every newspaper and notable critic condemned the
work. The story of Gervaise Macquart's rise and fall as a laun-
dress in a Paris backstreet, of her marriage with Coupeau, who
dies of *delirium tremens* and drink, and with Lantier, who initially
abandons her and then returns only to live on her meagre earnings
before taking up with another woman, and the scenes of Gervaise
and another washerwoman fighting in the washhouse, of Cou-

peau's drunkenness, and the sexual violence that ensues as well as the use of working-class slang were clearly too much for a reading public used to the romance and exoticism of Hugo and the idyllicism of George Sand.

A battle thereupon began between the more conservative critics with a taste for the Romantic 'idealistic' literature of the past and the younger and more progressive supporters of the new realism or 'Naturalism' with its pseudo-scientific stress on the physical aspects of Man in his environment. While the battle raged between Zola and his friends and most of the press and literary critics of the period, his sales continued, however, to rise. Some thirty-eight printings of *L'Assommoir* were made in 1877 alone. By the time Zola's other notorious novel *Nana*, which described the powerful role of the prostitute Anna Coupeau, daughter of Gervaise, as a devourer of men during the Second Empire, appeared in March 1880, well over eighty editions of *L'Assommoir* had been sold. As the articles and pamphlets of both sides continued to assert their points of view with equal vehemence, Zola grew richer. In 1878 he was able to move from his Batignolles flat to a comfortable but small apartment in the Rue de Boulogne in Paris as well as to acquire a country home at Médan near Triel on the outskirts of the capital.

Zola had by his journalism, his novels and the dramatisations of his works made 'Naturalism' a household word in literary circles; sex, low-life, medical abnormalities and slang had become the order of the day for the new generation of writers; and as a result of the battle waged and the triumph eventually gained, Zola had become the leader of a small circle of writers who were later to be referred to as the 'Médan Group'. Among them was Maupassant who, as has been seen, was at this time gradually abandoning the Romantic interests in history and idealism of his early drama for the contemporary realism and crude cynicism of *Des Vers*.

Maupassant had met some members of the Group prior to their association around Zola at Flaubert's and Catulle Mendès's social gatherings in the Rue Murillo and Rue de Bruxelles as well as at

the *République des Lettres*, to which some of them, like himself,
occasionally contributed. Paul Alexis had known Zola ever since
his arrival in Paris from Provence in 1869. He had become his
most intimate friend as well as the one who most resembled him
in looks – both of them being tall and plumpish, with oval faces,
dark, closely cut hair, and wearing pince-nez, but with the simple
difference that Zola had a full beard and Alexis a bushy moustache
– and had attended Flaubert's Sunday afternoons with Zola for
some time. Although a zealous supporter of both Zola and the
Impressionist painters and an enthusiast for literature and the
theatre, Alexis found it extremely difficult to write and apart from
a number of short plays and stories written in what he believed to
be the 'Naturalist' manner, his chief claims to fame were his
biography of Zola of 1881 and his satirical articles in the press
later published under the pen-name of Trublot. Partly because of
their common origins in Provence and largely because of Zola's
close friendship with him despite his poor literary output, Alexis
was devoted to the founder of Naturalism and remained so long
after Zola's popularity had declined. He was a lively even if
temperamental person who led a somewhat bohemian existence
with his mistress and young child and whose writings contain a
mixture of disillusioned idealism and salaciousness similar to
Maupassant's.

Another member of the Group, whom Maupassant had
probably got to know at the *République des Lettres*, was Léon
Hennique, who had published an epic melodrama on a seventeenth-century Protestant fanatic *Les Hauts Faits de Monsieur
Ponthau* in 1876. Born in Guadaloupe of a military family,
Hennique had been a law student at the Sorbonne before turning
to writing poems and plays. It was as a playwright rather than as
a poet or novelist that he was to make his name and that he first
attracted the attention of Mendès, who introduced him to the
literary world. Although this small, slim man with dark, wavy
hair and a rather military air with his 'cavalier' moustache and
beard and penetrating look behind his pince-nez joined the
'Naturalists', his works were from the start anything but

'Naturalistic'; they seem to owe more to Balzac and Flaubert in their exaggerated characterisation and social criticism than to Zola.

The other two members of the Group were Henry Céard and Joris-Karl Huysmans, who had been acquainted with each other through a mutual friend just after the events of 1870–1. Céard had at first been a medical student but had soon left this career to become a journalist on the paper *Les Droits de l'Homme* prior to joining the bureaucracy of the Ministry of War. Endowed with a clinical mind and an analytical literary talent, Céard is usually considered the theoretical brain behind the 'Naturalist' movement. He was also, apart from Alexis, the person who provided much of the documentation for Zola's novels and often stood in for him at theatre shows the novelist was supposed to be attending as drama critic for the paper *Le Voltaire*. Like Alexis, Céard was not a prolific writer and produced only two long novels in his entire career; the first of them, *Une Belle Journée* of 1881, is, however, a masterpiece of psychological analysis and critical irony. Although it owes much to Flaubert, it was considered supremely 'Naturalistic' in its simple plot and analysis of a couple who go off to the country one day to commit adultery but are prevented from doing so and spend a wet, monotonous and disillusioning afternoon together in an inn doing nothing in particular instead.

The remaining member of the Group, Huysmans, with his bushy hair and beard and dreamy gaze, provides quite a contrast with the clean-shaven look and sharp eyes of Céard. A civil servant in the Ministry of the Interior, and of Dutch origins, Huysmans had, unlike most of the other Naturalists, published quite a few works before joining the Group. An ardent supporter of Zola's 'Naturalism', Huysmans had not only written a pamphlet defending Zola's *L'Assommoir* but also published a collection of prose poems and a novel on 'Naturalist' lines – *Le Drageoir à Epices*, in 1874 and *Marthe*, the story of a prostitute, in 1876. More such novels were to follow – *Les Sœurs Vatard* in 1879, set in the bookbinding trade, *Croquis Parisiens* in 1880 on life in the capital's streets and bars, *En Ménage* in 1881 and *A Vau l'Eau* in 1882 – all well-documented and vigorously written with the appropriate realism and slang. Although Huysmans had sent Flaubert and Zola copies of his novel *Marthe*, it was Céard who introduced its author to Zola on his second visit to the Rue de Boulogne.

These then were the main members of the Group which gathered round Zola after 1877, though occasional visitors such as the young Swiss novelist Edouard Rod, the Provençal painter Numa Coste, the playwright and critic Octave Mirbeau, the story writer Gabriel Thyébaut, and Zola's friend Marius Roux also attended many of the circle's meetings. Usually the group and any other visitors to Zola's house would dine together on Thursday evenings in the back of a small restaurant owned by Mme Machini, which Hennique had discovered at the corner of Rue Coustou and Rue Puget in Montmartre, prior to going on to Zola in the Rue de Boulogne.

Occasiorally, however, they went on to the house of one of the group, including Maupassant's flat in Rue Clauzel, which was so small that the chairs for such gatherings had to be stored in a cupboard. On such occasions Guy would often invite in prostitutes who were his neighbours to share in and liven up their merriment. As Huysmans related in the *Revue Encyclopédique* on 1 August 1893, the food and wine, like the conversation, were often fairly crude but the atmosphere was youthful and lively, and Maupassant, above all, was, as always in company, the life and soul of the party. After 1878 these dinners came to be called the 'Dîners du Bœuf Nature' after the type of food that was served and the kind of atmosphere that prevailed. From Mme Machini's they had by then moved to Procope's on the Left Bank and Joseph's near St Lazare and the company included not only the followers of Zola but also the novelist Paul Bourget, the poet François Coppée, and many of the Impressionist painters such as Cézanne and Manet. From these 'dinners' the circle of friends would move on to Zola's plush apartment with its varied furnishings of Flemish tapestries, Oriental vases, and antique furniture in assorted styles. Madame Alexandrine Zola would serve her husband's guests with plenty of drink and snacks and the young men would go on discussing literary and other matters with the slightly senior, famous novelist well into the night.

One of the more significant gatherings of Zola's young followers was the dinner offered to not only Zola but also the older precursors of the new 'Naturalism', Edmond de Goncourt, Flaubert, and his friend Turgenev at the Restaurant Trapp, just beside Paris's St Lazare station on 16 April 1877. The idea of such a dinner was not in itself very original; it was common practice among literary and artistic figures to meet and chat over a meal or drink either at their own homes or studios or at particular restaurants. In the 1860s Flaubert, Sainte-Beuve, Taine and other writers like Renan and Goncourt had regular dinners together at the Magny Restaurant, and beginning in late 1874 Flaubert, Daudet, Goncourt, Turgenev and Zola had met together each month at the Café Riche and elsewhere for a dinner they called the 'Dinner of the Hissed Authors' since they had all had plays performed which had been hissed off the stage.

The young followers of Zola also often met at many literary or artistic gatherings other than purely 'Naturalist' ones. Those at Flaubert's and Catulle Mendès' have been already mentioned. Others of a less formal or significant nature were given the names of the cafés and bars where the participants met: the *Lion d'Or*, the *Bons Cosaques*, the *Chat Noir*, etc. What made the dinner at Trapp's in April 1877 so important was that it was held by the young 'Naturalists' in honour of the movement's precursors and therefore was seen as the consolidation of the new 'school' following Zola's triumph with *L'Assommoir* earlier that year. Edmond de Goncourt recorded in his diary that evening:

'This evening Huysmans, Céard, Hennique, Paul Alexis, Octave Mirbeau, Guy de Maupassant – all the young men of Realism or Naturalism – acclaimed us – Flaubert, Zola and myself – as the three leaders of modern literature during an exceptionally lively, friendly dinner given for us. This is the formation of a new literary army . . .'

Neurotically sensitive and egotistic, Goncourt enjoyed the dinner in his honour, but was in fact annoyed at what he saw as Zola's plagiarism of elements in his technique and work and was to become increasingly jealous of the younger writer's immense success. Moreover, the fact that Flaubert attended must in large part have been due to Maupassant's powers of persuasion since the 'Hermit of Croisset' did not believe in literary schools or movements and had openly criticised Zola's ideas on 'Naturalism', often to his face. Zola's stress on the physical aspects of life, particularly low-life, and apparent lack of emphasis on artistic form and expression would hardly appeal to the conservative, chaste aesthete of Croisset. Indeed, Zola had, as a tribute, dedicated *L'Assommoir* to Flaubert 'in defiance of good taste'! Nevertheless, Flaubert had found certain parts of the novel powerfully moving and even if he disagreed with Zola's principles and polemic in the press about 'Naturalism', he could not deny that the thirty-six-year-old author of *L'Assommoir* had talent and success.

In any case, Flaubert immensely enjoyed literary dinners both because he liked good food and because he liked to escape the hermiticism of his work among jovial, comradely company. This is why he allowed himself to be encouraged by his disciple to attend the Trapp dinner during his short stay in the capital for the publication of his *Trois Contes*, despite his reservations on Zola's 'Naturalism'. Certainly he must have felt his efforts rewarded when he saw advertised in the press that several courses on the menu had been named after his novels – Bovary soup, chicken and truffles à la Saint-Antoine, and artichokes au Cœur Simple! – even if some of the other items were named after characters or novels of Zola and Goncourt – salmon à la Fille Elisa, parfait naturaliste, Coupeau wine and liqueur de l'Assommoir!

By having the elders of contemporary French literature at the dinner and by achieving a certain amount of press coverage – particularly in Mendès' *République des Lettres*, which announced the great event on 13 April in a spectacular way – Zola and his young followers gained a lot of publicity and came to be recognized as a new but powerful influence in the cultural climate of the late

1870s. No longer did it seem that 'Naturalism' was the outrageous cry of one man; the author of *L'Assommoir* was widely
supported by the young generation of writers as well as their
elders; the triumph of 'Naturalism' was not just the success of
Zola himself but the promise of success of a whole movement
and its followers.

It was this hope of success that encouraged Maupassant to
associate with Zola and his circle just as he had earlier played
more than a little on Flaubert's feelings for Laure and Alfred Le
Poittevin in order to benefit from the famous novelist's assistance
to him. Apart from a common enjoyment of the sensuous and the
erotic and a certain shared desire for realism, Zola's 'Naturalism'
had not much appeal to a young poet being taught to pay
attention to individual form and expression in verse and the novel
by Flaubert and trying out his talents in historical plays and
moralistic poems; the 'Naturalists' were not primarily concerned
with style or the morality and psychology of their characters.
Maupassant realised this difference between himself and Zola's
followers from the very start.

When his play *Histoire du Vieux Temps* was staged in February
1879 he realised, as he reported to Flaubert, that Zola and the
young 'Naturalists' were not very enthusiastic about its Romantic
period setting and aristocratic location, which were at odds with
their desire for contemporary, lower-class realism. Henry Céard
wrote later of the performance: 'We were polite but without being
enthusiastic about it. We climbed on to the stage and congratu-
lated Maupassant, and then together we went to the Ambigu
theatre where they were playing the 40th performance of *L'Assommoir*.' [25] Maupassant thus went along with the 'Naturalists'
and, instead of openly departing from Zola, he decided to exploit
for his own benefit the publicity 'Naturalism' had gained by
trying to conform more to the 'Naturalist' ethic. Zola's movement would provide a useful stepping-stone to his own success;
he wrote to his friend Pinchon in February 1877, when Zola's
L'Assommoir was all the rage and he himself was still finishing his
historic drama *La Trahison de la Comtesse de Rhune*:

'I am part of a literary group that disdains poetry. They will serve as a springboard to other things; it's not a daft idea; I am pressing for Naturalism in the theatre and in the novel because the more of that kind of work one does, the more people are taken in to accept it . . . and that's alright for the others. But look out for a reaction against it, my friends! . . .'

It was clearly this desire of Maupassant to profit from the publicity 'Naturalism' was gaining that largely prompted him to stress the erotic side of his imagination in the poems he wrote at this time. *La Dernière Escapade, Au Bord de L'Eau, Vénus Rustique, Le Mur* as well as the repetition of the obscene farce *A La Feuille de Rose* – arranged according to the invitation, especially for Zola, Goncourt and Daudet – were undoubtedly calculated not only to display Maupassant's apparent friendship for Zola and adherence to his cause but also to provoke some of the same sort of publicity for their author as *L'Assommoir* had gained. To some extent they did establish Maupassant as a poet of risqué verse and a lively participant in literary gatherings; and Zola was pleased to recognize Maupassant's realism as 'Naturalistic' when he mentioned the poem *Au Bord de l'Eau* in an article in *Le Messager de l'Europe* of February 1878.

Unfortunately a new wave of protests arose in early 1880 as a result of the publication of Zola's novel *Nana* and there was a desire among the more reactionary public to take action against 'Naturalism' including censuring papers like Alis' *Revue Moderne et Naturaliste* to which Maupassant had contributed two poems. He was not so keen then on being considered a 'Naturalist' and, as has been seen, sought Flaubert's help in extricating himself from the awkward situation by referring to his poem's artistic value. Maupassant's 'Naturalism' was, then, fairly shallow; he went through the motions of it without fully committing himself. He attended the meetings of the Group, he went to the premièies of the dramatisations of Zola's novels *L'Assommoir* and *Nana* on 18 January 1879 and 29 January 1881 respectively, and he was a guest at the dinners at Brebant's following these performances, as well as at the fancy-dress one celebrating the fiftieth edition of *L'Assommoir* in April 1878. He even helped Zola buy a boat, which, with the help of Léon Fontaine and Hennique, he sailed the 49 kilometres from Bezons to Zola's country home in July 1878 and that he suggested should be called 'Nana' after the prostitute in the novel because 'everyone will be able to board her'! Furthermore, he regularly received complimentary copies of Zola's works as they appeared and would have contributed to the paper the 'Naturalists' were going to found in 1880, *La Comédie Humaine*, if lack of finance had not prevented it appearing.

He did, however, contribute to Zola's publicity campaign in favour of 'Naturalism' by writing on the group and on Zola himself in the newspaper *Le Gaulois*, where the author of *L'Assommoir* gained him entry in 1880. One of the first articles he had published each week in *Le Gaulois* and later collected together as *Les Dimanches d'un Bourgeois de Paris* was in fact devoted to a visit he made with his friend Léon Fontaine to Zola's country-seat at Médan. Zola had acquired this small property – so small he referred to it as a 'rabbit-hutch' – in the summer of 1878, and had added to the size of the house by building a square tower-like structure next to it, from where one could overlook the river at the foot of the garden. Now that he was fairly well-off Zola spent much of his time out at Médan, often inviting his young followers to visit him or dine with him there so as to read them parts of his next novel and discuss literary matters instead of in Paris. Occasionally, the group would go along the river on *Nana* or on Maupassant's *Feuille de Rose* to land on the islet not far from Zola's property. The hospitality of Médan thus became a substitute for Croisset as Flaubert buried himself more and more in his novel, and Maupassant was obviously pleased to be able to combine his literary pursuits and his love of the countryside on his visits to Zola. He describes his arrival at Médan as follows:

'A large, newly built square building that was very high seemed to have given birth, like the mountain in the fable, to a tiny white house lying at its side. This latter building, the original property,

was put up by the former owner. The tower was built by Zola.
They rang the door-bell. An enormous dog, a cross between a
Pyrenean and a Newfoundland, began to bark furiously . . . but a
servant came running out, calmed *Bertrand* down, opened the
door and took the journalist's card to his master . . . The servant
came back shortly afterwards and asked them to follow him . . .
The door opened into an exceedingly large room, with a high
ceiling, that was kept bright by the light of the long window overlooking the garden. Antique tapestries covered the walls; on the
left, flanked by two stone figures, there was a monumental fire-
place which would have consumed a whole oak-tree if it was lit
all day. There was also an enormous table piled up with books,
newspapers and sheets of paper, that occupied the middle of this
vast, grandiose apartment and so attracted one's attention as one
came in that it was only after a while that one noticed the man
lying nearby on an Oriental divan large enough to seat twenty
other people.

'He came towards them, greeted them, offered them two seats,
and sat down again on his divan with one leg folded underneath
him. A book lay by his side and he held in his right hand a paper-
knife in ivory, the sharp end of which he kept on peering at from
time to time with one eye since he had to keep the other one closed
because of his short-sightedness . . .

'His dark gaze was a penetrating one and often ironical; one
felt that behind it an active mind was working furiously, seeing
through people, interpreting their words, analysing their gestures
and laying bare their hearts. This round, powerful-looking head
was well suited to his short, concise surname with its two striking
syllables on two stressed vowels.'

In this portrait of Zola, Maupassant stresses two particular
qualities in the 'Master of Médan', as he came to be called: a
certain epic powerfulness and a clinical desire for precision and the
truth. The first is implied by the description of the building itself
and its furnishings – which in fact became more and more baroque
in their number and diversity as time went on and more and more

alterations were made to the house. The second of these qualities is virtually symbolised in Zola's gaze and his persistent contemplation of the paper-knife. Together, these two aspects of Zola comprise the epic social scientist that the author of the *Rougon-Macquart* series of novels wanted to be.

Maupassant's picture of Zola conformed, then, to the image of himself Zola wanted to sell to the public, usually through the articles and pamphlets of his young followers. Maupassant, like Huysmans, Hennique and Rod in their articles and essays, adds the third aspect of Zola's public image later on in the same account of his visit when he mentions how proud Zola was to show his guests over his new property; the author of *L'Assommoir* and *Nana* is depicted as a respectable, bourgeois property-owner and not the revolutionary socialist many reactionaries feared and therefore desired to suppress. In a period when memories of the 1871 Commune rising of the workers were still vivid and in which, as has been seen, censorship could still be used as an effective weapon against what was deemed by particular parties to be against their interests, the public image of a respectably bourgeois Zola was a salutary precaution. Even if, however, Maupassant's portrait of Zola at this time conforms to the image of the inhabitant of Médan that many others of the followers of 'Naturalism' produced, his actual views of Zola's zest for the powerful and scientific exposure of society in his novels did not.

Maupassant's latent disagreement with Zola can be estimated from a letter he wrote to Flaubert on 24 April 1879. In it he criticised the Master of Médan's overwhelming and rather arrogant campaign in the press to establish himself as the literary scientist of his age, and 'Naturalism' as the most modern scientific instrument in literature that no proper writer could do without and which contemporary society would have to accept. Zola had claimed, furthermore, that, as the product of a scientific age, 'Naturalism' aimed at revealing the ultimate truth about Man and his environment; truth could no longer be distorted or suppressed in works of imagination and idealism but had to be shown with scientific accuracy in current literature. Maupassant commented on all this to Flaubert:

'What do you think of Zola? I find what he says quite ludicrous. Have you read his article on Hugo? His article on present-day poets and his booklet *The Republic and Literature*? "The Republic will be Naturalist or it will not exist at all" – "I am simply a scientist" (Just that – what modesty!) – "an investigation into Society" – "the live evidence" – and the whole series of formulas . . . We'll soon see on the back cover of books: "A great novel according to the Naturalist formula"! But "I am simply a scientist", that really takes the cake . . . And yet nobody laughs . . .'

A more profound criticism of 'Naturalism' itself as a movement rather than simply of Zola's polemic about it in the press can be found in a letter of 17 January 1877 that Maupassant sent to another unnamed member of Zola's circle, usually, but somewhat improbably, identified as Paul Alexis. In it he expounds Flaubert's concepts of the originality of the individual writer by his interpretation of his material and his mode of expression. He sees all literary attitudes and movements as phases in the continuous evolution of literature through the ages, a concept that reflects perhaps his early interest in natural evolution. He considers the realistic or 'naturalistic' no more vital to a literary work than the imaginative and fantastic and believes 'Naturalism' is therefore being as restrictive by its stress on particular aspects of life as the Romantic movement of the 1820s and 1830s was in its emphasis on the emotional and exotic. Since movements and their particular principles were only phases in an unending evolution of literature, leaders of these different movements like Hugo and Zola were really just outstanding examples of individual talent:

'I do not believe any more in Naturalism and Realism than in Romanticism. These words in my opinion mean absolutely nothing and only create arguments between people with different temperaments and outlooks.

'I do not believe that the natural, the real, and the true to life are conditions *sine qua non* of literary works. They are just mere words.

'The Essence of a work derives from something, not named and unnameable, that one can recognise and yet not analyse like electricity. It is a literary fluid which we recognise for some reason as talent or genius. I find the people who stress the idealistic and deny the realistic in literature as blind as those who stress their realism and deny everything else . . .

'Let us rather be original, whatever the nature of our talents . . . let us be the originator of something. Of what? It matters little provided that it is beautiful . . . Plato, I think it was, said: "The beautiful is the splendour of the truth"; I absolutely agree with this and if I believe that the writer's perception should always be precise, it is because I think this is necessary if his interpretation is to be original and really beautiful. For real power, talent or genius in literature are all in the interpretation. The thing perceived by the writer passes through his mind, taking on a particular colour, shape, value and implication according to the fertility of his imagination . . . Everything can be beautiful whatever the period, country or literary school, because it is derived from writers of all different temperaments and outlooks.

'The Classical Period of the seventeenth century thought it had found the supreme and definitive formula for literature, but what remains of their works? A little of Corneille, some Boileau, some Bossuet!!

'The Romantics made a great cry of victory to which everyone responded. They had discovered, they thought, the supreme form of art. What remains of it? Some texts of Hugo, which are some of the best ever written in poetry; but a few pieces only – they survive, however, because Hugo was a magnificent poetic genius, not because he created the Romantic movement. It just happened that Hugo created Romanticism because that was the essence of his genius; he alone was Romanticism.

'Another school now comes along that calls itself Realist or Naturalist. It will be incarnated in some writers of talent and will then pass away. What will remain? Some beautiful works by a few men of talent.

'Today Zola happens to be a magnificent and striking figure. But his outlook is only one manifestation of art and not its sum-total just as the temperament of Hugo was another manifestation of the same art. Their view of the world and their interpretation are different, but neither of them have really set literature on a definitive path forever; they both thought they had, because they both incorporate their particular genius. After the Naturalists will come, I am convinced, the opposite extremists – the Arch-Idealists – for literary reactions alone are a logical part of literary evolution – history shows us this and it is not going to suddenly change any more than human nature. . . .

'This letter must not go outside our little circle, of course, and I would be upset if you were to show it to Zola whom I like very much and deeply admire, because he might be offended by it . . .'

Zola did not have to read the letter, however, for within a year the volume *Soirées de Médan* containing Maupassant's *Boule de Suif* was to appear and make plain the divergences within the Naturalist camp. Moreover, many of these views were to reappear in Maupassant's study of Zola, published in the *Revue Bleue* and by Quantin in 1883. Here he dismissed Zola's desire for absolute truth in literature by referring to individual interpretation; he stressed the discrepancy between Zola's precepts and his writing; and concluded that Zola was not, despite his realism, as revolutionary in practice as in theory, since a review of the *Rougon-Macquart* novels often revealed a poetic symbolism and epic exaggeration similar to that in many Romantic works. Zola was thus in Maupassant's eyes not the supreme revolutionary in literature he liked to think but rather a highly talented and individualistic product of literary evolution, owing much to both the past and his own originality.

The six stories written by Zola and his five principal followers

and collected together in the volume *Soirées de Médan* were published by Charpentier on 16 April 1880, complete with a short
preface stressing the theme of the 1870 war running through the
stories, defying further hostile criticism of Zola and his followers
and asserting that: 'Our sole concern has been to affirm publicly
our real friendship for each other and at the same time our
common literary outlook.' The next day Maupassant contributed
an article – one of his first – to Arthur Meyer's newspaper *Le
Gaulois*, to which Zola had introduced him, pointing out with
less stress than in the preface the friendship and similar outlook
of the group's members and explaining how the six writers had
come upon the idea of publishing their stories in one volume:

'We have no pretension to being a school. We are simply some
friends whom a common admiration has brought together at
Zola's house and that, in turn, a similarity of temperament, of
views on a number of things, and of philosophical outlook has
brought even closer together . . . There has been revealed in all of
us, however, an unconscious and fatal reaction against the
emotionalism of the Romantics for the simple reason that literary
trends follow one another and are dissimilar from one another . . .
    'Now for a few details about our collection of stories.
    'We were together at Zola's house at Médan during the
summer. During the course of the lengthy meals we had there (for
we are all of us self-indulgent gourmets and Zola himself eats as
much as three normal writers) we began to talk among ourselves.
Zola told us of the books he was going to write and his opinions
and ideas on all sorts of literary matters. Now and then he took
up his rifle and being short-sighted shot at clumps of grass which
we told him were birds while he was chatting, so that he was surprised when he could find no body from his prey. Sometimes we
went fishing. Hennique was good at this, much to the annoyance
of Zola who could only catch old boots. I would laze on the boat
Nana or I would swim for hours while Paul Alexis lurked
around savouring his obscene imagination, Huysmans would
smoke and Céard became bored with the countryside.

'That's how we spent the afternoons; moreover since the evenings were lovely and warm and full of the scent of the surrounding greenery, we used to go each evening on to the island opposite the house. One moonlit night we began speaking of the short-story writer Prosper Mérimée and the ladies exclaimed: "What a charming story-teller he was!" Huysmans then retorted something to the effect that: "A short-story writer is someone who, not knowing how to write, expresses himself pretentiously on insignificant things."

'We began then to run through all the famous short-story writers and to point out enthusiastically the merits of such writers, the most marvellous of whom to our mind is the great Russian who has almost been adopted by France, Ivan Turgenev. Alexis claimed it was difficult actually to write a short story; Céard, always cynical, was looking up at the moon and said quietly: "Now here's a nice Romantic scene you could use . . ." to which Huysmans added: "Yes, it's good for some slushy, sentimental stories." But Zola saw something in the idea and thought we should tell each other stories. The proposal made us laugh at first but then we accepted the idea and to make it more difficult we even agreed that we would all keep to the framework chosen by the narrator of the first story and simply use it for our different plots . . .'

The description of Zola and his followers sitting in the moonlight telling each other stories like Chaucer or Boccaccio's groups of narrators is amusingly fanciful but untrue; like Paul Alexis' satirical article on the Médan circle in the paper *Les Cloches* a week later, Maupassant's account of the volume's composition was designed to make the whole matter appear more exciting and comradely than it was and to promote the volume's sales by publicising its origin in this way. A less distorted version of the truth – it has since been claimed that Hennique first suggested the volume – can be found in the letter Maupassant wrote to Flaubert on 5 January 1880:

'I see you have forgotten what I mentioned to you on my last

visit to Croisset about our volume of short stories and so I hasten
to explain it to you again. Zola has had published in Russia and
then in France in *La Réforme* a story on the 1870 War called
L'Attaque du Moulin. Huysmans had printed in Brussels another
tale entitled *Sac au Dos*. Finally, Céard has sent to a Russian
review, to which he contributes, a very strange and rather violent
story about the siege of Paris called *Une Saignée*. When Zola
heard of these two other works about the War he said to us that
in his opinion they would fit in well with his own story in a
volume that would not be particularly chauvinistic but would
be distinctive in its message. Thereupon he asked Hennique,
Alexis and me to each write a story so as to complete the volume,
which would have the advantage of selling well since it had
Zola's name on it and could bring in one or two hundred francs
for each of us . . .

'In writing our stories, we did not have any anti-patriotic
intention or any intention in particular; we only wanted to try to
give in them a true picture of the War, leaving aside the chauvin-
ism preached by Déroulède and the false enthusiasm that it is
usually thought necessary to include in any story dealing with
soldiers and guns. In our work generals, instead of all being
superb mathematicians filled with the noblest feelings and gushing
with ideals, are seen as mediocre beings like everyone else except
that they wear braided képis and have more people killed, not
through any evil intention on their part but through mere
stupidity. Our integrity in appreciating military matters gives the
whole volume a curious quality and our intended detachment in
appreciating those topics which necessarily arouse passionate
feelings in people will exasperate the bourgeois far more than a
full-scale attack on them. The volume is not, however, anti-
patriotic but just truthful; indeed, what I say about the people of
Rouen is far short of the truth . . .'

Maupassant was clearly pleased to be able to appear in print and
earn some money from a volume published in Zola's name; moreover, as he told Flaubert in a letter of late April 1880 when the

volume had appeared, he would gain publicity from it to sell his collection of poems that Charpentier was bringing out shortly.

Maupassant began writing his contribution to the volume, *Boule de Suif*, in late 1879 though he had probably thought of and written parts of it prior to then. The story was based on what had actually happened during the war to a Rouen prostitute, Adrienne Legay, an acquaintance of Guy's uncle Charles Cordhomme – called Cornudet in the tale – who had been obliged to sleep with a Prussian officer while on her way to try to bring comfort, food and messages to her lover and his soldier friends in Le Havre. The incident had probably either been mentioned to Guy by his uncle or told him by his mother or his cousin Louis Le Poittevin. Although according to Maupassant the stories of Zola and his young friends were not meant to be antipatriotic, there was clearly more than a little criticism of the bourgeois and the army implied in them, as is shown by Guy's reference to the tale he is writing in his letter to Flaubert of 2 December 1879: 'I am working hard at my short story on the people of Rouen and the War. I will from now on be obliged to carry some pistols in my pockets when I walk in Rouen!' By early January 1880 Maupassant sent his manuscript to Charpentier and by the end of the month the first set of proofs were on their way to Croisset for Flaubert's inspection. On 1 February the Master of Croisset replied to his disciple, hailing the work as a gem, and including just a few comments to make it even more perfect:

'But I am longing to tell you that I consider *Boule de Suif* a masterpiece. Yes, a masterpiece, young man! Nothing more nor less than the work of a master. It is totally original in theme, excellently conceived throughout and in a superb style. The scene and the characters come across clearly and your psychological understanding is great. In short, I am delighted; in fact, I laughed aloud two or three times . . .

'I have put down on a piece of paper for you my comments as your supervisory reader. Take note of them because I think they are valuable.

'This short story of yours *will* last, you can be sure of that! What wonderful faces you give your bourgeois! Not one that is not perfect. Cornudet is great and marvellously true to life! The nun with the pock-marked face is perfect and so are the count with his "my dear child" and the ending! The poor girl crying while the other chap sings the *Marseillaise* is sublime. I could hug and kiss you for a good quarter of an hour for writing like this! Really, I am delighted by it! I enjoyed reading it and am full of admiration.

'However, precisely because the theme is rather sordid and embarrassing for the bourgeois, I would take out two things, which are not really bad but which might cause some bother with certain fools because they seem to say: "I don't care a fig." First, the manner in which the young man hurls mud at the national coat of arms; and secondly, the word "tits". If you see to these two points, even the most prudish reader will have nothing to reproach you with. Your tart is a charming lass, but you would please me if you could make her tummy less protruding at the beginning!'

Flaubert's comments were, however, more than mere stylistic trimmings if it is recalled that at this time Maupassant was still extricating himself from the trouble he had got into with his poems in the *Revue Moderne et Naturaliste*; Flaubert might use salacious language and slang in his correspondence, but for both literary and political reasons he never used it in his work. Besides, Flaubert was a peace-loving conservative bourgeois at heart and he did not himself want all the upset and publicity of the trial over *Madame Bovary* all over again. Maupassant had some of the impetuous defiance of a frustrated and disillusioned youth, unlike his more experienced sixty-year-old master. He only took fright when it was too late and his very livelihood at the Ministry was threatened, as it was later in February 1880.

By April, however, Guy had been rescued by Flaubert from impending scandal and prosecution and although when the *Soirées de Médan* volume appeared it was often unfavourably received as a product of Zola's 'Naturalism', all but the more reactionary critics such as Le Reboullet in *Le Temps* and Albert Wolff in *Le Figaro* hailed at least *Boule de Suif* as a small masterpiece. Edouard Rod, a friend of Zola and his group, praised Maupassant's interpretation of reality and his humour in *Le Voltaire* on 20 April and the next day in *Gil Blas* Jean Richepin pointed to the vigorous poetic qualities of Maupassant's style. Maupassant wrote to Flaubert at the end of the month:

'*Boule de Suif* is enormously successful . . . ! ! Catulle Mendès came to see me especially to congratulate me; and he told me, as you did, that in his opinion this short story would last and that they'll still be talking about it in twenty or thirty years time. That pleased me immensely because Catulle is a genuine literary artist. I have also received lots of compliments from other people whose opinion I value . . .'

The volume went through eight reprints in a fortnight and Guy was pleased not only with the publicity it gave him for the imminent publication of his poems but also to find that he had talent and could earn money by drawing on it. It was not long therefore before he was up in Charpentier's offices inquiring about the sum he was going to reap from the book's sales. Unfortunately, his share of the profits – about 500 francs in all for each of the first few months – was the same as that of the other five contributors despite the greater popularity and the literary superiority of *Boule de Suif*. This and the fact that the title of the volume – chosen by Céard as a tribute to Mme Zola's hospitality at Médan – tied Maupassant to the 'Naturalist' group were, however, the only disadvantages in his success. In every other way, *Boule de Suif* was a stepping-stone to his fame and fortune.

Out of the six stories in *Les Soirées de Médan* Maupassant's is clearly the best both with regard to theme and in matters of technique and style. In comparison with Zola's tragic idyll on the fate of a girl and her father and brother in a mill that is taken and then lost by the enemy; with Alexis' tale about a widow who collects

her husband's body from the battlefield and gives a lift on her
return home to a young priest with whom she falls in love; with
Huysmans' fairly autobiographical and amusing account of his
experiences as a soldier who prefers to be a patient suffering from
dysentery in a number of hospitals than in the army; with
Hennique's gruesome story of how a band of soldiers take a
bloody revenge on the inmates of a brothel where one of their
comrades has been badly treated; and with Céard's tale of an
incapable general's infatuation with his patriotic but vicious
mistress during the siege of Paris, Maupassant's *Boule de Suif* is
in a class of its own.

From the very first page with its harrowing description of the
tattered, disorganised army in retreat and the bourgeois shopkeepers of Rouen making themselves scarce (and, unlike the
Norman peasants, putting up no resistance to the Prussian
invaders who soon arrive), to the last pages with the self-sacrifice
of *Boule de Suif* to the Prussian officer and her subsequent tearful
isolation in the coach by her fellow-travellers, Maupassant relates
the fate of both France and the naïve but patriotic prostitute to
the selfish attitude of the bourgeois. Cornudet's singing of the
Marseillaise serves finally as a tribute to *Boule de Suif*'s naïve
patriotism in resisting the Prussian officer's demand and her
generous submission to the will of her bourgeois companions.
It is also an indictment of the egoism and smug passivity in face of
the enemy of her respectably moral and religious fellow-travellers.
For Maupassant the simple Norman peasant who throws a stone
or takes a shot at the enemy is far worthier of our admiration than
any of these more sophisticated types, who would prefer to
sacrifice their country just as they do *Boule de Suif* rather than
abandon or harm their commercial interests and own well-being.

By relating the different strands of his theme by a series of
juxtaposed contrasts of people, situations and symbols of these –
techniques used by Flaubert for implied comment and irony –
and by making his characters representative types by brief, deft
touches of parody while remaining at the same time individual by
his selection of their particular thoughts and actions, Maupassant

manages to convert what is a simple episode from the realities of 1870 into something highly critical and symbolic. It is the more humble, low-life realism desired by the 'Naturalists' since it is concerned with a prostitute and the lust of a Prussian soldier, but neither low-life nor vulgar language is included and the actual sexual implications are kept to a minimum and are only referred to when relevant. Maupassant's view here of reality is thus a very discriminating and concise one – unlike that of most of the other followers of Zola or of Zola himself.

Background details, description of the setting and physical particulars and psychological analysis of characters are kept to a compact minimum – a compactness that Henry James so admired that he wanted to copy it and wrote in the margin of his note-books that '*A la Maupassant* must be my constant motto'.[26] Furthermore, Maupassant's attitude to the situation and charac-ters he is describing is far from being 'scientifically' detached and impersonal as was prescribed by 'Naturalist' precepts. As with Flaubert's attempts at objectivity in his novels, it is quite clear from his structuring of the story and his depiction of the charac-ters what is Maupassant's attitude towards his creations; no one could mistake his preference for the plump, rosy-cheeked Elisabeth Rousset. And it is equally clear and pointed what moralistic inference is to be drawn from the tale's depiction of *Boule de Suif*'s plight.

It was because Maupassant was so deliberately discriminating and pointed in his particular interpretation of reality that he needed to follow Flaubert's instruction on being precise and care-ful in his choice of words and mode of expression, even though he did not share in this pursuit the masochistic conscientiousness of the aesthete of Croisset. An individual interpretation of reality and an individual technique and style had evolved, as Flaubert could now gladly perceive, in his 'disciple"s writing; they were the talents of neither a Romantic nor a 'Naturalist' but, as Maupassant himself desired, they were the tools of a writer.

CHAPTER 5

Sorrow and Success

While Maupassant was still receiving compliments for *Boule de Suif* and *Des Vers* and the *Soirées de Médan* volume was being reviewed in the press, the tragic news of Flaubert's death arrived. He had died suddenly on 8 May 1880 only three weeks after he had seen *Boule de Suif* hailed as a small masterpiece and barely five days since he had written to his celebrated disciple asking to see clippings of press reviews of the work. No one had suspected that this great literary giant would vanish so suddenly and so soon when he · had entertained Goncourt, Zola, Charpentier and Maupassant at Croisset for the Easter weekend in late March 1880; or when, a few weeks later on 27 April, Mme Pasca, the Lapierres, and Mme Brainne had gathered at Rouen to enjoy the annual dinner in honour of St Polycarp (the patron-saint who Flaubert had adopted because of the similarity in outlook between himself and the ancient bishop of Smyrna who had bitterly complained to God for allowing him to be born in the century he lived in). Like the Easter weekend at Croisset this dinner had been even merrier than normal, for Flaubert felt relieved both that his niece's financial problems were virtually settled at last and that the first part of his last great novel on the antics of two bourgeois bachelors, *Bouvard et Pécuchet*, was near completion after years of arduous research and labour. Moreover, at Croisset he had been playing host to close literary friends and his beloved and now successful disciple, and at Rouen he had been surrounded by three of his favourite women friends – Mme Brainne, Mme Lapierre, and Mme Pasca. The fact that these two occasions had been so lively and enjoyable and that there seemed nothing amiss and everything looked so much brighter for Flaubert than for years only made the news of his death all the more of a shock.

Maupassant received a telegram informing him of Flaubert's apoplectic attack in the late morning of Saturday 8 May when he arrived at Bezons for his afternoon's rowing and immediately returned to Paris to get a train from St Lazare to Croisset. The rest of his journey and the circumstances of Flaubert's death can be found in the following letter Maupassant sent to Turgenev on 25 May:

'I met the Commanvilles (Flaubert's niece and her husband) at six o'clock at the station. On my way I had called at my flat and found two telegrams from Rouen telling me that Flaubert was in fact dead. We therefore made that terrible journey after dark plunged in our sombre and cruel grief. At Croisset we found him laid-out in his bed, little changed except that the attack of apoplexy had made his neck swell with dark blood. It was then that we learnt the details of his death. He was perfectly well on the preceding days ... On the Friday he had dined well, he had spent the evening reading out lines of Corneille with his doctor and neighbour Monsieur Fortin, had slept all right until eight o'clock the next morning, then taken a bath, dressed, and read through his mail. It was then that he called his housekeeper because he did not feel well; as she did not come up immediately, he opened the window and called to her to fetch back Monsieur Fortin, who had just that minute left on the ferry. When the housekeeper came to him, she found him still on his feet, rather stunned but not showing any need for anxiety. He told her: "I'm going to have one of my attacks. It's lucky it's happening today for it would have been terribly embarrassing if it had occurred in the train to Paris tomorrow." He opened a bottle of eau de Cologne, dabbed some drops of it on his forehead, lay down gently on a large divan muttering: "Rouen ... we are not far from Rouen ... Dr Hellot ... I know the Hellots well ...", and then flopped on to his side, his face convulsed with an onrush of dark blood, his hands rigid, struck down by a death blow which he had not foreseen for a moment ...'

It was then that Guy revealed how attached and close he had been to the great novelist who had taught him so much by his example in the art of literature and from whom he had never hesitated to ask favour after favour. Maupassant might have been selfish and ambitious in his relations with Flaubert but he had also cherished the older man's affection for him over the years and brought back for him the intimate happiness of his friendship with Alfred and Laure Le Poittevin. Moreover, for Guy, Flaubert had been an even more affectionate, intimate father-figure than Bouilhet; unlike Gustave de Maupassant, Gustave Flaubert could tell him about writing and literature, and he was fond of both Guy and his mother. For Flaubert, young Maupassant represented a reincarnation of Alfred and of his childhood with the Le Poittevins to enliven and bring consolation to him amid the labour and problems of his last years, as well as a chance to be generous with his affections and father a literary son in his lonely toils at his desk. Had he not written in a copy of his novel *La Tentation de Saint-Antoine* sent to Guy in 1874 that he 'loved him like a son' and had Maupassant's dedication of *Des Vers* to 'my paternal friend' not made him recall the Le Poittevin family and brought tears to his eyes?

Because of the mixture of respect and intimacy and the similarity of thought and humour that came to exist between them, as can be seen from their correspondence with its moments now of formality and flattery and now of emotion and obscenity, it was Guy who with Dr Fortin and Dr Pouchet prepared Flaubert's body for burial: washing it, bathing it in eau de Cologne, dressing it in silk underwear and a suit, complete with waistcoat, cravat, and skin gloves, and brushing the famous moustache and long locks of blondish hair that had made people refer to Flaubert as 'the Viking'. Guy also stood vigil over his Master's coffin just as the latter had years earlier watched over Alfred's and Bouilhet's and received all the callers to the famous house.

The funeral itself took place on Tuesday 11 May, a warm spring day, first at the nearby parish church of Canteleu, about a third of a mile from Croisset, and then at the family grave in the city cemetery at Rouen. Zola, Goncourt, Daudet, Banville and many young men of letters and artists were present, but hardly any of the elders of nineteenth-century literature such as Hugo, Taine or Renan, and few of Flaubert's intimate friends such as Maxime Du Camp and Edmond Laporte. Furthermore, it was a funeral such as Flaubert himself would have described with much satirical humour and many misanthropic comments, for the spectators from Rouen barely knew who the deceased was, most of the journalists and many of the so-called mourners were more interested in seeking favours from each other and inquiring about the meal to follow than in the service itself, and when it was time to lower the coffin, it was found that the grave was not long enough and Flaubert was initially laid to rest head-downwards. Perhaps amid his sorrow and tears, Maupassant recognised the less depressing side of this superb example of what the author of *Madame Bovary* and *Bouvard et Pécuchet* called 'the stupidity of mankind' and might himself have enjoyed guffawing over with his young disciple.

Flaubert's passing-away at this moment in Maupassant's life, just when he was beginning to be successful and fulfil both his own and his 'paternal friend's' dreams, hit Guy hard; now he would only have himself to rely on for inspiration and criticism; he would no more be able to look to Croisset for these or for the enthusiastic assistance he had received so far towards the realisation of his literary ambitions. Moreover, with the passing of Flaubert, the spirit of the past with its childhood memories of Alfred and Laure Le Poittevin and the equally idyllic friendship of Alfred and young Gustave, which Laure had instilled in her son and which the novelist of Croisset had enjoyed recognising in him, had to a large extent died away too.

Suddenly deprived of the affectionate father-figure and critic he had become used to and could always turn to for advice or a favour, Maupassant continued for some time to be obsessed by his memories of Flaubert. His criticism in the press of Maxime du Camp for revealing the epileptic fits Flaubert suffered from and his help to Flaubert's niece and Turgenev in revising *Bouvard et*

Pécuchet and placing it in Mme Adam's *Nouvelle Revue* as well as his participation in the committee headed by Hugo and Turgenev for a Flaubert memorial were only in fact to prolong his grief. He had written to Zola in late May 1880: 'I cannot tell you how often I think of Flaubert; he haunts my mind and I think of him constantly'; and at about the same time, on 24 May, he had described his own and his mother's reactions to Flaubert's death in very similar terms to the novelist's niece:

'The farther the death of poor Flaubert recedes in time, the more his memory haunts me and the more my heart is grieved and my mind is at a loss. His figure is constantly before my eyes, I see him standing there in his vast brown dressing-gown that swelled out around him as he raised his arms in speaking. His every movement comes back to me, all the intonations of his voice ring in my ears, and I can hear all those words he used to use as if he was still saying them to me. It is the beginning of those harsh separations, that breaking-up of our existence, in which all those we love, who recall the past for us and with whom we could be most intimate, pass away. Such blows bruise our hearts and leave there for always a wound that we will continue to feel in our thoughts. My poor mother, down there in Etretat, was terribly shocked and it seems she remained alone in her room for two whole days crying. For her it means the loss of her last friend from the past; there will no longer be any echo of the happy times of her youth and childhood in her life; she will never again have someone to keep asking "Do you remember this?" and "Do you remember that?" I feel at this moment in an excruciating way the futility of living, the uselessness of all one's efforts, the monstrous monotony of everyone and everything and that moral and spiritual isolation in which we all live but from which I suffered less when I could chat with him; for he had like no one else that understanding of philosophical thought which opened up new horizons on everything and kept one's mind at a sublime level from where one could look down on the whole of mankind and realise the "unending wretchedness of everything".

'These are saddening matters but such sad thoughts are more valid than indifferent ones when one's heart is heavy . . .'

Flaubert's death thus aroused Maupassant's latent pessimism as well as leaving him both more lonely and more insecure than before. It had clearly also had a terrible effect on his mother's already neurotically emotional sensibility in her equally lonely life at Etretat. In both cases the emotional shock and strain caused an aggravation of the nervous disorders Guy and his mother suffered from. Laure had been consulting specialists in Paris for some years now about her debility and her eyes, but so far no real diagnosis or solution had been found. The upset of Flaubert's death and the fact that her younger son Hervé had taken to leading a profligate life – he had run away from home on one occasion and was constantly in debt and obliged to beg and borrow from everyone, including Guy who sent him 300 francs in October 1880 – only served to make her nervous condition worse. As a result she was urged by her doctors to escape from the emotional strains and financial pressures of Etretat for a while and relax somewhere quiet. She chose Corsica, with its warm climate and unspoilt countryside, and left for there in the late summer to avoid the heat earlier in the season. Meanwhile, Maupassant's condition had also worsened, with the greater strain on his nerves and eyes that his entry into literature and journalism entailed. Already at the beginning of March 1880 he had written to Flaubert:

'I have a paralysis in the movement of my right eye and Dr Abadie considers this condition virtually incurable. I shall just have to wear a pince-nez with a special lens to get normal vision. But my other doctor who is a professor at the Faculty of Medicine (Dr Rendu), while admitting openly the existence of my condition, affirms that it will be cured. He thinks Abadie has not unravelled at all as yet my pathological condition. I am, according to him, suffering from the same illness as my mother; that is, a slight irritation of the upper part of the spine. Thus, heart palpitations, my hair falling out, and the trouble with my eye would all be caused by the same thing and all these symptoms could all equally well disappear to make way for others, you see. I think he's right . . .'

Flaubert was concerned for his young disciple and let him consult his own doctor, Fortin, when he joined the Easter party at Croisset on 17 March 1880. It was as a result of this consultation that Flaubert wrote to Turgenev on 7 April: 'As regards de Maupassant, his condition is not as serious as I thought. He's got nothing organically wrong with him but is extremely gouty, ultra-rheumatic and completely neuropathic.' [27] With the emotional shock of Flaubert's passing and the greater pressure on him to write after the success of *Boule de Suif* and *Des Vers* Maupassant decided, however, in June 1880, for medical reasons as well as no doubt to have time to write, to apply for sick leave from the Ministry of Education and the Arts:

'Sir, a nervous condition from which I have been suffering for some years has assumed rather worrying proportions in the last few weeks, attacking my eyes and making me suffer violent migraine. As the attached certificate shows, my doctor, M. Rendu, believes only a complete rest can cure me.' [28]

In the certificate Rendu wrote as follows:

'This young man has been suffering from a persistent nervous condition giving rise to constant headaches and congestion in the brain which have several times endangered his health. This condition, though only slightly worsened, persists together with violent heart palpitations that come on at certain times and are accompanied by digestive disorders. Finally, M. de Maupassant has been suffering for the past few weeks from a paralysis in the movement of his right eye coinciding with violent neuralgia in that part of his head. Because of the persistence and intensity of these troubles which very often prevent M. de Maupassant from applying himself to his work in the office, I think it would benefit him to take as complete a rest as possible and have a leave of some three or four months.'

Clearly, Maupassant needed some escape and relaxation from his work because of his medical condition; but when two months later Guy again applied for leave before his first quota had expired, it would seem that his nervous disorders were really only an excuse, albeit a fairly valid one, for him to get more time off from the Ministry so that he could continue his writing of articles for *Le Gaulois*, some more short tales and odd episodes for his later longer novels. Besides, his mother was planning to go to Corsica and Guy not only wanted to visit her there but also thought the island a fine subject for some articles. He therefore wrote to his Minister once again on 3 August:

'Minister, you were kind enough in the month of June to grant me three months paid leave to enable me to improve my poor health. Despite my careful attention to my condition I am still in a hardly satisfactory state even now, as the enclosed certificate from Dr Rendu testifies, and I should like to ask you to prolong for a further three months the leave you granted me. The advice of my doctor is that I have a complete change of air and go to a spa . . .'

Leave was granted again and young Guy, certainly ill but not wanting to cure himself at the cost of his literary projects, soon arrived, not at a spa, but in Corsica and then only for a few days. He wrote from Vico on 29 September to one of his friends from Médan, Léon Hennique:

'You know I made this trip to Corsica so as to spend some time with my mother whose state of health has forced her to leave France. I found her a little better than she was, but she wanted to follow me on my excursions at a distance in a carriage in order not to be away from me during the few days I am here. Now she has

fallen ill at Vico no doubt through sheer exhaustion. I have therefore been looking after her here since last week since I cannot even
move her to Ajaccio. As soon as I am able to leave, I will take the
boat back without completing my touring, which is a pity because
I will perhaps never return to this magnificent country; and I will
have spent a lot of money for nothing since I have only made one
excursion because of the ill health of my mother who is filled with
despair at the thought of my leaving so soon.'

Despite what he told Hennique, Maupassant seems to have seen
quite a lot of the island and got to know a fair amount about its
history and way of life, as his articles on it in *Le Gaulois* in
October and December 1880 and his use of it in his novel of
1883, *Une Vie*, eloquently testify.

For Maupassant, when he landed on Corsica after the overnight voyage from Marseilles, the island represented not only an
escape from depression and work to warm sunshine and the
possibility of adventurous excursions, but also the chance to see
the birthplace of Napoleon and the life of the famous 'maquis'
known for its family vendettas and bandits. It was the Bona-
partist past and the sun-drenched, unspoilt naturalness of the
island which impressed him when he reached the capital Ajaccio:

'The town, beautiful and clean, seems despite the early hour to be
crushed already under the burning glare of the southern sun. The
streets are planted with magnificent trees; there is almost a smile
of welcome in the very air filled with those mysterious perfumes, pungent aromas and wild scents of Corsica that the great
Napoleon still longed for when he was dying far away on St
Helena.

'One soon recognizes that one is in the country of the Bona-
partes. Everywhere statues of the First Consul and Emperor,
busts, pictures, inscriptions, street names recall the history of the
family...

'The town of Ajaccio, so prettily situated in a gulf of blue sea
and surrounded with olive trees, eucalyptus, and fig and orange

groves, only needs now the indispensable development that will transform it into the most charming winter resort on the Mediterranean . . .'

It seems strange that Maupassant, who so enjoyed the tranquillity and wildness of unspoilt Nature, should want to change Ajaccio into a Trouville or Nice but he clearly desired both naturalness and comfonrt, ope spaces and full amenities. Perhaps this was an indication of his contradictory temperament, which enjoyed both solitude and company in turn and a sign already of his sophisticated self-indulgence later when he liked to socialise at Cannes and Menton.

Since Corsica was not yet converted into a winter resort Maupassant had to content himself with its unspoilt charms, which he in fact liked immensely. On a visit by mule to the remote monastery of Corbara to see Father Didon, whom he had met at Flaubert's, he took the mountain road through the beautiful forests of Aïtone and Valdoniello, into the awe-inspiring Niolo valley, and past the rugged peaks of the Piana range and stopped at night in the village of Létia where he found hospitality in the homes of the Paoli and Arrighi families, who arranged some excursions around the region for him. There were no hotels and no cafés; only the sun, the mountain peaks, and the little hamlets in the crevices of the hillsides. So impressed was Maupassant by the unspoilt beauty and wildness of the Corsican landscape that he sympathised with Father Didon's lack of desire to return to Paris from his monastery on a lonely promontory amid the coastal range and told him: 'If I ever become old and wish to become a hermit, which I doubt however, it is up there on your mountain that I will come and pray.' Unfortunately, the more famous and sophisticated Maupassant was to have to abandon all thoughts of solitude and peace as he entered farther into the fashionable world of high society. For the moment Maupassant enjoyed the untamed wildness of Corsica and was excited on one of his excursions to actually see a real Corsican bandit, whom his party of guides were escorting over a mountain pass where the

police were on the look-out for such outlaws; Maupassant
described the incident as follows:

'The Corsicans, alert, with their rifles on their shoulders, kept on
stopping as they were accustomed to doing at all the streams and
fountains to have a mouthful of water before continuing. As we
approached the top of the mountain their pace gradually slowed
down and they spoke under their breath to each other in their
local dialect which was completely incomprehensible to me.
However, I did manage to catch the word "policeman" every so
often. Finally, we halted and a tall, bronzed fellow vanished into
the surrounding undergrowth. A quarter of an hour later he
returned; we started off slowly again but only to stop again two
hundred yards farther up and another man dived into the bushes.
Full of curiosity I asked my guide what was happening. He
replied they were waiting for a "friend" . . . Suddenly, however,
as quick as a goblin jumping out of a box, a small, dark, stocky
figure dived with a great leap into our midst from out of the
undergrowth. Like all the Corsicans he had his loaded rifle on his
shoulder and looked at me most suspiciously. He was ugly,
gnarled like an olive-tree, very dirty of course, and his eyes with
their blood-shot edges seemed to squint a little. He was soon surrounded, fêted, and questioned by the rest; everyone seemed to
love him like a brother and respect him like a saint. Then, when
they had all had their say, we got going again at a very slow pace
with one of the mountain guides walking some hundred yards
ahead of us as a scout . . . As we arrived at the mountain pass a
sort of anxiety came over the party. Eventually we were over it . . .
A look of relief and happiness could be seen on everyone's face
and we began our descent . . . Then, after about an hour, the
mysterious person who had joined us so suddenly turned and
shaking all our hands bid us farewell before leaping back into the
undergrowth of bushes.'

Maupassant, with his writer's imaginative interest in the exciting
adventures of bandits and Corsica's history of family vendettas,

could not resist finding out aoubt the life and deeds of the famous Bellacoscia brothers, who had committed dozens of murders for the sake of love and family honour and been outlawed but not caught by the police for years. He also mentions in his account of the Bellacoscias how a young girl from Paris, who was intrigued by the romantic adventures of the Corsican bandits, sought a meeting with one of the outlawed brothers and soon fell in love with such a daring, hot-blooded fellow:

'What a dream come true! To have a real bandit to oneself for a whole day from dawn until evening. He told her Corsican stories of love and adventure in which the stiletto plays no little part; he told her of a schoolteacher who had fallen in love with him; and the soft dough that she like many other women had in place of her brains was so excited by all this that at nightfall she did not want to leave her bandit and asked him to come back for supper with her at the house she was staying in, where the beds were already prepared.'

This aspect of Corsica as a wild, unspoilt land where daring, virile men still fought and died for love and honour was to be used by Maupassant in his novel *Une Vie*; his main characters, Jeanne and Julien, spend their honeymoon in Corsica – Jeanne enjoying its romantic associations, like the Parisian girl Maupassant described, and Julien finding its wild landscape a stimulant for his untamed sexual desires. The fact that Jeanne's disillusionment and depression and Julien's dissatisfaction with her commence after they return from their honeymoon in Corsica might well reflect Maupassant's own mood on leaving the island's sunshine and rugged naturalness for the monotony of his labours in Paris.

For the rest of the winter after his return from Corsica Maupassant worked hard at his writing. His ill health continued largely no doubt because of his greater concentration and he told Flaubert's niece in January 1881 that he had not replied sooner to her letter because of the terrible neuralgia he had been suffering for the past week in his head and eyes. The same month he wrote to his mother, who was convalescing in the south of France, from their home at Etretat, where he was busy, despite the cold he had and the bleak, wintry conditions outside, finishing a short story which he thought 'to be at least as good as *Boule de Suif,* if not better' – *La Maison Tellier.* This letter gives ample description of Maupassant's solitude and depression when he was involved in the process of writing and had not the company of his mother, Flaubert or his friends to raise his morale amid the problems of composition and his troublesome health:

'The cold wind blows under the doors, the lamp keeps flickering as if to go out, and the fire lights up the room with its brightness, though – fierce as its heat feels on your face – it does not really warm the place. All the antique furnishings are around me looking gloomy and sad and not a sound comes from the village which lies dead under the winter snow. One cannot even hear the sea. But I am chilled more by the loneliness of life itself than by the solitude of the house. I feel as if the world has disintegrated around me; the emptiness of life bears down upon me. And amid this vanishing of everyone and everything, my brain continues to function lucidly and precisely and dazzles me with the vast Nothingness of life . . .'

Much of this sense of solitude and pessimism was to find its way into Maupassant's later novel *Une Vie,* episodes of which he composed and published as separate stories at this time. For the moment, however, Maupassant's pessimistic mood had not reached its nadir and was not reflected in his work. Indeed, the volume of stories entitled *La Maison Tellier,* which he completed after applying for another period of leave from the Ministry in December 1880 and after another couple of months of comparative solitude by the river at Sartrouville in the spring of the following year, was anything but gloomy when Victor Havard published it in May 1881. It showed the sentimental, ironically and slightly licentiously humorous side of Maupassant instead, and completely hid the pain and anguish of his personal life just as his reputation as a jovial, bawdy sailing-man concealed the quieter, more poetic and idealistic side of his nature.

It is said that Maupassant heard of the incident that *La Maison Tellier* is based upon – the visit of the inmates of a Rouen brothel to the first communion of the proprietress's niece and the consequent closing of the brothel for the day – from Flaubert's friend Charles Lapierre; he had simply moved the location of his story from Rouen to Fécamp to avoid scandal and embarrassment. As in *Boule de Suif,* the prostitutes are treated kindly by the author. In the very first line he refers to the men of Fécamp visiting the brothel as naturally as they would a café; and he is at pains throughout to show how maternal yet efficient Madame Tellier is in running her house and how naïve and basically honest the girls are in supplying the natural needs of men, whether they are the more respectable bourgeois who want an odd evening of sensual pleasure, the sailors who flock there from the port, or the commercial traveller in the train and old Joseph Rivet in the village.

Rosa's sleeping with the first communicant because the latter is frightened alone in her bed before the great day, and the infectious crying of the brothel's inmates in the church during the service serve to show that same naïve honesty in them despite their profession as in *Boule de Suif.* While the latter is compared to a nice, rosy apple in her Norman robust naturalness, the innocent inmates of Madame Tellier's house are symbolically related to the ducks in the basket carried into the train compartment by some local peasants. But whereas in *Boule de Suif* Maupassant is critical of the bourgeois betrayers of France in the 1870 war and offsets the prostitute's character against his ironic parody of her respectable companions in the coach, here in *La Maison Tellier* there is no real criticism of any character. Maupassant laughs gently at the bourgeois men who are startled to find the brothel closed because of the first communion of the proprietress's niece and are as annoyed at being deprived of their evening's pleasure as the rowdy groups of sailors whom they otherwise disdain. He laughs compassionately at the prostitutes' crying in the church; and he enjoys laughing at the commercial traveller's playfulness with the girls, for it is Norman and natural.

Of course, although there is little explicit criticism in the story, the fact that Maupassant chooses prostitutes for his main characters and that they receive such favourable treatment in the story is an implied criticism of society's attitude towards them. While the Norman peasants in their innocence and ignorance accept Madame Tellier and her friends and treat them as honoured guests in their church, the crafty bourgeois of the town such as those depicted full of frustration at the story's opening prefer to disdain them according to social convention, while at the same time slinking off in the evening to visit the brothel. It is this slight, ironic comment on social values that governs both his very choice of subject and also the structure and style of Maupassant's stories – the use of contrast and juxtaposition of characters and episodes, the use of symbols, and a concise expression that is calculated to provide just the right amount of simple detail and psychological explanation.

If *La Maison Tellier* follows *Boule de Suif* and many a 'Naturalist' novel of the period in using a prostitute as a protagonist with the purpose of commenting on conventional society's values, the other stories in the volume are also based on aspects of life that can be used as models for ironic criticism of social habits. Both *Le Papa de Simon* and *Histoire d'une Fille de Ferme* concern the problem of the illegitimate child and the unmarried mother; *En Famille* is a humorous account of a couple's attempts to benefit from the death of a parent; and *La Femme de Paul* describes how Paul commits suicide when he discovers his mistress with a lesbian friend appropriately named Pauline. The problems of paternity and illegitimacy, of the disruptions caused in family relations by money or ambition, and confusion or deviation in sexual behaviour are favourite, almost stereotyped subjects in Maupassant's work. This is not only because they could provide him with short, episodic and gossip-like tales which appealed to his respectable readers who liked to read about the non-respectable and non-conventional in their daily routine; but also because such subjects allowed Maupassnt to poke a critical finger in an ironically humorous and amusing way at the hypocrisy and superficiality of the established social system of conventional habits and respectable morality of the world about him.

The fact that Maupassant's work did prick at the established order's social and moral conscience can perhaps be seen in the booksellers Hachette's initial refusal to sell *La Maison Tellier* at its railway kiosks all over France because it was thought an obscene book! Of course, *La Maison Tellier* was no more obscene than *Boule de Suif*; Maupassant is extremely discreet in his references to sexual matters in both and seems in fact to assume the reader's broader understanding of what is only implied in this context in the stories. Indeed, his brothel-keeper and prostitutes are rather too respectable to be true and it could well be objected that he has veered away from realism in depicting them in an idyllically Romantic way – partly perhaps from a fear of further censorship. Unfortunately, the more explicit emphasis on sexuality in many 'Naturalist' works such as Zola's *La Curée, La Faute de l'Abbé Mouret* and, of course, *Nana* had already caused more conservative readers and critics to protest at the unashamed pornography of 'Naturalist' writers, and since Maupassant's name featured in the *Soirées de Médan*, his stories tended often to be unfavourably treated by the opponents of Zola and his movement, whether they deserved it or not.

Despite this reaction on the part of more conservative critics – mostly the same ones who had already misjudged or condemned *Boule de Suif* the year before – *La Maison Tellier* was on the whole well received. Turgenev, to whom it is dedicated partly out of friendship and partly perhaps because it had been he who had suggested that the story's drunken English sailors would in such a situation sing *Rule, Britannia*, rather than *God Save the Queen*, praised the work and recommended it to Tolstoy who was similarly enthralled.[29] Pierre Loti, the celebrated novelist of the exotic, believed it to be the finest short story in French literature. And when Zola wrote a short article on Maupassant in *Le Figaro* on 11 July 1881 – in which, much to many people's indignation, he coupled an account of Maupassant with one on the slow-worked and unfruitful talents of Paul Alexis – he praised the *Maison Tellier* volume for the simplicity of its realism and psychological analysis. Above all, *La Maison Tellier* showed both Maupassant's friends and his critics that the talents he had displayed in *Boule de Suif* and *Des Vers* were not just accidental and that he could write further works with the same approach, style and readability. It showed he was well on the path to fame and fortune and only needed to press on with his writing to achieve them.

Maupassant did press on with his stories and his novel *Une Vie* as well as with his contributions to the paper *Le Gaulois* during the rest of 1881. It was partly because he wanted the time off for his writing and partly because his concentration on his literary work had a damaging effect on his latently bad health that he sought unpaid leave from the Ministry once again. This time he took to living on the river at Sartrouville in the white house on the quayside he shared with Léon Fontaine while a new apartment he had acquired in Paris at 83 rue Dulong was being renovated.

Then, in early July 1881, while *La Maison Tellier* was still being reviewed in the press and praised in literary circles, Maupassant left France with his adventurous friend from the *Revue Moderne et Naturaliste*, Harry Alis, for Algeria. Whether it was Arthur Meyer, the editor of *Le Gaulois*, or Alis who suggested the visit or whether it was Maupassant who wanted to combine a recuperative trip to the sun with some current affairs reporting is not known. Certainly, Algeria had been in the news recently at this time. Large numbers of Spanish settlers in the southern desert areas of Oran province had been massacred by the insurrectionist Arab chieftain Bou-Amama's nomadic tribesmen, who had so far eluded the French colonialist army sent out from the coastal areas to find them. And certainly, to judge by the preface Maupassant wrote for *Au Soleil*, the volume edition of his articles on his journey published in *Le Gaulois* in late 1881 and the *Revue Bleue* in 1883–4, he desired to get away to Algeria, as he had earlier to Corsica, so as to escape from the depressing monotony of his rather too industrious existence at home:

'When one is weary, weary of crying from morning till night, weary of not having the strength to get up to have a glass of water, weary of seeing the same friends too often so that they become tedious, the same odious, passive neighbours, and the same monotonously familiar things – one's house, one's street, the maid who asks "what would monsieur like for dinner?" and leaves the room lifting up with an unseemly kick of her heels the tattered edge of her filthy skirt, one's all too faithful dog, the unchanging blotches on the wallpaper, the regularity of one's meals, sleeping in the same bed, doing the same actions each day . . . : when one is tired of oneself, one's voice, the things one keeps on endlessly repeating, the narrow circle of one's ideas, one's own face in the mirror and the expressions it has when one is shaving or combing one's hair, then it is necessary to leave and experience something of a life that is new to one and full of change. A journey is a kind of gateway through which one passes from the reality one is already familiar with to an unexplored reality that seems like a dream.'

Maupassant and Alis set sail from Marseilles on the *Abd-el-Kader* for Algiers on 6 July 1881. They did not stay long in the capital, however, and soon left on an exhausting and often dangerous tour that took them first west through the Chélif valley to Oran and down south with a military convoy that was going to bring supplies through to the garrison near Saïda; they then set off through the desert wastes of the Zahrez and the Ouled-Naïl range and visited the Saharan settlements of Boghari and Bou-Saada with two officers exploring the region before returning north via Constantine and over the plains of the Kabylie province to Bône, whence they left on the *Kléber* for France. The whole journey was to take some two months and cover many hundreds of miles.

Once they had left the white houses, the Europeanised amenities and busy casbahs of Algiers and Oran they found themselves, as they headed south towards the Atlas mountains and the Sahara, in empty desert under a scorching sun; they travelled on horseback with Arab guides, sharing the hospitality of local chieftains as they went and sleeping under canvas with only the sandy wastes, the stars and the vultures, vipers and scorpions to keep them company. It was no wonder that the French army could not keep track of the tribes that had revolted against colonial rule or trace the elusive chief who planned the insurrection, Bou-Amama; for only the nomadic Arabs of the desert could find their way in such a wilderness of sandstorms, mirages, and rotting carcasses and they were not hindered like the French troops with equipment and provisions:

'The Arabs in these circumstances have an advantage over us which we strive in vain to overcome. They are the fruits of this soil. They live on a few figs and a few grains of flour and, not worn out by this climate that exhausts us Northerners and mounted on horses which are as steadfast and as insensitive to the heat as themselves, they can travel a hundred or a hundred and thirty kilometres in a day. Not having any baggage, convoys or provisions to drag along with them they can move about with astonishing speed, pass in between two camped garrisons to go and attack a village that thought itself safe and then vanish without trace, coming back suddenly when they are thought to be miles away.'

Maupassant's experiences in the desert made him realise not only the basic primitiveness of the nomadic tribes who were too often on the move to create a proper culture – he was surprised, for example, at the poor state of their tents and utensils when they had such fine carpets to sleep on and jewellery for their women – but also the duplicity of the Arab character. Already when in Algiers and Oran he had deplored the dirt and squalor of the casbahs and the use of children to obtain money from visitors, and remarked on the empty mechanical gestures of those praying in a mosque. Now out in the remoter areas he heard the local tribesmen bringing their complaints about their relatives or neighbours to the French army officers for settlement and realised after listening to the several different versions of each case the craftiness and untrustworthiness of the plaintiffs; indeed, he feared that even the very tribal chiefs whom the French trusted and relied upon might well not be as loyal as had been supposed.

He was shocked too at the many tales of homosexual practices he heard about among the Arab chiefs and their sons, although he was less shocked and more intrigued by the open prostitution of the girls of the Ouled-Naïl tribe at Boghari with their spectacular hair-styles and use of gold jewellery. Maupassant's view of the Arab population in Algeria was thus far from sympathetic; he was not taken with their character nor with their lack of culture and comfort; and he realised the gulf that existed between the French colonialists mainly resident in the coastal cities of Algiers and Oran and the tribesmen of the hinterland.

Nevertheless, despite his reservations about the Arabs, his main criticisms were aimed not at them but at French colonial policy. He blamed the French method of appropriating Arab land and leaving the Arabs without the means of obtaining food as one of the principal reasons for tribal insurrections and the support Bou-Amama found among the desert tribes. He sympathised with a French woman he met in the sun-baked town of Saïda, who, having emigrated with a claim on a plot of land sold her by the French government, now found she could grow nothing on it, and realised how she and her family were suffering from the harsh climate. And, finally, he blamed the French colonialists for putting so much trust on the *aghas* or tribal chiefs and for allowing the natives of the coastal Kabylie province to keep guard over forest areas there while suspecting them of being the instigators of the vast forest fires the province suffered in summer! Maupassant was not, however, alone at this time in criticising France's colonial policy, which was approaching its heyday in the

1880s, and many other writers were to condemn the government's action not only in Algeria and West Africa but also in South-east Asia two years later.

Despite his criticisms Maupassant enjoyed his visit immensely. He wrote to his mother from Saïda in August 1881:

'Just a short note, my dearest mama, to let you have my news which is excellent. I have just been out there as far as the chotts without a sign of Bou-Amama ... I can easily stand the heat. And I can assure you it's pretty unbearable up there on the high plateaux. We went a whole day with the sirocco wind blowing like fire in our faces. You could not even touch the butts of our rifles without burning your fingers. Under every stone you come across a scorpion. And we have also seen jackals and carcasses of dead camels being devoured by vultures ...'

And he was to write in his account of his travels how much he enjoyed the escapist remoteness and peacefulness of the desert when he lay in his tent under the stars after the day's trek in the unending expanse of the Sahara:

'And if you knew how far-away from the world, from life and from absolutely everything one feels oneself under this small, low tent through the holes in which one can see just the stars above and from under the flapping sides of which there can be seen but the vast sandy wastes!

'This land is monotonously unchanging, always dead and dusty; and yet it is here that one desires nothing, one regrets nothing, and one aspires to nothing. This peacefully still landscape, desolate and dazzling with light, satisfies the eye, sates one's thoughts and appeals to one's senses and one's dreams, because it is complete, it is *absolute*, and one could not imagine it otherwise. The odd bit of vegetation even shocks one here like something out of place, irritating and intolerable.

'It is every day the same spectacle at the same hour: the fiery globe devouring the earth; and as soon as the sun has set, the moon in its turn rises over the endless wilderness. But each day, little by little, the silent desert enters into your soul, penetrates your mind just as the harsh sunlight pierces your skin; and one feels one would like to become a nomad like these tribesmen who change their surroundings without changing their homeland amid this endless expanse which is virtually always the same.'

The silence and endlessness of the desert allow Maupassant to escape the pressures and anguish of his life at home. Unlike the nomadic tribesmen he cannot, however, escape for long; and when he moves on, it is back to the civilised world of nineteenth-century France with its industries, its science and its social and religious upheavals and not to another peaceful haven in the silent remoteness of the unchanging desert.

Symptomatic of the changes and consequent conflicts taking place in France at this time was society's reaction to 'Naturalism', which has been seen to have been quite violent among the conservative critics of *Au Bord de l'Eau* and the *Soirées de Médan*. When the fruits of Maupassant's labours after his visit to Algeria were collected together and published in the volume *Mademoiselle Fifi* in May 1882 (many of them having already appeared in the paper *Gil Blas* under Guy's *noms de plume* 'Valmont', borrowed from his ancestor's name, or 'Maufrigneuse' from December 1881 onwards) Maupassant was accused, like many of Zola's other followers, of concentrating in his work on the vulgar and pornographic. However, as has been observed in the cases of both *Boule de Suif* and the *Maison Tellier* stories, the more mature Maupassant was, despite his interest in pornography and reputation as a libertine, neither vulgar nor pornographic in his writing. It was because of his association with Zola and the 'Naturalists' that his work was all too readily taken as a target for conservative critics' attacks; they could not bear that another writer besides Zola himself should show that the 'Naturalists' were successful and talented.

The real reason for certain people's antagonism to Zola and 'Naturalism' lies in the fact that the theories and practice of

'Naturalism' represented in the literary field changes that were evolving in society as a whole in the 1870s and 1880s. 'Naturalism' was a progressive movement reacting against the illusions and idealism evoked in the Romantic writers' sentimental and exotic views of life; it looked to scientific theory and accuracy and not to the ideals of religion and morality for its depiction of Man; it thus took away the veneer of conventional respectability and illusion that disguised life both in reality and in the novel, and aimed to reveal the real, naked human being underneath. By reacting against the past and its religion and morality 'Naturalism' was, however, merely developing in literature what mechanised industrialisation and the scientific theories of Berthelot, Claude Bernard, Pasteur or Darwin had done in real life by making Man appear more materialistic and self-sufficient. 'Naturalism' was thus a product of its age in both a moral and spiritual sense as well as innovatory in the literary sphere.

It represented for its critics a general reaction against the established order that preferred scientific theories to Christian morality and consequently reduced Man from a being of conventional manners and tasteful appearances to an independent creature conditioned by the pressures outside and within himself such as heredity and instinct. To attack 'Naturalism' for its pessimistic view of Man as such a creature, by saying that the novels of Zola or Maupassant were sordid and pornographic, was in fact to criticise the evolution of social life and thought of the age they mirrored. The clash of 'Naturalist' writer and reactionary critic was then symptomatic of the conflict between progressive and traditional elements in French society itself in the early 1880s.

The original volume of stories entitled *Mademoiselle Fifi* has indeed extremely little that could be termed vulgar or pornographic in it. Its publication by Henry Kistemaeckers of Brussels, who had brought out many of the more forthright 'Naturalist' works of Huysmans, Rod, Alexis and Bonnetain, prepared the critics, however, for the worst. Moreover, Maupassant knew when he suggested the story of *Mademoiselle Fifi* itself to Kistemaeckers on 25 March 1882 that it would 'create a stir' and no doubt hoped to gain some publicity from this; but this 'stir' was to derive not from anything actually vulgar or pornographic but from the social implications of the tale, as in the case of *Boule de Suif* and *La Maison Tellier*.

Mademoiselle Fifi again recalls an incident in the Prussian occupation of France after the 1870 war; some Prussian officers are occupying an old French château and trying to overcome their boredom on a rainy afternoon by first destroying the valuable works of art and tapestries in the château and then inviting some prostitutes from Rouen for the evening. It is, however, when the Prussians' contempt for the French, so far seen in their attitude to the château and the local population, reaches its climax and one of them, nicknamed Mademoiselle Fifi by his companions, because of his coquettish disdain of the French, proposes a toast to their conquest of all the women of France that Rachel, the Jewish prostitute on his knee, stabs him. Her heroic action and escape to the bell-tower of the local church and her ironic ringing of the knell at the Prussian's funeral signify as in *Boule de Suif* the superb patriotism of the prostitute. The fact that the story closes with her courageous survival in the church tower until the war is over and her marriage to a wealthy husband who makes out of her 'a lady as good as many others' was clearly intended to be as critical of the passive Christian middle classes of the locality in 1870 and of women in general as the examples of Elisabeth Rousset and the inmates of the Maison Tellier had already been by similar implication.

In the other stories of the volume – apart from the amusing tale in *Un Réveillon* of a Norman peasant couple's removal of their father's corpse from his deathbed so that they can use the bed over Christmas – an equally critical view of women is presented and a largely pessimistic impression of life and love is given. *Marocca* shows the violent lengths to which a woman will go to receive the sexual pleasure she requires – in this case an Algerian beauty in Bougie who is ready to kill her husband with an axe to prevent him discovering her affair with the narrator – and stresses the sensual attractiveness of such a woman. *La*

Bûche, with its account of how a log falling from a fire prevented the narrator from being found in the arms of his friend's wife, states that women are unfaithful and exploit their appeal to men to pursue their own curiosity of adventurous romance. Indeed, Maupassant goes on to say in this story that men and women are so unequal by nature that the two can never remain in harmony in marriage and that the close, confiding friendship of one man with another is far superior and more permanent since one is not possessed and then abandoned by a faithless wife nor bothered with children who desert one in one's old age:

'You see, Madam, whatever love it is that welds a man and a woman together, they always remain strangers to each other in their mind and soul; they remain like two sides at war with each other; they are of different races; one of them must always be the master and the other the slave; one the trainer, the other the one trained; at one time it is one, another time the other in each of these roles; they are never equal. They might clutch at each other in ardently passionate embraces but their throbbing hands never meet in that same broad, strong and loyal clasp which opens two men's hearts and allows each to confide in the other in a sincere feeling of deep, virile affection. Wise men, instead of marrying and producing for their consolation in their old age children who will abandon them, should seek out a good and faithful friend and grow old with him in that mutual exchange of thoughts which can only exist between two men.'

Further pessimistic views of women and love are found in *Une Aventure Parisienne* and *Mots d'Amour*; in both love is seen as an illusion to blind us momentarily to true reality, a mirage on the horizon of our lives. In the first, a provincial wife with that same perfidious curiosity of romantic adventures as is described in *La Bûche* goes to Paris under the pretext of a social visit in search of love and excitement in the capital. She comes across a celebrated writer in a shop, pursues him all day, and finally succeeds in sleeping with him, but only to discover that he is more interested in sex than passion and to realise how ordinary and ugly he is; her dreams of the romance and of the vice of the capital are thus swept away like the refuse being swept into the gutters by the street-cleaners she passes on her way back to the country.

In *Mots d'Amour* a man writes to his mistress that she should be silent when they are together for 'in matters of love one is always evoking dreams and so that the dreams may be fully evoked, you must not interrupt them'. Such disillusioned idealism, reminiscent of some of the poems in *Des Vers*, also permeates the story *Le Lit*, in which the narrator finds in an old cassock he buys some letters from an elderly lady to her former lover, a priest, describing how she sees her old bed that has witnessed so many births, marriages and deaths through the ages including her own as a symbol of life; 'nothing is nice outside one's bed' she concludes, implying that the rest and comfort of a bed provides Man with one of the few consolations and shelters he has from life's processes, whether he is in pain or apparent happiness.

Similar pessimistic views can be found in the articles Maupassant published in *Le Gaulois* on 20 and 28 July 1882 in reply to the critics Albert Wolff and Francisque Sarcey's complaints that he, like other Naturalists, only concerned himself with the baser aspects of society and with the habits of prostitutes. While recognising in his reply to Wolff that there has been too great a concentration on low-life, Maupassant asserts that 'the persistent depictions of the "lower depths" is in effect but a protest against the secular theory of everything being ideal and poetic' and that if writers have concentrated so much on the baser aspects of society it merely shows the strength of their protest against Romanticism's idealisation of life. No one class, no established morality or systematic propriety is to prevent the writer of the 1880s taking a detached, penetrating look into all aspects of society; if life is not full of poetry and idealism, then literature should not be either and must show the cruder sides of existence with the better ones. Maupassant's reply to Sarcey, defending his interest in prostitutes, follows on from this rejection of conventional idealisation and propriety in the novel and reveals quite clearly his pessimistic view of women:

'The real reason for literature's interest in the prostitute is this: literature has now veered towards accurate observation of life; Woman has in effect two functions in life: love and maternity. Writers, perhaps wrongly, have always regarded the first of these roles more interesting for the reader than the second and they have primarily depicted Woman in the exercise of the professional role for which she seems to have been born. Of all subjects for writers love is that which most touches the public. And it is the woman of love whom they like most.'

Maupassant goes on to assert that unlike men women are classless and of not very different ability from one another; their human role is limited and because of this and their intellectual incapability they climb the social ladder only according to their lover or husband's status; a prostitute like any other woman can thus become a most elegant and proper wife, as Maupassant had said at the end of *Mademoiselle Fifi*. Earlier, in *Le Gaulois* of 30 December 1880, he had expressed similar views when considering the opinion on women of the German philosopher Schopenhauer, some of whose work had recently been translated into French by Maupassant's friend Jean Bourdeau. Agreeing with Schopenhauer on women's lack of intellectual and literary ability and asserting that we should not seek to find this in women since this is not their role in life, which is the love-making and maternal one, Maupassant blames Christianity for making women aware of their influence over men and idealising them:

'It was then that she realised her true power, showed her real talents, and cultivated her rightful domaine – that of Love! Man had intelligence and brute force; but then she made him her slave, her thing, her toy. She made herself the inspirer of his actions, the hope in his heart and the ideal of his dreams. Love, that bestial function of all creatures, that trap of Nature, became in her hands a terrible weapon for her domination. . . . Mistress of our hearts, she became that of our bodies . . . And if modern civilisation is so different from ancient civilisations and Oriental societies that disdained ideal, poetic love, it is due to the special genius of women and their secret, sovereign domination of us . . .'

Maupassant's degradation of women is then indicative of his revolt against the values of contemporary society and life in general. He was not alone in this attitude in the early 1880s for the defeat of Napoleon III in 1870 and some recent trade slumps and bank crashes had undermined people's confidence in France's apparent prosperity and power. Furthermore, a growing scepticism among intellectuals, produced firstly by the effects of 'Naturalism' and scientific theories that had reduced Man's role to a product of evolution, molecules and instincts, and secondly by the increasing gulf between an ever wealthier commercialised society and the ever more sophisticated, introverted world of the literary artist, had caused many writers and thinkers to view life with gloom. The values of the past in the political, moral, spiritual, and artistic spheres had all been undermined and were in process of being revised. There was a climate of change and uncertainty that inevitably gave rise to feelings of despair and doom, when the new sceptical and evolutionary approaches of thinkers to contemporary society seemed to suggest that life was founded on a series of unproven assumptions and principles, and that France had perhaps passed her prime and was declining in a welter of soul-less over-civilised sophistication.

It is not surprising that in such a climate the pessimistic views of Schopenhauer, his fellow German philosophers Büchner and Hartmann and the Englishman Herbert Spencer flourished. Similar ideas were propagated by the composer Wagner and the Russian nihilists, recently made known by Turgenev in his novels *Virgin Soil* and *Fathers and Children* and mentioned by Maupassant in his article on the Russian writer in *Le Gaulois* of 21 November 1880. These ideas were made known largely through the many abridged translations and articles in the press by Caro, Bourdeau, Cantacuzène, Challemel-Lacour, and writers like Maupassant himself that appeared at this time. For a sensitive and sick novelist like Maupassant who had long periods of depression and frustration, whose confidence in man had been sapped by his interest in the theory of evolution and whose trust in society's values had been undermined by his own experiences and by Flaubert's attitude, Schopenhauer's metaphysic of the relativity of Man's knowledge of reality and of life as a continual desiring, delusion and suffering, which can only be escaped by suppression of the will and contemplative, neo-Buddhist isolation, had a great appeal. This can be judged to some extent by the tale *Auprès d'un Mort*, which Maupassant published in *Gil Blas* on 30 January 1883, on the death of the German philosopher; the hideous, cynical smile of Schopenhauer's corpse caused by the frame of his false teeth, which falls out later as the body decomposes, serves as a macabre symbol of the philosopher's sceptical overturning of all hopes, ideals and beliefs in life.

It was in this climate of Schopenhauern pessimism, which at this time produced Zola's *Joie de Vivre* and Huysmans' *A Rebours* (highly praised by Maupassant) as well as Paul Alexis' *Le Besoin d'Aimer* and Edouard Rod's *La Course à la Mort*, that in 1883 Maupassant published his first novel, *Une Vie*. It was serialised in *Gil Blas* in late February and early April 1883 and appeared at Victor Havard's, who had brought out *La Maison Tellier*, that same month. Turgenev, whose death Guy was to mourn later in the year, had persuaded the editor, Strassulevitch, to serialise the novel at the same time in the *Messager d'Europe* of St Petersburg. *Une Vie* was dedicated to Flaubert's close friend Mme Brainne, who had always been so hospitable to 'little Guy' as she used to call him. However, she clearly disapproved of the gesture, to judge by Goncourt's diary account of the way she reprimanded Maupassant at Zola's house on 10 April. Perhaps she feared that people would see more in her relationship with the young writer than was the case, as had happened with her friendship with Flaubert years before, and disliked the notion; or perhaps she did not want to be associated with a book that Hachette had again banned from its railway kiosks and that had aroused much scandal in the press against which Guy anonymously and in vain tried to protest through letters to various newspapers.

Maupassant had not written the whole novel in one supreme effort but over quite a number of years. Indeed, it is said that it was his plans for this novel which he discussed in many of his letters to Flaubert, who approved of them with great enthusiasm. He certainly mentioned the idea of a novel in a letter to Flaubert of 10 December 1877, but it is clear that he had not yet started on it and was not to do so for some time to come because of his work at the Ministry and his concentration on his poems and dramas. His anxiety about changing his job, his ill health, and his other interests prevented him adding much to the novel during the following year, and on 13 January 1879 he complained to Flaubert that his work and his drama *Histoire du Vieux Temps* were stopping him continuing his novel: 'You see, I have very little free time. I am getting farther and farther parted from my poor novel. I rather fear the umbilical cord between us has now been cut. . . .' However, as his work situation improved and his stories gained success, Maupassant no doubt returned hopefully to the idea of his novel. Two episodes in it were to appear separately entitled *Le Saut du Berger* and *La Veillée* in *Gil Blas* on 9 March and 7 June 1882, indicating not only Maupassant's writing of the novel at this time but also the episodic way in which it was completed; and extracts from his account of his trip to Corsica were also added to it later that year. It was then during the months that Maupassant spent in his study at the house he rented with Léon Fontaine at Sartrouville on the river Seine that he completed the novel after his return from Algeria. It had taken some five to six years to write and its pessimism was not just a product of the contemporary moral climate but also the fruits of Maupassant's own experiences and thought over these years: the fruits of his own family background, ill health, frustration at work, boredom in love, annoyance with society and politics, as well as of his contact with the sceptical 'Hermit of Croisset', who shared and fermented these views of his young disciple with his own misanthropic, anti-social opinions and example.

Une Vie is a novel of gloom and disillusionment. The life described in it is that of Jeanne de Perthuis des Vauds, whose early idealism and hopes are constantly crushed by a disillusioning fatality as cruel as that which Flaubert had applied to his frustrated Romantic heroine Emma Bovary. Like Emma, Jeanne has left her convent school innocent of the harsh facts of life and full of Romantic notions about the world; when she is brought home to the old mansion beside the sea called *Les Peuples*, she is 'ready to grasp all the happy things in life which she had dreamed of for so long'; her vitality and innocence are reflected in the descriptions of the sea and countryside about her just as her aspirations for love are symbolised in the old tapestries in the mansion's drawing-room, depicting the passion of Pyramus and Thisbe. When she meets the handsome, dominating Julien de Lamare she thinks she has found the passion and lover of her dreams; this is shown through their conversations on exotic places – reminiscent of Emma Bovary and Frédéric Moreau's similar ones in Flaubert's novels – and their sailing together along the coast near Etretat. Her ideals of love and hopes for married life are indeed confirmed for a while after their marriage when they spend their honeymoon in Corsica, and Jeanne's imagination is fired by the island's exoticism and awesome landscapes.

Their return to *Les Peuples* accentuates, however, the disillusionment which had been indicated at the novel's beginning by the rain falling, by the picture of the dead lover Jeanne looks at and by the lover's receding footsteps she imagines hearing. It had been illustrated above all on the couple's wedding night, when Julien had savagely deflowered his virgin bride. Julien's continued thirst for sexual satisfaction coincides with Jeanne's disillusionment in her dreams of love and married life. His liaison first with Rosalie the maid and later with a neighbour's wife, Gilberte Fourville, mark Jeanne's gloom and despair in her monotonous existence, symbolised in the autumnal colours and snowy silence of the surrounding countryside. The horrible way

Rosalie gives birth to Julien's child shatters Jeanne's dreams of conjugal love and maternity completely.

As if such incidents were not sufficient to bring Jeanne to despair, her mother suddenly dies and she discovers that the latter, who had instilled all the Romantic notions about love in her daughter, had herself committed adultery. This now makes Jeanne realise the futility of human existence and the unpleasant realities about it; she sees that all her dreams and ideals were based on false premises; death denies the significance of life and love is but a pretext: 'All things in life culminated merely in misery, sadness, misfortune and death. Everything was a deception, a lie, the cause of suffering and tears.' This pessimistic view of life is shortly afterwards symbolised in the ascetic priest Tolbiac's savage attack on a dog having pups, Count de Fourville's killing of Julien and Gilberte by pushing the caravan used by them over the cliff and Jeanne's miscarriage on hearing of this.

With this destruction of Jeanne's hopes for a second child and the death of her husband, Jeanne can look to neither the past nor the future for consolation. Only her affection for her first child, Paul, had raised her spirits during all her disillusionment and now he too deserts her in her hour of need and becomes involved in financial disasters and an unfortunate liaison in Paris that drain her of money and force her to sell *Les Peuples*. Her last inspection of the old, empty and now dilapidated mansion from which her parents have departed and where her own dreams have been shattered provides a gloomy epilogue to this novel of disaster and disillusion. Only the arrival home of Paul and his baby son after his mistress's death adds a final note of possible vague optimism on the very last page: 'Life, you see, is never so good nor so bad as you think.' This dictum, reminiscent of what Flaubert had written in a letter to his young disciple on 18 December 1878, does little to diminish the general gloom and pessimism of the work which stem not only from Jeanne's disillusionment but, above all, from the crude and horrible events in the novel. The rape of Jeanne on her wedding night, the maid's giving birth, the priest's attack on the dog in labour, and the death of Julien and

Gilberte were highly 'Naturalistic' in showing the seamy side of life, particularly the sexual aspects, but they are rendered here especially horrifying by the sadistically crude realism with which they are described.

If, as has been claimed, the characters of Jeanne and Julien have affinities with Maupassant's own parents and if *Les Peuples* can be identified with the Château de Grainville and *Les Verguies*, then the ugly violence of the novel's events could be seen as an expression of the author's own deep frustrations and revolt against his father and all ideals in love and life; only compassion for Jeanne as a mother is allowed to stand, perhaps as a tribute to Laure. It would be unwise, however, to speculate too much about the biographical accuracy and psychological implications of the novel since it is a work of fiction. What can be said, nevertheless, is that, whatever the autobiographical extent of the work, *Une Vie* represents Maupassant's pessimistic view of the disillusioning futility of human existence and a denial of its ideals.

Similar themes to those in *Une Vie* can be found in the dozens of short stories that Maupassant published at this time – a further indication of the episodic mode of composition of the novel. Most of them appeared first in *Le Gaulois* or *Gil Blas* in 1882 and 1883 and were then collected together in the volumes *Contes de la Bécasse* and *Miss Harriet* of 1883 and *Clair de Lune* of 1884. With the one theme or situation Maupassant thus managed to reap a triple income and with the constant flow of stories he wrote in these years this income increased by leaps and bounds.

The same devastating effect of sexuality and intensity of passion that shatters Jeanne's marriage in *Une Vie* and seems to defy social convention and morality can be found in *L'Enfant*, *Une Veuve*, and, by symbolic implication, in *Madame Cocotte* and *Le Loup*; always it brings tragedy and death – in the case of the pregnant widow in *L'Enfant*, her gruesome end in an attempt to abort her child merely serves to shock the reader into accepting the doctor/ narrator's view at the story's opening that such sexual passions are not for the conventional bourgeois. Such intense desires have equally tragic results when they go unrequited as in the cases of the peasant spinsters in *La Rempailleuse* and *La Reine Hortense* and of the religious English woman in love with a painter at Etretat, *Miss Harriet*.

Two other aspects of this theme of extra-marital sexuality that defies social conventions are the relationship between the husband's wife and mistress and the problem of the illegitimate child. They are very much to the fore in *Le Pardon*, where the wife forgives her husband and even lays flowers on his mistress's grave, and in *L'Enfant*, where the wife, like Jeanne with her son's child in *Une Vie*, agrees even on her wedding-night to bring up the child of her husband and his dying mistress. More tragic circumstances can arise later, however, if paternity of the child is not claimed at its birth; the drunken peasant lad in *Un Fils* whom an Academician later recognises as his son by a Breton maid he met thirty years before has led, like the equally unattractive subject of the later tale *Duchoux*, a futile, anonymous existence precisely because of his lack of paternity – a situation Maupassant will exploit again in later stories such as *Le Père*, *Monsieur Parent*, *Adieu*, and *L'Abandonné*.

A difficult situation can also occur if, years after the child is born illegitimate, paternity is suddenly discovered such as in *Le Testament*, where, rather like in a later tale *Hautot Père et Fils*, a wife leaves all her wealth and one of her sons to her former lover. Incestuous relationships can arise in such circumstances as in *Monsieur Jocaste* and *L'Ermite* where fathers unknowingly possess their own daughters. In all these situations the unconventional challenges the conventional pattern of life and the natural urges of men disrupt the established order of things, whether it is a case of disguised adultery as in *Les Bijoux* or something more perverse like the incestuous relationship of *Monsieur Jocaste*, and macabre like the lover embracing his putrefied mistress in her grave in *La Tombe* and the woman picking up distressed lovers in the cemetery in *Les Tombales*. In most of the stories it is a sudden revelation or a disillusioning incident that forms the plot and gives rise to the criticism of the characters.

The few tales of the 1870 war – *Un Coup d'Etat* and *L'Aven-*

ture de Walter Schnaffs - serve this same purpose of showing up
the bourgeois for their vanity and presumptuousness through the
revelatory situations they find themselves in; while the two or
three ghost stories – *La Peur, Conte de Noël,* and *Apparition* –
again defy the established understanding of life by conveying
uncertainty and mystery instead. In contrast to the implied
criticism – often suggested by the indirect narration and pre-
facing of tales – of the bourgeois in town and country, Maupassant's stories on peasant life are largely descriptive, sentimental
and humorous. Only occasional glimpses of Norman country life
and the coastal scenery were given in *Une Vie,* but in *Miss
Harriet* there are long descriptions of the Etretat area and in
Contes de la Bécasse there are quite a number of illustrations of the
Norman character. *Farce Normande* shows the region's love of
gaulois fun – a bridegroom is tricked into missing his wedding-
night – and *Un Normand* the local brand of irreverent humour;
Saint-Antoine provides an instance of peasant craftiness from the
1870 Prussian occupation; *Les Sabots, Aux Champs, En Mer,*
and *Pierrot* describe, like *Le Diable* later, the Norman's concern
with money and his meanness in their tales of children being
bartered for money and a man's arm and a dog being sacrificed to
save expense. Thus, while the stories involving the bourgeois
class have moral and social implications, the tales about the
Normandy peasants are basically centred on purely human
qualities and failings.

What is interesting about all the stories is, however, the way
Maupassant manages to use the same situation time and time
again merely by altering the circumstances in some small way – a
change in the location, a difference of age, a switching of relationships, or a fresh perspective from a new angle. This was partly
due to the fact that he often kept the basic ideas of his long stories
or novels in his mind for a long while before he wrote on them in
a definitive form and used them meanwhile in shorter tales to
prefect his presentation of them as well as to continue to make a
living. Whether it is the short tale or a larger novel, however, the
themes and interests of the writer remain the same: he criticises

the same people and conventions and he laughs at the same human antics and foibles.

How far Maupassant's actual interest in what he described was genuine it is difficult to judge; no doubt his own sexual desires and activities and his Norman background determined to some extent the nature and treatment of his basic material just as his concern with both town and country life reflects his own participation in both, but there is no hard evidence to prove any greater auto-biographical involvement. It seems in fact more likely that he exploited bourgeois situations and peasant happenings that he heard talked about because they invited scandal and gossip and, using the inventive and imaginative talents he displayed in company as a boastful storyteller, he based his tales on them to please his reading public, who similarly enjoyed such matters presented in an open and respectable literary form. The conventional bourgeois of the towns and cities savoured the slight taste of naughtiness in his work with a sly relish and enjoyed the exotic flavour of his tales of the countryside with a townsman's curiosity.

Moreover, apart from his tales about peasant life, he did not follow Zola in describing the working class and its vices, but wrote about the bourgeois in town and country as well as the rural aristocracy – the two classes, in fact, with which his readers were familiar and could identify. In short, Maupassant exploited not only the social and geographical division between town and country but also the very hypocrisy and egotism of the conventional, selfish bourgeois that he deplored in his work; indeed, he used the scandal he aroused for his publicity. But he did not care about this as long as he prospered; for he had decided to resign from the Ministry and rely on his writing for a living.

And prosper he certainly did, working away so hard into the night to produce the flow of material – some seventy stories and two novels in 1883 alone – for *Gil Blas* and *Le Gaulois*, until he was immobilised by neuralgia and nearly blind. He wrote to Zola in 1883 that his eyes were so weak he could hardly see to read or write and was forced to ask his friends to do his proof-reading for him. He was thus obliged on 19 March 1883 to consult another doctor, this time an ophthalmic specialist Edmond Landolt, who in fact diagnosed that his eye condition was related to his contraction of syphilis. But it would seem that he did little to prevent his condition from worsening apart from taking more baths and powders and, increasingly, some pain-killing drugs including ether, which also had the advantage of giving his tired mind a greater lucidity when he was writing.

As long as the editors asked for more stories for their readers, and the publishers – Charpentier, Havard, Rouveyre, Kistemaeckers, Monier, and so on – clamoured for his works and sought sole rights over them for enormous sums which Maupassant enjoyed continuously raising, he did not stop writing. Having become involved in literature because of emotional ties and for aesthetic reasons and having found it first a worthy haven for escape from the outside world and then a subterfuge from the cruel realities of life, Maupassant now exploited his talents to become a slave of his own desires for fame and money regardless of the consequences. Underlying these materialistic ambitions were, however, his sceptical pessimism and his ill health; under the appearance of the man of fame and fortune there lay the mind of the cynic and the body of the invalid that he carefully hid.

PART THREE

THE CÔTE D'AZUR

CHAPTER 1

The Fruits of Fame

With the success of his first novel, *Une Vie*, and the continuing popularity of his short stories, which maintained his earlier reputation gained by *Boule de Suif*, *La Maison Tellier* and *Mademoiselle Fifi* and kept his name constantly in the public eye, Maupassant's way of life began gradually to change. He could now afford much more luxury and sophistication in his home and in his social engagements and, if he carried on working away to continue to have wealth and fame and fell ill in doing so, he could at least spoil himself with the best treatment and cures available for his ailments. After 1883 Maupassant still spent his mornings writing at his desk, but his afternoons and evenings were increasingly taken up by his sporting activities and his round of engagements in high society.

However, while the first of these depended on his own volition and was as welcome as ever as a source of recreation and relaxation, the second was more of an imposition from outside and at first resented by the shy, conscientious writer in him. Maupassant knew nevertheless that his fame depended to a large extent on his sociability, and therefore came to concede more and more time to the claims of his many admirers and high-ranking hostesses. A life of luxury and pleasures thus began to intrude on his rather solitary existence of toil and illness. This change was not only a natural consequence of his fame but also a reflection of the society he lived in; it too had gradually sought more and more escape in luxury and pleasure from the complex industrial and commercial world it had created as the nineteenth century came towards its close.

In the 1830s and 1840s Balzac had shown the moral and social effects of ambition and wealth which were arising from the commercial expansion of the cities and towns. By the 1860s and 1870s other writers were to comment on the further developments of commerce by industrial mechanisation and speculation at home and colonial expansion overseas. France was catching up on Britain as an industrial, highly urbanised state. Her newly rich commercial and industrial upper middle class now replaced what remained of her former aristocracy and tried to imitate its innate tastes and luxuries by its acquired wealth and assumed habits. The more one earned, the more pleasures and luxuries one afforded and the higher and more genuinely aristocratic the society one frequented.

As Taine showed in his *Vie et Opinions de Frédéric-Thomas Graindorge* of 1867 and as Zola depicted in *La Curée* of 1872 – and later in *La Débâcle* and *L'Argent* – upper middle-class wealth founded on ambition and speculation brought in an era of pseudo-aristocratic pleasure and luxurious self-indulgence which Balzac had foreseen decades before. Strangeness and variety became the order of the day in the formation of new tastes and styles to satisfy the increasingly more lavish and sophisticated demands of such a society as the competition of business infiltrated into the realms of pleasure; and these desires were answered by the eclecticism and cosmopolitanism of literature and thought as well as by the exoticism of the late nineteenth century. Foreign gods, foreign writers, colonial furnishings and overseas flora were all the rage. Silks and furs, orchids and tropical birds, marbles, mosaics and mazurkas were the trappings of this *fin de siècle* world of money and pleasure that acclaimed alike the Rothschilds and the Lafittes, Sarah Bernhardt and Réjane with equal fervour. Thanks to his success and the receptivity of the public to his work, Maupassant too now had the money to indulge like the rest of society of the 1880s in some of its tastes and pleasures; the *'industriel des lettres'* ('industrialist of literature'), as Maupassant called himself, was to have his share in the sophisticated high life of the Paris *salons* and the aristocratic elegance of the Côte d'Azur.

Signs of Guy's new prosperity and of changes in his mode of existence could already be seen in 1883. As a result of the profits from his stories in *Gil Blas* and *Une Vie* he had his recently acquired apartment in the rue Dulong renovated, bought a yacht which he named *Louisette* and kept moored near La Salis along the Côte d'Azur where his mother spent the winter and where he often came to visit her, and had a country house built by Touzat on a plot of land at Etretat owned by Laure near the village of Criquetot. This house, which Maupassant renamed *La Guillette* from the feminine diminutive of his own name, was – apart from the various rooms he hired along the Seine at Chatou and Sartrouville and on his visits to the Côte d'Azur – to be his retreat for much of the rest of his life. It was far from the bustle of Paris and less frequented than the resorts of the south and it provided Maupassant with the sea, fresh air and Norman country-side of his youth that he loved. Here he could go swimming and boating around the picturesque coast with his cousin Louis Le Poittevin, could entertain some of his friends with the help of his Belgian valet François Tassart, whom his tailor had recom-mended to him in November 1883, and, above all, sit in peace and write.

The house itself, a single-storey construction consisting of two wings joined by a wooden balcony and an out-house, that was formed out of an upturned boat or *caloge* supported on brickwork and served as a bathroom and as Tassart's quarters, had a grand view of the sea and was surrounded by a large garden. Here Guy planted poplars and ash-trees and lots of flowers, with the aid of his local gardener and custodian, Cramoyson, and cultivated beds of strawberries and a few vegetables. He also had a goldfish pond constructed; and so as to have fresh food, kept a whole poultry-yard of chickens and ducks, enjoying feeding the fish and chickens and taking pride in the virility of his cock-fowl. He also liked to practise shooting at a special target he had put up and occasionally went out hunting with his two basset hounds. According to the description of him given in *The Woman's World* of 1889 by one of his visitors at *La Guillette*, the American

Blanche Roosevelt, Guy's rustic appearance and tough, ruddy look made him seem particularly at home there:

'In personal appearance Guy de Maupassant is of medium height, solid, well-built, and has the bearing of a soldier; he has a fine characteristic Norman head, with the straight line from neck to crane which we see in the medallions of the old Conquest warriors; his forehead is low, rather too heavily lined; and his hair, brown and wavy, is now combed straight back in the fashion of modern Roman youth. In short, M. de Maupassant has such a look of cheeriness that he reminds one of a clear autumn day – an agreeable harmony in russet colours and russet tints: dark brown laughing eyes, a shapely mouth half concealed by a heavy brown moustache, an olive skin mantled with red and a general healthy ruddiness give this character and warmth to his physiognomy.'

However, while the head and complexion – as well as, quite often, the untidy and old clothes he wore – remained those of the rural Norman, the sensual mouth and moustache were already those of the 'Bel Ami' of society, which he desired to be and that later made Goncourt refer to him in his *Journal* on 9 July 1892 as being 'vulgarly handsome' in his attractiveness to society women. In the same way, despite the rustic setting of *La Guillette*, its interior was to become increasingly sophisticated as Maupassant penetrated further into high society and its shelves became cluttered more and more with antiques and bibelots. A special guest room was also prepared for those of his guests who could not or did not want to return home after a dinner there.

François Tassart has left in his memoirs [30] brief accounts of these anonymous guests and the gatherings they attended; how clear his memories of them were after thirty years and how truthful his accounts of Maupassant's love life and of the hoaxes played on many an admirer and guest are after being published by a journalist ghost-writer is hard to tell. Did Maupassant take his revenge on one young lady by having her seduced by an apparently wealthy and certainly lecherous Spaniard, trick another into believing one of the guests was an Italian count, seek to spite another by sending her a box of frogs, and enjoy fooling a group of young ladies by trying to pass off to them a schoolmistress in masculine attire as an effeminate youth? Certainly, Guy always liked playing tricks even in childhood and there is no reason to suppose he grew out of this habit, although much of the detail of the hoaxes is open to doubt. As for his love-life, he no doubt satisfied his appetite with some of the many young ladies, female artists and actresses who visited him or whom he met in Paris and brought to Etretat. No exact records are available, however, and therefore too much should not be presumed or read into Tassart's memoirs.

Several of the women who came to *La Guillette* were neighbours like Mme Hermine Lecomte du Noüy and Clémence Brun. Hermine, tall and golden-haired, had abandoned her architect husband in Rumania, where he worked, to return to France. As an intellectual and occasional story-writer she was good company for Guy and he in turn was pleased to have her help in the writing and distributing into volumes of his stories, particularly when his sight began to fail. Clémence Brun, the chestnut-haired wife of a coffee-merchant, was also of great service to him in this respect. Many of his other guests were visitors to Etretat with whom he merely chatted and invited to a game of bowls or croquet just as he would often go out shooting with his male guests, calling at Ernestine Aubourg's inn on their return. Apart from these excursions and the occasional dinner-party, Etretat was essentially a retreat for Guy; much of his novels *Bel-Ami* and *Pierre et Jean* was written in the peaceful garden of *La Guillette*; and he found here for many years, even after he had been attracted by the better climate of the south, a place of comparative solitude and relaxation dear to his Norman heart.

Another sign of Guy's greater opulence and sophistication was his moving on 3 April 1884 from the rather cramped apartment in rue Dulong he had inhabited for a couple of years to a suite on the ground floor of a block left by the painter Eugène Le Poittevin to his nephew the landscape artist Louis Le Poittevin at 10 rue Montchanin (now rue Jacques Bingen) a few streets away. The well-known hostess of literary gatherings, Mme Aubernon, lived opposite at number 11, Mme Adam had her *salon* nearby and from here the peace and greenery of the small, elegant Parc Monceau were but a hundred yards away. Guy was now also somewhat nearer the fashionable *salons* and residences of the famous avenues leading towards the Arc de Triomphe from the north of the city – Wagram, Friedland, Foch and Malherbes.

And so here the robust yet stolid Norman, who gave away apples and eggs to his neighbours at *La Guillette*, offered a local beggar at Etretat, Marie Seize, a few francs, and provided a fire-work display for the locality every August 15, showed the more sophisticated side to his character in his choice of decorations and furnishings. A well-known painter and decorator, Kakléter, was given the task of painting the dining-room in deep red, the lounge in Louis XVI blue, the bedroom in yellow, and the conservatory in olive green. Rows of bookshelves were installed for the writer's hundreds of volumes and an antique chair and wide desk took up most of one side of his study. Both here and in the other rooms the walls and table-tops were cluttered with all kinds of antique and exotic objects and subtropical plants adorned every corner as well as filled the indoor garden of the conservatory. Statuettes of angels and a bust of Flaubert vied with a large golden statue of Buddha, Rouen vases with Chinese porcelain, Louis XVI objets d'art with fashionable Japanese bibelots. The acquisition of a bearskin rug and of a cat, Piroli, added a touch of sensual softness to the sophisticated décor, while a ceiling in stained glass by Mme Lecomte de Noüy's brother, Camille Oudinot, that was illuminated by gas lighting, was put up in January 1885 and bathed the writer's lounge in the strange hues of its mottled reflections.

The variety and exoticism of the suite's furnishings were to a large extent the result of the eclecticism and bizarreness of con-temporary thought and taste as well as of Maupassant's own garishness and lack of discrimination – a fact which made

Goncourt, who prided himself on the vast, precious collection of art and bibelots of his own apartment, disdainfully comment that the writer's study looked like the 'lodging of a negro pimp'. Moreover, while the highly contemporary mixture of sensuality and sanctity provided by the furs and flora on the one hand and the religious trappings on the other revealed in particular the hedonist and the sceptic in their owner, certain other fittings betrayed the heavy toll on his health that such luxury cost him. Because of the deteriorating condition of his eyes, particularly after long bouts of writing, the amount of light in his rooms had to be limited; as he did not want the windows shuttered, which would have prevented him getting the fresh air he liked to have, he had curtains fitted and drawn so that only a restricted amount of daylight filtered through. And to ease the migraine and also the palpitations he suffered, he had a shower installed in November 1884 to replace the tub of ice-cold water he bathed in every day at midday. This was usually followed by a massage with eau de Cologne, performed by his valet François, on the couch that, rather significantly, stood opposite the desk in his study.

It was also because of his health and because it was fashionable that Maupassant went more and more often to stay with his mother convalescing in the warmer climate of the Côte d'Azur. Here, he could escape the worst of the Paris winter, see his mother and brother and go sailing on *Louisette*; he could also keep in close contact down there with his friends in high society. For in coming to the Côte d'Azur, Maupassant was following a social trend that first of all saw Europe's royalty – including Queen Victoria and the notorious Prince of Wales – and cosmopolitan aristocracy visiting and settling there because of the mild climate, pleasant scenery and elegant atmosphere; then the wealthy bourgeois had arrived in imitation of their superiors and also bought villas and yachts along the coast. Less well-off than either of these groups, Maupassant merely rented a flat in Cannes overlooking the sea in early 1884.

According to his valet's memoirs, Maupassant would work there until midday, go pistol-shooting, sailing or visiting in the afternoon, and had his mother and brother to dinner each evening. He had always hated the darkness and cold of winter in the north and became more and more attracted to the sunnier and less depressing climate of the Midi so that in November 1885 he rented a villa at Cap d'Antibes from a sea captain named Muterse, who was to provide him with another sailor for his yachting excursions as well as with the craft that was a year later to be called *Bel Ami*.

As Guy became more established on the Côte d'Azur, he bought his mother a separate house called *Badrine* on the Antibes–Cannes road, and provided a farm near Antibes for his brother who had taken up horticulture. It seemed as if Maupassant had thus satisfied his own and his family's interests by escaping as often as possible to the sunny sophisticated south; unfortunately, neither money nor luxury could ward off the fatal sickness that was eventually to overcome all three. Indeed, in Maupassant's own case, the continual need to earn the money to finance his homes and yachts as well as the finer clothes he wore and the entertaining he now did served only to aggravate his condition. In 1884 he wrote to Zola that he had not written to him because 'I have had to produce so much material to pay for my house at Etretat that I really have not had two hours to myself'; and on 22 July that year he told the photographer Félix Nadar's niece that he had postponed his visit to the spa at Châtel-Guyon and was relying on his next novel to cover his debts:

'I have underwritten bills that I must pay month after month right up to next January; and I will only be able to pay them by borrowing. I was well off two months back, but 12,000 francs for house-moving and 5,000 francs for hunting expenses, which had to be paid at once, have forced me to take drastic measures. I am sorry to bother you with these intimate details of my finances but I wish to explain to you how it is that I am completely unable to do the favour you ask since I am reduced to the strictest of economies until the publication of my next book, on which I have already taken out a loan . . .'[31]

The 'industrialist of literature' as Maupassant called himself thus became a victim of his own success and fame; the more material he produced, the more money he gained, the more of a celebrity he became, and the more of a socialiser he had necessarily to become whether he really wanted to or not. Maupassant was not in fact, despite his success as a rather salacious joker in an informal group of fellow rowers or artists, a very sociable person suited to more formal society. The writer in him was shy, the pessimist indifferent and the Norman sceptical and cautious; his rather tough, muscular, military bearing was belied by a docile inner placidity and his pose as a libertine by his chaste conversation. This was how the dramatist Georges de Porto-Riche described him as he was in 1885 in *Le Figaro Littéraire* of 16 March 1912:

'He does not look like a man of letters. Guy de Maupassant is a fellow of thirty-five, fairly slim, of military bearing, and neatly dressed. Seen from a distance, when he does not see you looking, he has something harsh and insolent about his face, but as soon as you talk to him, his expression changes; the insolence of a moment ago gives way to a polite niceness that seems quite natural. A smiling docility comes over him from head to foot. His gaze is perhaps still suspicious but his voice is exceptionally soft. His gestures are reserved and lack familiarity. His whole manner is cautious and extremely modest . . . His conversation is careful and calculated. He only speaks a bare minimum and very seldom mentions himself. He does not make any verbal attacks on anyone but his retorts can be dangerous . . .'

If his sudden outbursts of acid comment and the occasional lively jest revealed the more passionate nature beneath his calm exterior and occasionally involved him in fierce argument or playful controversy, his docile shyness, slight stutter and polite manner appealed to women and, with his latent, accentuated sensuality, made him particularly vulnerable to their advances. Thus, although he was not by nature particularly suited to socialising and had little time for it in fact because of his writing, he was increasingly driven by his reputation as a writer on the one hand and his docile affability as a guest on the other into indulging in it for publicity purposes. It was a vicious circle which was to take a strangle-hold on him when his diseased and anguished body and soul could no longer find any escape from its grasp.

Guy's fame did have its compensations, however. He received a large fanmail and acquired a number of female admirers of different kinds. Among these his correspondence with a young invalid in Paris, Marie Bashkirtseff, who wrote to him anonymously in April 1884 asking to become his secret *confidante*, provides an amusing and revealing episode. At first, Maupassant was both irritated by and suspicious of her anonymity; he was by nature suspicious and diffident and having been tricked by the hoaxes of other correspondents he was not very inclined to accept Marie at her word. He told her, moreover, that he was not in the least as she probably imagined him, being without a poetic soul and indifferent to his work:

'I have not a pennyworth of poetry in me. I treat everything with indifference and spend two thirds of my time being utterly bored with myself. I spend the other third of it writing material that I sell at as high a price as possible, regretting having to do this wretched type of work that has brought me the distinction of being known and famous for you!'

Marie was not to be put off, however; her reply, teasing him with her anonymity and answering his assertions about his indifference and venality by pointing out he was not the first writer to complain about his work and write for money, was even accompanied by a sketch of how she thought Maupassant looked – a corpulent man dozing in an armchair under a palm tree at the seaside with a glass of beer and a cigar on the table in front of him! In turn, Maupassant teased her in his letter of 3 April by saying he believed her to be a college teacher or prefect and treating her as such in a satirical manner. He also commented on her sketch of him:

'Your sketch does indeed look like me. I would, however, like to
point out a few errors:

'1. I'm not so fat.

'2. I never smoke.

'3. I drink neither beer nor wine and alcohol, just water.
Therefore dreaming in front of a glass of beer is not my favourite
pose. I am more often crouched in Oriental fashion on a divan.
You ask who my favourite painter is among contemporary
artists? – Millet. Among musicians? I hate music! I prefer in
reality a pretty girl to all the arts. I would put a good dinner – a
really good one – a rare one – almost on the same level as a pretty
girl.

'There's my creed, my dear professor . . .'

Clearly Maupassant was exaggerating to some extent just as he
was in his earlier letter – he liked to boast of his libertine desires
and his indifference to his work to conceal his basic shyness and
devoted conscientiousness from other people – but his disillusionment with life as a whole, his attempts to escape from it in
recreation and some self-indulgence and the resulting boredom
when his escapism was too temporary to satisfy him were completely true. Was not Céard to remark to Goncourt on 20 July
1892 that Maupassant was the most indifferent man he had known
and yet at times he could also be the most passionate? It has
already been mentioned that Guy was both idealistically sentimental and ruthlessly objective in his views of life; the contradictory mixture in him of the sensualist and the misogynist, of the
moralist and the cynic and of the socialiser and the loner, which is
also often found in the fusion of Romantic sentiment and
'Naturalistic' realism in his work, was to become increasingly
unsatisfactory. For he was seeking an ideal woman when he
despised womankind, longing for love when he believed in the
individual's alienation, writing for a society he scorned and
enjoying the pleasures of a Nature he deplored.

Marie Bashkirtseff was not deterred by Guy's offhand comments, however, and she replied pretending she was a college

prefect and ticking Maupassant off for the sensuality of his works and his preference of women to art. This time, however, her teasing aroused his irritation; sensitively aware of his contradictory nature and suspicious of her intentions, he clearly did not like being called 'a devourer of women' in so facetious a way nor having his indifference and self-indulgence dismissed as that of 'a good joker'. Marie had gone too far this time and Maupassant was no longer going to play the game. His cynicism and mistrust of women were aroused and his reply was sharp and bitterly sarcastic; he maintained he was bored and indifferent as he said and that if she wanted someone more exciting and poetic she should write to Victor Hugo instead. Finally, he dismissed her interest in him as merely an attempt to get his valuable autographs and declared he saw little point in continuing to write to the hoaxer that she clearly was.

Marie was hurt and told her famous correspondent so; she had expected understanding from someone she had admired so much; that was why she had written to him in the first place. The kinder, sentimental Maupassant replied, this time saying he was sorry to have offended her and assuring her that 'I am not as brutal nor as sceptical and improper as I have seemed to you'. In a last letter to him Marie confessed she was ill and upset by what had transpired between them, and on 23 April Maupassant tried to smooth over their disagreement and proposed a meeting. Whether such a meeting took place is uncertain particularly as Marie died not long afterwards. The correspondence with Marie does however show, despite its brevity, both the playful and the sceptical, both the kind and the harsher sides of Maupassant's character in his dealings with his unknown admirer.

In contrast to the capricious, bedridden Marie Bashkirtseff, whose overtures to Maupassant were probably motivated by a naïvely girlish desire to give her restricted life and intimate thoughts some greater significance by her contact with a famous writer she admired, the figure of Gisèle d'Estoc is much more flamboyant and perverse. A sculptress from Nancy, originally named Marie-Paule Desbarres, she had espoused all the feminist ideals of George Sand and the future suffragettes and possessed certain lesbian tendencies that made her an admirer of strong female historical figures. It was these same tendencies that involved her in a number of love affairs with other young women; one with a certain Marie-Edmée Pau in Nancy caused such scandal that she was obliged to move to Paris, where she continued to work as an artist and in fact was herself painted by Manet; a later affair with a circus star, Emma Rouer, resulted in a duel in which Gisèle stabbed her opponent. A further example of the masculine prowess of this young hero-worshipper of Joan of Arc, who dressed in men's clothes as a schoolboy, naval cadet or ship's officer, was provided in 1894 by her attempt to blow up the satirical writer Laurent Tailhade, who had repulsed her overtures, by planting a bomb in a bunch of flowers at a Paris café!

Gisèle d'Estoc was, then, a totally different woman from the naïve, teasing Marie Bashkirtseff; she was despite her fine complexion and attractive female body as forceful and tough as any man; indeed, her interest in sculpture, her love of fencing and shooting, and her writings in books and articles on female emancipation and the super-women of history all derived from her lesbian role. Why then she was keen to get to know Maupassant with his chauvinistic views on women and feminism it is difficult to imagine. Did she hope to convert him? Or was she merely curious to see the famous opponent of all she stood for in the flesh? Whatever her precise reason, she wrote to Maupassant in 1881 or 1882 seeking to meet him. As with Marie Bashkirtseff, Maupassant is suspicious and sceptical about himself in his reply:

'If it is true that you are just an inquisitive woman and not a mere hoaxer among my friends who is having me on, I declare I am ready to reveal myself to you when you want, where you want, as you want, and in whatever circumstances you like! You will most certainly be disillusioned; so much the worse for us. Since you are expecting a poet, allow me to soften the blow and tell you some unfavourable details about myself. Physically, I am not handsome and I have neither the manner nor the appearance to appeal to

women. There is absolutely nothing elegant or even neat about
me and the cut of my clothes is a matter of complete indifference
to me. My whole attractiveness has the coquettishness of a
labourer or butcher's boy and consists of strolling along the banks
of the Seine in summer in my boating costume to show off my
brawny arms. Quite vulgar and ordinary, isn't it?'

His next letters to the mysterious correspondent whom he calls
his 'unknown Diana' continue to emphasise that he is sensual
rather than sentimental and prefers Schopenhauer's misogynism
to all ideals of love and romance; he tells her: 'I am not made for
seducing women except those of simply a sensual or corrupt kind'
and in the same letter he adds: 'I love the flesh of women with
that same love as I have for the grass, the river, and the sea'.
Despite his reservations, Gisèle visited him at rue Dulong and
Guy soon afterwards sent her Carjat's photographic portrait of
him. This first meeting was followed by several others on the
Seine at Bezons and Sartrouville and for the next few years he
wrote to her from wherever he was – Paris, Cannes, Algeria –
signing his letters 'Ton Guy' or simply 'Guy'. This close relationship between the shy sensualist and the masculine lesbian
seems to have lasted until Maupassant accused her of being the
author of a scandalmongering anonymous letter about their
relations and asked her to end their meetings and to collect her
belongings from his rooms at Sartrouville.

An account of this strange relationship is to be found in a document published by the critic Pierre Borel in 1939 purporting to be
Gisèle's diary.[32] Although the references in it to Maupassant's
muscular strength, his fears, his belief in the alienation of the
sexes, his migraine and syphilis, and his seeing his double are, like
the allusions to his visits to Corsica and Algeria, quite credible,
the incorrect dating and confusion in the chronology of events
tend to make the reader extremely suspicious of accepting the
details given of more intimate, private incidents in the couple's
relationship. Like the memoirs of Maupassant's valet, to which
reference has already been made, this supposed diary of Gisèle

d'Estoc has all the faults of a journalistic concoction produced
some time after the events it is said to depict.

Many parts of the letters [33] are in fact extracts from Maupassant's works, added to the text of the correspondence to make it
longer and, perhaps, more credible. How far we can believe the
reported statement of Maupassant to Gisèle that 'I have never
loved any woman. But you, I love you madly with all the powers
of my being', or the fact that Maupassant is said to have procured
girls from along the river to satisfy Gisèle's lesbian tastes is hard
to judge; both details seem equally exaggerated and sensationalist
particularly in the context of the somewhat suspect document as
a whole. Gisèle and Guy may have shared a close relationship and
she may have picked up one of the many girls at the river landing
stages, just as there is some truth in the events described in the
diary and some credibility can be lent to the two largely pornographic poems which appear in it and vaguely resemble those of
Maupassant elsewhere; but caution still needs to be exercised in
accepting Gisèle's diary as hard evidence rather than as a piece of
semi-fictitious journalism.

Maupassant's other correspondents and admirers were on the
whole less pathetic than Marie Bashkirtseff and not quite so perverse as Gisèle d'Estoc. Moreover, whereas Marie came from
fairly wealthy bourgeois stock like Maupassant's own and Gisèle
may be seen to represent that artistic *demi-monde* of not very well-
to-do aesthetes and actresses that Maupassant liked because of
their amoral liveliness and sensuality, his other admirers were
drawn from the high society of particularly the financial world: a
world of luxurious apartments in fashionable residences both
along the best avenues of Paris and in the best places along the
Côte d'Azur, where the architecture and furnishings reflected in
their glistening array of marble, gold, silks and velvet the vast
wealth of their financier owners, which in turn could be seen as a
sign of the country's economic prosperity. For this was the era of
the sumptuous Paris Opéra of Garnier, of the Hôtel Païva in the
Champs Elysées, of the majestic Palais de Luxembourg built for
the exotic 1889 World Exhibition, of the imposing residences of

the Boulevard Haussmann and of the florid architecture of piers
and hotels of the Riviera at Nice, Cannes and Antibes. When
industry, finance, and colonial development were flourishing,
there were no limits to the self-indulgence of the wealthy in their
vain, sophisticated relations with others in the upper echelons of
society. Style, menus, guests and attitudes all had to be as novel
and exclusive as possible in the competitive pursuit of sophisticated pleasures and the ambitious conceit of impressing one's
fellow-men. These were the years when Pierre Loti gave his
exotic parties – medieval, Arab or Breton – at Rochefort; when
Sarah Bernhardt received her visitors in a swan-skin-lined coffin
guarded by parrots, lizards and a pair of panthers; when Robert
de Montesquiou, Jean Lorrain and many others acted in real life
with all the bizarre, pederastic dandyism of the hero of Huysmans'
novel *A Rebours*, and it was all the rage to converse about
Wagner, Tolstoy, D. G. Rossetti, Ibsen, and everything new and
exotic from Darwinism to Angkor Wat.

It was into this sparkling, hedonistic world founded on the
finances of a booming industry and commerce that success and
fame brought Maupassant. He was a success, he was known, and
therefore he had to be invited by the hostesses of the *salons* in
Paris and on the Côte d'Azur to enhance the significance of their
list of guests and decorate their dinner-tables. To have the author
of the highly controversial novel *Une Vie* and of those sensual
tales *Boule de Suif* and *La Maison Tellier* at your weekly evening
of social entertaining was a prize worth pursuing. And so, as well
as being invited to the homes and dinners of other writers, artists
and journalists such as Mme Adam, Mme de Nittis, Mme Brainne,
Bourget, Anatole France, Goncourt, Zola, Daudet, Mirbeau
and so on, Maupassant now found himself being asked more and
more into the luxurious residences of the wealthy.

One of these was that of the Countess Emmanuela Potocka, an
Italian princess – a daughter of the Duke of Regina – married to
the Polish Count Nicolas Potocki, attaché at the Austro-Hun-
garian Embassy in Paris. Their luxurious residences at 27 Avenue
Friedland and 7 rue Tronchet – nicknamed the 'Credit Polonais'

9 Marie Kann by Bonnat

10 Countess Potocka

11　Madame Straus by G. Boldini

because of their richness – were the meeting places for a vast number of writers, doctors, artists and aristocrats of the most cosmopolitan variety. They included the novelist Paul Bourget, the diplomat and promoter of the Russian novel in France Viscount Eugène de Vogüé, the British ambassador Lord Lytton, the dandy Robert de Montesquiou, the portrait-artist and friend of Proust, Jacques-Emile Blanche, the Byzantologist Schlumberger, the philosopher Caro, and many lesser known artists such as Gervex, Jean Beraud, and so on. It was through his journalist friend Georges Legrand and the latter's fashionable gambling and well-to-do wife Clotilde, an ardent admirer of Guy's work, that Maupassant was introduced to the Countess.

Emmanuela Potocka had the reputation of being a capricious siren both because of her slender, finely proportioned even if rather small figure and her deep, dark eyes with their wild, sensuous gaze and because of her husband's wealth, which enabled her to indulge her every whim. Modestly draped in black velvet and a sable stole, she had been painted by Bonnat and had had a perfume called 'Shaw's Caprice' specially prepared for her. While her husband was otherwise occupied with his mistress, she played hostess to the cream of Parisian society, being known to her admirers and often signing herself as 'La Patronne' on notepaper bearing the motto 'Quid non Dilectis'. Robert de Montesquiou recorded later how the Countess completely dominated the Count in his saying 'La Comtesse Potocka/Qui son Potocki plaqua' and in his description of how the temperamental Emmanuela had once left home like the heroine of Ibsen's *Dollshouse* after a dispute with her husband over a servant.[34]

It was not long before this capricious hostess, who was pleased to have such a prize guest as Maupassant, and the ambitious writer, who was delighted to find a society personality keen to promote his work, were good friends. Clearly, Maupassant was quite attracted by her and enjoyed her capricious, lively temperament, but as in his other correspondence with women his attitude tends towards a flattering masochism and his feelings for them are curtailed by his scepticism with regard to their sincerity. Writing to show her his gratitude for her promotion of *Une Vie* in 1883 he signs off: 'It is on my knees that I want to thank you for this.' And when he sent a letter from Cannes on 13 March 1884 he was at pains to point out how he preferred her frankness to the snobbish, convention-bound aristocracy of the Côte d'Azur, but at the same time wondered whether her friendly feelings were motivated by a genuine sympathy or mere caprice; the letter is casual and humorous in tone and reflects the familiar even if cautious nature of Maupassant's relations with her:

'But now I think of other kinds of people I like chatting with. Perhaps you know one of them? She has not the normal respect for the "Leaders of Society" (what an expression!) and she is open in her thoughts (at least I think so), in her opinions and her dislikes. And that's probably why I think so often of her down here. Her thoughts leave me with an impression of an impetuous, familiar, seductive frankness. They are full of surprises, filled with the unexpected and possessing a strange charm. Unfortunately I cannot believe (I do not know why) that her friendship is very constant.

'That, however, is what I would like to know, what I should like to discover. The friendship she has for people, does it come from a momentary distraction of her boredom, a whim of the imagination that is satisfied, or from something deeper and more human, from that bond of minds that makes relationships more durable and that ineffable harmony of spirit that turns even the shaking of hands into a subtly delicate physical and mental pleasure. I am expressing myself very badly. You understand me often when I say nothing, so can you understand me too when I use words that are not sufficiently well-chosen?

'I have forgotten to tell you that I shall perhaps have the pleasure, the great pleasure, of kissing this lady's hands in a few days' time when I will probably be obliged to come and spend twenty-four hours in Paris to settle some matters . . .'

This cautious, mutually beneficial flirtation continued for quite a few years. The Countess liked to indulge her caprices and, whimsical and dominating, she enjoyed playing with the hearts and vanities of her male guests. Her capricious playfulness appealed, moreover, to the equally playful Maupassant and he was a willing participant in her fantasies. On one occasion she sent him, no doubt with a certain contemptuous sarcasm, a number of dolls representing some of the female guests she was going to invite; Maupassant, with his usual sense of somewhat vulgar fun, returned them to her with enough stuffing in them to make them appear pregnant! Although the Countess enjoyed the joke after Guy had mollified its effect by his apologies, the Count did not and was not too pleased to see Maupassant at Avenue Friedland in July 1884. Guy wrote to Nadar's niece that month: 'I went to dine the other day at the Countess's. The Count, however, gave me such an unpleasant look that I intend never to set foot there again . . .' [35]

The break was but a temporary one, however, and Guy was to continue to be a favourite guest of Emmanuela Potocka for several more years, even attending some of her 'Maccabee' dinners. These Friday evening banquets named after the Judean martyrs of long ago were devised for male guests who were supposedly willing to die for love of their beneficent hostess; each of them received a sapphire badge with the motto 'A la Vie, à la Mort' inscribed on it, which they were asked to wear at the dinner. Maupassant, Bourget, Lord Lytton, and many other well-known writers of the day submitted to the Countess's whims and enjoyed the orgiastic festivities that usually followed the banquets. It is said that on one such occasion the Countess threatened Jacques-Emile Blanche with a revolver to urge him to paint her portrait and that on another the lesbian daughter of the notorious Duke de Morny performed a trapeze act above the dining table! In a social climate where luxury, self-indulgence and novelty were vital, such functions soon became notorious and adventurous young men as well as more celebrated personalities came to attend and seek the favours of their hostess by their flattery and antics. The crazy fascination the Countess exercised through such caprices can be judged from a letter of Mme Straus to Maupassant during the summer of 1886, in which she reports to him the latest news of the 'Maccabees':

'I have not heard much of the Maccabees. I believe they have borne the summer heat fairly well except for young Dubois de l'Estury and Ignace Ephrussi who appear to me to be a little more "far gone" than the others and should have been consigned to some well-known mental-institution doctors. It is certainly time! Ignace has fortunately had the bright idea of walking completely naked through the Paris streets for this brought home to his family that he was rather odd and needed looking after. The beautiful Countess has a double effect. She acts both on the heart and on the mind of her guests!' [36]

It was said that her hold over her would-be suitors was such that when one suitor threatened to shoot himself if she continued to resist his advances, she merely replied: 'You have been promising me you would do it for so long now,' and that the philosopher Caro, who had offended her and been banned afterwards from the 'Maccabees', died from the upset this caused him. The 'Patronne's' parties and the excursions the Countess organised in the country and on the river did give Guy, however, a moment of pleasurable escape from his work and the problems of his life, but more and more he found he had little free time and his only true escape was being alone in the country or at sea and he attended less and less the events of the 'Maccabees' while nevertheless maintaining his flirtation with the temperamental Emmanuela.

It was at the Potockas' that Guy met another woman who was to play an important part later in his life: the thirty-year-old Mme Marie Kann. Like the Potockas, Jewish and of Slavic ancestry – her maiden name was Warshavska – she, her husband Edouard and her sister Loulia, who was married to the composer and dramatist Albert Cahen d'Anvers, lived together in an upper-class district of Paris at 118 Rue de Grenelle. Here, Maupassant found many of the same guests as in Avenue Friedland – the writers Bourget, Goncourt, Anatole France, Edmond Rostand, and many minor figures such as the painter Bonnat, the translator of Schopenhauer, Bourdeau, and the lawyer Joseph Reinach. Here too he found many other members of the cosmopolitan Jewish high society of the capital, who had become wealthy and risen in social rank through their participation in banking, investment and speculation – activities that the country's industrial expansion had encouraged but which certain racialist and anti-Semitic elements in the rest of society such as the author of *La France Juive* (1886), Edouard Drumont, Daudet, and many smaller financiers viewed with envy and displeasure until a decade or more later the Dreyfus Case allowed them to give vent to their feelings.

Maupassant, although he was no doubt somewhat envious of their wealth and as a writer did not share their preoccupation with finance, enjoyed the wit, novelty, exoticism and glamour of the Jewish society of the aristocratic Faubourg St Honoré with its cosmopolitan sophistication and found their company useful in the promotion of his books and reputation. He thus had no objection to meeting the Rothschilds, Foulds, Sterns, Ephrussis, Bischoffsheims, Morpurgos and Péreires at Mme Kann's and, in turn, being received by them, despite his occasional criticism of Jewish characters in his novels on account, not of their faith, but of their representative and successful interest in finance. Indeed, in the luxurious decorations of his several homes and the industry he created out of his writing he seems later to have tried to imitate them.

The Kann residence was as splendid as the Potockas' and its hostess as fascinating as the capricious Emmanuela; Marie and her sister had read most of European literature in their childhood and were fluent, dominating conversationalists. Moreover, despite an increasingly pallid complexion due to various ailments, the Kann sisters – aunts of Ida Rubinstein – had a unique seductive charm; Goncourt, though slightly biased by his somewhat anti-Semitic envy, has left this description of Marie in his diary entry of 7 December 1885:

'On a sofa Mme Kann sits nonchalantly with her large, deep-set eyes filled with the languorousness of all those of a brunette colouring, her tea-rose complexion, her black beauty spot on her cheek, her mouth with its disdainful expression, her bosom with its pale whiteness, her languid gestures, now slow and separate and now made in a feverish manner. This woman has a quite unusual charm at once delicate and mocking which is combined with that peculiar seductiveness of Russian women – the intellectual perversity of their eyes and the beguiling chattering of their voices...'

For the moment, Maupassant merely saw her at the Potockas' and visited her at Rue Grenelle or at Saint-Raphaël on the Côte d'Azur. She, for her part, was delighted to be able to flirt with a tall, robust writer with the exotic look of a countryman instead of with the frail Paul Bourget whom she called 'Plante Brisée'. He was not, however, to fall completely under the spell of her Slavic-Oriental charms until some two years later, when Bourget had virtually broken with her.

Another society hostess who needs to be mentioned is Mme Géneviève Straus, to whose *salon* Marie Kann is said to have brought Maupassant after their meeting at the Potockas; Jewish – her father was Halévy the composer – and well-to-do like Emmanuela Potocka and Marie Kann, she was to become one of Maupassant's keenest visitors and most ardent correspondents. When Guy first met her, it was some seven years since she had lost her first husband, the composer Georges Bizet, and it was to be a couple of years or so before she actually married the wealthy lawyer Emile Straus, a relation of the Rothschilds and one of their legal advisers, in 1886. At once, he was attracted by the liveliness and intelligence of the young widow and the aristocracy of both society and intelligentsia that frequented her *salon*; though of a dark, Spanish complexion with black shiny hair and sparkling eyes she was not particularly pretty, as were his hostesses in the Avenue Friedland and Rue de Grenelle, but she was extremely friendly, sensitive and witty – sufficiently so for Guy to invite her to dinner in May 1884:

'I know it is hardly right for a woman to go to dinner at the home of a young bachelor, but I do not understand why it should still be shocking when this woman by herself meets other women there whom she knows, do you? . . . Moreover, if I were to give you a list of the people who came to dinner both at Cannes and at Étretat or here, you would see it was long and had lots of distinguished names on it! . . . In short, you would make me very happy if you accepted and I would promise not to say a word about it in my *Gil Blas* column . . .'

She replied full of enthusiasm to see him but still mindful of her other obligations from which she could not easily escape; however, she does suggest he comes to see her even if she cannot manage to accept his invitation:

'I do not know if it would be incorrect; what is certain is that I would like to say yes straightaway; what is sad is that my Saturday evening is so booked-up that I do not see a way of disengaging myself from my commitments in at least a fairly honourable manner that would satisfy me. Not only am I engaged for dinner but I have sent out invitations for that ghastly evening at the Opéra-Comique and I have actually got people daft enough to accept. I have been in vain seeking a way out of all this by various ingenious permutations since yesterday; but I'm afraid I am powerless when faced with so many complications. Please do not suspect me of making sacrifices on the altar of *social conventions*. I am not thinking at all of *Gil Blas* and I would even accept quite courageously a word of censure from Arthur Meyer. Come and see me on Saturday all the same; you will give me great pleasure. . . .' [37]

The relationship between the author of *Une Vie* and one of the future models for Proust's Duchess of Guermantes in his famous *A La Recherche du Temps Perdu* was to become an extremely close and familiar one; this can be seen from the following flattering letter from Guy to Mme Straus, inviting her to Chatou for a trip on the river and either lunch or dinner afterwards and asking to be allowed to see her sometimes privately at home:

'Would it therefore be possible to meet you sometimes at home outside formal visiting hours? If you find me a bore, just say so. I will not be offended. Really my request is very modest and is only wrong in not being in verse. For is it not natural for one to ask to see more often and alone those women under whose seductive spell one falls, so as to appreciate them better and savour their charm and grace? . . . I would like to come and see you when I know I will be expected, I alone will be looked at and listened to, and only I will be there to find you beautiful and charming. I will not stay too long, I promise . . . I realise now your attractiveness, I recognise how much I like, enjoy and will continue to enjoy more and more each day the essence of your particular personality . . .'

The same familiarity can be found in a letter from her of 1886 apologising for not writing sooner:

'I have found myself so overburdened with letters to write these last few days that I have sworn to write no more to anyone. Naturally I am quick to depart from my resolution in writing this, but that's because it's for you! You should be grateful for that because I am terribly lazy! Next year I shall take the wise precaution of quarrelling with almost every one of my friends so as not to have to reply to them. I can of course confess this to you since you would not be on such a list. Only don't betray my idea . . .' [38]

The luxurious house with the circular *salon* at 137 Boulevard Haussmann and its lively hostess with the dark, sparkling eyes and quick nervous gestures, as Goncourt described her in his *Journal* on 28 March 1887 and as Delaunay and Moreau painted her, were to welcome Guy de Maupassant as well as young Marcel Proust and his friends for many years to come.

Maupassant's entry into high society and his increased acquaintance with its scandals and business deals as well as with its varied hostesses and their equally diverse entourages were reflected in his next novel, *Bel Ami*. Already in 1882, shortly after the publication of *La Maison Tellier* and *Mademoiselle Fifi*, the philosopher Hippolyte Taine, whose work had contributed so much to Zola's theories of 'Naturalism', had advised Maupassant not to limit his 'Naturalistic' approach just to the lower classes but to depict the upper echelons of society too. So far, there had been little sign of such a change in Maupassant's work; his long short story, *Les Sœurs Rondoli*, that had appeared in *L'Echo de Paris* from 29 May to 5 June 1884, was still concerned with the better side of prostitution – this time in Italy, where the narrator meets a girl on his train to Genoa, stays with her, and when she vanishes finds her home and discovers the reasons for her passivity in a love affair she had had in Paris. The longish tale *Yvette*, adapted from an earlier short story and published in *Le Figaro* from 29 August to 19 September 1884, also deals with the sad plight of the prostitute in its analysis of how a young girl full of ideals about love is eventually forced to accept the libertine male society which comprises her mother's moneyed clients.

Although neither story has the broader theme or the social backcloth of the novel that was soon to appear – *Les Sœurs Rondoli* harps on both the narrator's and the prostitute's loneliness and *Yvette* depicts the libertine life along the banks of the Seine – it is just possible to see in the narcissistic, sex-conscious personalities of many of the men in the latter story some of the traits of the protagonist of *Bel Ami*. Moreover, Maupassant began writing the novel immediately after finishing *Yvette* in the summer of 1884 because he needed to earn money to pay for his moving into his new home and the decorating he had had done there. It was perhaps because he so needed the money from the novel that, despite the many other stories he was writing and the grave state of his eyesight, he managed to finish *Bel Ami* by late February 1885. It appeared in *Gil Blas* from 8 April to 30 May, at the same time as its publication by Victor Havard and its serialisation in the St Petersburg *Messager d'Europe*.

Bel Ami is the story of the blue-eyed, blond-haired Georges Duroy's climb up the social and political ladder by means of the various women he seduces. At the beginning of the novel he has just returned to Paris from the army in North Africa. He is jobless and relies on the prostitutes of the *Folies Bergère* for the satisfaction of his desires. At the novel's close he is being married at the famous Madeleine church to the daughter of one of the richest families in the capital while being promised a baronetcy and a seat in Parliament very shortly. What happens inbetween is a series of seductions. They begin with the lonely, frivolous Mme de Marelle, a friend of his army friend Forestier who offers him a job on his newspaper *La Vie Française*, continue with the calm, cautious Madeleine Forestier whom he marries after her husband's death, reach their peak with the reluctantly conventional but ardent wife of the wealthy magnate Walter, and conclude with his blackmail of his wife to gain a divorce and his kidnapping of Suzanne Walter to make a rich, political marriage. The stages in his rise to success and wealth are measured by the reflections of himself Duroy sees in the mirror on the landing of the Forestiers' house, by various symbols such as the portrait in the Walters' garden of Christ walking on the water that resembles him and the goldfish in the pond there which bite at the bait he feeds them, and also by the role of his interest in North Africa first for articles on his army experiences and later for use in financial speculation and political manœuvring.

As elsewhere in Maupassant's work, the action is swift and episodic – a procedure appropriate to newspaper serialisation and related to the moralistic concision of his short stories. Both the seduction scenes – described in the most discreet way – and such incidents as Duroy's duel with a slanderous fellow-journalist, his visits to centres of low-life with Mme Marelle, Forestier's death, his honeymoon with Madeleine Forestier in Normandy – a good opportunity to depict Norman peasant life once more – and his meeting with Mme Walter in the Trinité church almost exist as separate entities in their shrewd psychological analysis of character and succinct impressionistic realism. Only occasionally the action is too swift between chapters and the characters' thoughts too blatantly ready-made; Bel Ami's sensual narcissism about his moustache, reminiscent of the tale *La Moustache*, and the poet Norbert de Varenne's pessimistic views of life, though essential to the novel's theme, tend to be rather too emphatic and obvious. Hence it is no surprise when at the end of the novel Duroy sums up its message and tells the cuckolded M. Marelle: 'Strong men always succeed whether by one means or by another', and Norbert de Varenne comments at Bel Ami's marriage to Suzanne Walter: 'The future lies with those who are crafty and smart!'

Underlying and contrasting with this rise to power and wealth of the crafty, libertine Bel Ami there is, however, the novel's pessimism no doubt reflecting much of Maupassant's own. Throughout, Norbert de Varenne points out the futility of Man's efforts in every field – 'Breathing, sleeping, drinking, eating, working, dreaming, all that we do, is part of our progress towards death. Living is, in short, part of death!' he says to Duroy; and Bel Ami himself is suddenly confronted with the nothingness of life and human effort and turns away in terror at the deathbed of M. Forestier:

'For a few years he [Forestier] had lived, eaten, laughed, loved, and hoped like everyone else. And now it was all over for him, over for ever. A man's life! Just a short time and then it's over and done with! One is born, one grows up, one is happy, one hopes, and then one dies . . . The planets, the animals, men, the stars, whole worlds come alive and then die and are changed. But never does a person, an insect, or a planet return to life!'

The sexual prowess and consequent success in journalism and politics of Bel Ami might be the main theme of the novel, but as elsewhere in Maupassant's work there is a note of the futility of all human effort and the final nothingness of death for all men which counterbalances the more positive side of Duroy's spectacular career just as it did in Maupassant's own outlook.

Although the sales of *Bel Ami* were at first not as high as

Maupassant anxiously hoped for, partly because public attention was diverted just then by the death of the great poet Victor Hugo, they soon improved and within four months the novel had reached its thirty-seventh edition. Brunetière, a leading critic of the age, who was greatly opposed to the crudeness and immorality of 'Naturalism' as a whole, considered it the most remarkable product of 'Naturalism' in its artistic use of a discriminating realism devoid of vulgarity for its depiction of not just low-life but of the society, press and political world of the period. Duroy's progress is, as in a typical 'Naturalist' novel, due to his sexual conquests, but it is not these that wholly dominate the novel. Instead, it is the intrigue surrounding and issuing from these affairs, reminiscent of a Balzac novel, which gives the work its interest; for it is through this that Bel Ami makes his way up the social ladder and the novel is filled with glimpses of contemporary society from the inside – the string-pulling and ghost-writing of the journalistic world, the adulteries behind the scenes of press, finance and politics, the speculation scandals of leading bankers and politicians, and implicitly the whole hypocritical travesty that the established order of Church, State and Family actually is.

So realistic did it all appear that critics and readers at the time of its publication and since began treating it as a 'roman à clé' and trying to identify the characters and incidents with contemporary persons and events. Bel Ami was seen as Maupassant himself – an effect he himself encouraged by signing copies of the novel with that name – or identified as the journalist René Maizeroy and the writer Jean Lorrain among many others. Indeed, Lorrain threatened to challenge Maupassant to a duel over the matter and later got his own back by using Maupassant's reputation and name for one of his characters in his novel *Très Russe*. The identification of the ladies of the plot led to more than a little gossip and a few whispers among Maupassant's friends and hostesses in society. The speculation dealings related to the campaign in Morocco that Duroy becomes involved in with Walter and Laroche were eagerly compared to the recent French seizure of Tunisia with the aid of a government official named Roustan, the role of the Rothschilds in the collapse of the Union Générale and its shares in Tunisia, and the fall of the Jules Ferry government because of the scandal that ensued.

Clearly, like the dashing heroes of the tales *Madame Parisse, Mohammed-Fripouille, La Moustache,* and many others, Bel Ami was to a large extent Maupassant as he would have liked to have been rather than the shy sceptical sensualist he was. The Marelles and Forestiers were partly modelled on people Maupassant had met. The Walters owed much to wealthy Jewish financiers such as the Foulds, Erlangers, and Rothschilds in real life. The Morocco campaign was virtually based on the Tunisian one of 1881–2. And the insights into the press given in the novel obviously derived from Maupassant's own substantial experiences of newspaper offices and editors. In most cases, however, Maupassant's characters were conflations of those he knew including aspects of himself.

Nevertheless, because many journalists and certain writers had taken exception to some parts of the novel, Maupassant felt obliged to send a letter to *Gil Blas* on 7 June 1885 stressing that he had not aimed at depicting either all the press or any particular persons in the novel. He claimed that he had only used the press and a particular type of newspaper and certain types of people in it in order to portray Bel Ami's adventurous progress – 'I show from the very first lines that we have before us the seed of a species of rogue that will grow and flourish in the kind of ground it fell on. That ground is a newspaper . . . he uses the press as a thief uses a ladder.' Nevertheless, although he was not intending to depict all the press in the novel and he himself was not the rogue his character represents, there can be little doubt that 'Bel Ami''s ambitiousness was largely Maupassant's own and that his successes were in fact a reflection of Guy's own reliance on the press for his popularity and entry into society.

The controversy about the identity of the characters, together with the contemporary realism of the novel, helped, moreover, to boost the book's sales and raise even further Maupassant's reputation; as with his other works, conventional society enjoyed the perverse pleasure of being shown its unconventional side, its secret adulteries and scandals, and following the sexual adventures and amoral exploits of a contemporary Casanova.

Maupassant realised this only too well and henceforth relished applying the name Bel Ami to himself, not because it mirrored his own character which it did not as he well knew, but because he knew it appealed by its scandalous connotations to his public and thereby fostered his popularity and success. Thus, Henry James, while equating Bel Ami with his author as cads of a similar order, when he sent the novel to a friend, was quick to point out that while the character was just a cad and no more, Maupassant might appear a cad but he was one of undoubted genius. From now on, Maupassant was known all over Europe, from Paris and London to Berlin and St Petersburg, as the dashing, ambitious Bel Ami and looked upon as the very epitome of the restless, sophisticated French society of the 1880s, in which he and his author leapt to fame and fortune.

CHAPTER 2

The New Life and its Problems

If, according to historians and commentators on the *fin de siècle* period in France such as Nordau and Spengler, the seeds of that society's exhaustion and decline were already being sown by the excesses of its ambition, sophistication and cosmopolitanism, then a similar course may be traced in Maupassant's comparatively brief career. One of the great differences between Maupassant and his creation Bel Ami was that while the latter looked and actually was dashing and virile, Guy might appear sturdy and muscular but he was behind this façade of fitness an increasingly sick man. Moreover, as has been seen, the hard toil which eventually brought him success and the social pressures imposed on him as a result of his fame did little to improve his health. More consultations, more powders, more showers, and more drugs were hardly of much avail when he had tired himself out and exhausted his eyes during months of writing.

His pen was, however, his living and since his own expenses for his various homes, his yachts and his entertaining and his lending to his mother and brother were so high he was obliged to carry on writing to keep himself and his family out of debt. His only solution to the problem of keeping himself solvent and fit was to spend long periods writing, usually with the help of friends such as Clémence Brun, Blanche Roosevelt, Gervex, Hermine Lecomte de Noüy, and others, who transcribed and proof-read his work, and to go away for equally long periods of relaxation by himself or with a couple of companions. When this

solution proved to have little success and his health continued to
deteriorate, he decided that he had to cut down his output, and in
1888 he virtually emigrated from the north of France and thought
of selling his Etretat home to live in the sun of the Côte d'Azur
for the last few years of his life. There is thus after the success of
Bel Ami a continuing drop in the number of short stories he produced and a corresponding rise in the single longer works he published; and there is at the same time an increase in the travelling
he undertook to try to escape from his work and society and
improve his health.

In April 1885, just after the publication of *Bel Ami*, Maupassant
left for Italy with his journalist friends Amic and Legrand and the
artist Gervex. He had no doubt discussed much of his itinerary
with his mother who had travelled extensively along the Mediterranean, for it was to her that he expressed his disappointment
with Venice – apart from the work of Veronese and Tiepolo he
saw and admired – and Rome, where he liked what he saw of
Raphael but called Michelangelo's *Last Judgement* a 'fairground
canvas' and referred to St Peter's as 'the grandest monument in
poor taste that has ever been constructed'. On this and later
visits he was, however, attracted by Pisa and Florence; he was
struck by the harmonious proportions of Pisa's Duomo and
marvelled at the art of Renaissance Florence, particularly
Raphael's Madonnas and also Titian's reclining nude that no
doubt appealed to his sensual eye.

The highlight of Maupassant's trip seems to have been not
mainland Italy, however, but Sicily. Its hot climate, its unspoilt
natural beauty, its Greek, Roman and Norman monuments, and
its swarthy, fiery people who reminded him of the Arabs of North
Africa, were all to Guy's taste for the exotic, the sensual, the
morbid and the harmonious, which feature so much in his work
and outlook. The harmonious proportions and equally harmonious setting of the Greek temples at Segesta and Agrigento
and of the amphitheatre at Taormina left him enraptured and he
was deeply impressed by the artistry of the gold and marble
mosaics of the Palatine Chapel and Monreale in Palermo and the

12 Guy de Maupassant, Madame de Broissia, Vicomte Eugène de Vogüé,
Madame Straus (with umbrella), General Anenkoff

13   Guy de Maupassant in about 1890, by Nadar

cloister of San Giovanni degli Ermiti nearby. In the archaeological museum in Syracuse the sensualist in him was attracted by the famous statue of Venus emerging from the sea 'of which I dreamed at every moment before even seeing her'; he wrote in *La Vie Errante* that for him she represented real, sensual Woman, not a mystical ideal: 'she is Woman as she is, as one loves her, as one desires her and wants to embrace her'. Another aspect of Sicily which Maupassant the energetic swimmer and rower enjoyed was climbing over the hills and mountains and scaling the volcanoes. He wrote to Mme Lecomte de Noüy on 15 May 1885 when he was at Ragusa:

'I get up at four or five o'clock every morning, go off in a carriage, and then do some walking on my own two feet. I am seeing monuments, mountains, towns, ruins, exciting Greek temples in unusual landscapes, and also volcanoes – small ones throwing up mud and other larger ones erupting with fire. In an hour's time I leave to make an ascent of Etna. . . . My stomach is not functioning at all well and my eyes are in bad shape. As for my heart, it is going with clockwork regularity and I am able to climb the mountains without it having the slightest effect.'

Not only did Guy climb Etna but he also descended a little way down into the seething crater of the island volcano named Volcanello while visiting the Lipari isles and Stromboli! Back on land, he encouraged his companions and some local villagers to make the arduous climb to the Castellaccio fortress high above Palermo and made a visit to a sulphur mine, from where he brought back a large sample of the mineral as a souvenir. Maupassant's energy and vitality during his trip hid, however, as elsewhere his latent pessimism and morbidity, which became manifest on his visit to the Palermo catacombs. He was fascinated, even amused, by the strange, grotesque sight of the dozens of fully attired skeletons left to hang down there and dry out and, like Bel Ami at Forestier's deathbed, was tempted to ask himself as he gazed at one of the empty figures: 'So this is what a man is. Eight years ago this was a man; it lived, laughed, spoke, ate, drank and was full of joy and hope until then. Look what he has become now!'

From Sicily Maupassant sailed over to Malta before returning to Naples, where he arranged to meet a female acquaintance Vera de Khanjonkoff, and then on to Rome. Here, he was invited to stay at the elegant residence of Count Giuseppe Napoleon Primoli, the favourite nephew of the Princess Mathilde, whom Guy had met at Mme Pasca's and at the Princess's villa at Saint Gratien in about 1880. Like his aunt, Primoli – or Gégé as he was known to his friends – was not only a wealthy dilettante in artistic and literary matters but also a writer and painter himself. He was in contact with all the great names in the arts and society all over Europe both through travelling to other countries and offering hospitality to any distinguished visitors – and there was no lack of these – to Rome.

A sensitive and well-informed guide to the Eternal City as well as on all matters concerning the arts and, in addition, being virtually the same age as Maupassant and endowed with a similar delight in the charms of the fair sex, Primoli was a most suitable host to Guy. In a letter written to Maupassant after his stay, Primoli was in fact to remind Guy of their visit to Sant'Onofrio with 'those two delightful young ladies who lent such a powerful charm to that peaceful, rather ascetic little convent'.[39] It is also said that he took Guy to a brothel in the Torre di Nina area so as to satisfy his guest, but whether this rumour is more valid than the false one reported by the psychologist Lumbroso,[40] which told of Primoli taking both Maupassant and Bourget to a Rome brothel and of how the former took full advantage of the opportunities offered while the latter merely waited around at the entrance, it is now impossible to say. A sensualist by nature and a confirmed bachelor, Maupassant could in any case hardly be blamed in a period when the most distinguished males escaped the constraint of domestic morality in the uninhibited climate of a brothel, for yielding to whatever temptations he was offered, if indeed they were. Far from being exceptional in doing so, Maupassant would merely have acted like most other men, particularly writers and artists, at the time. If tales of Maupassant's sexual appetite and performance have survived unlike the gossip about other men, it is partly because he was slightly more preoccupied with sex than they but largely because he wrote more about it and earned the reputation of being an insatiable Bel Ami. In actual fact, as has been seen, Guy appears to have been a shy, sensitive and rather sceptical lover, whose preoccupation with sex might well have derived from a combination of his nervous medical condition and a certain asceticism enforced by his work rather than from any insatiable craving for female flesh. Certainly, his acceptance of Primoli's offer in Rome, even if it were true, would not transform him into the sexual maniac many critics have sought to portray him as.

In early June Maupassant returned to France, stopping on his way to Paris to pay a visit to the dominating but neither particularly attractive nor intelligent female editor of the *Nouvelle Revue*, Mme Juliette Adam, at her villa at Gif on the Golfe Juan. Although she had years before refused one of Guy's poems for the *Revue* partly because it was a little too daring and partly no doubt because it reflected his association with Zola, to whom she was somewhat opposed together with her friends Daudet and Goncourt, she did accept his story *En Famille* in February 1881 and invite him to her *salon*, and she was now keen to claim Maupassant's work for her review since he was so well known. After all, Guy was no longer so closely associated with Zola, and his stories on the 1870 war appealed to her desire for revenge on Germany. Moreover, her firm, maternal attitude to her famous contributors such as Loti, Bourget and Anatole France as well as the financial reward she offered must have appealed to Guy, especially after 1886 when he had to seek a more lucrative alternative to *Gil Blas*, for the *Nouvelle Revue* published his account of his travels in Brittany, some of his tales such as *Le Vagabond* and *Le Rosier de Madame Husson*, and, later, his novel *Pierre et Jean*.

Maupassant had enjoyed his tour of Italy, seeing its artistic and historic masterpieces, and he promised Primoli he would try to help some of Italy's writers. In 1886 he sent Matilda Serao, the novelist and at that time editor of the *Tribuna di Roma*, the tale *Le Père Amable*, reviewed a certain Barzellotti's book in *Le Figaro* on 1 January, and proposed writing a preface for a French translation of the Sicilian novelist, Giovanni Verga's *I Malavoglia*. Maupassant was to return to Italy several times in the next few years to get some peace and sunshine, often sailing along the coast on his own yacht *Bel Ami*.

Although the sun and activity on his seven-week tour had done him some good, they could not cure the ills affecting his eyes and stomach. Therefore, after spending a month with his mother at Paris, he left on 18 July 1885 for Châtel-Guyon, a spa virtually owned by the consultant Potain in central France. While here he made several excursions into the mountains of Auvergne and, to escape the boredom that most of the patients apparently felt while taking the waters at the spa, he began to compose the novel *Mont Oriol*, which takes place in a setting resembling Châtel-Guyon. It was to finish this work, as well as to write some more tales for *Gil Blas*, that in October Maupassant fled the cold of the north and spent most of the winter of 1885–6 in Antibes on the Côte d'Azur.

Here he could work in peace, see his mother and brother every day and go sailing and hunting with his two dogs even in November and December. His life in Antibes was essentially a quiet, solitary one; he did some entertaining for some of his Paris acquaintances spending part of the winter in the south and also for his hunting companions, but in general he kept clear of too many social engagements. He disliked large numbers of people, feeling that his mental independence was threatened by them. Furthermore, his rustic look and coarse humour as well as a certain gaucherie in high society circles often made him feel ill at ease there. It was really only his need to be sociable for his publicity and his relishing his success and entry into social circles whose refined luxury he admired, that made him go into a world that had little intellectually to attract him. Commenting on the aristocratic society he found in Cannes in a letter to Countess Potocka of March 1884 he wrote:

'One finds little wit in the so-called fashionable society here and little intelligence either, in fact little of anything. A celebrated name and money are not enough. These people here make me think of terrible paintings in shiny gilt frames ... When one sees universal suffrage in practice and the people it elects, one feels like shooting the electors and guillotining its representatives; but when one sees close-up the princes who could govern us, one simply becomes an anarchist. They are simple and nice enough, it is true; full of childish playfulness, in fact afflicted with it, but what tiny brains! What conversation! What ideas! What thoughts! Oh, I shall never be a courtier ...'

Later, in March 1886, he was again to comment facetiously to Mme Lecomte de Noüy on the aristocratic, often royal society that flocked to Cannes at the appropriate season:

'Besides the two monarchs there are at least a hundred High-nesses, the King of Würtemberg, the Grand-Duke of Mecklen-burg, the Duke of Braganza, etc. etc. .... Everywhere there are Highnesses, all reigning over the salons of their noble subjects. I personally do not want to meet another prince, not one, because I dislike remaining standing a whole evening ... out of respect for His Royal Highness ...'

Although he could not help commenting in this way on the royalty and aristocracy he saw in Cannes, he was less critical of the upper-class *salons* he frequented in Paris, for in them he at least found some wit and humour as well as an opportunity to promote himself with many of his more distinguished readers and critics. It is then not quite so surprising as it may at first appear that when Ferdinand de Rothschild invited him to England in spring 1886, Maupassant accepted. He had heard a lot about England, particularly the Pre-Raphaelites, the Oxford and Cambridge colleges and the Savoy operas, from the novelist Paul Bourget, who had been there and stayed with Rothschild some years before. He now desired to see it for himself as well as visit some of his friends and admirers in London.

Most of the details of Guy's visit to London are provided by the letters he sent to Mme Straus and Count Primoli, who was already staying with the Duke of Bassano on the Isle of Wight and was similarly invited to the Rothschilds' country estate, a palatial mansion recently built for Ferdinand de Rothschild in the style of a Loire château at Waddesdon near Aylesbury, some thirty miles north-west of the capital, and superbly furnished and decorated with beautiful tapestries, rare paintings and exquisite furniture, carpets and clocks. The reason for inviting some distinguished guests from abroad such as Maupassant and Henry James was the large reception which was going to be held there on the first Saturday in August 1886. Among the guests were to be the son of the Prince of Wales, the future King George V, the Archbishop of Canterbury, the Prime Minister, Lord Salisbury, several important ambassadors, as well as many other social celebrities. In all there were to be some 300 guests. It was clearly a gala occasion even by Waddesdon standards. Guy stayed some days in London in the Piccadilly apartment of Ferdinand de Rothschild before proceeding by train to Aylesbury where he was conveyed from the station by carriage to the mansion itself a few miles away in a country village. No account exists of the reception itself but some impression of it can be gained from Maupassant's letter to Primoli, who was due to arrive a day later, on 4 August:

'I am here in an English mansion, surrounded by Englishmen – the Archbishop of Canterbury, the Prime Minister, etc., etc., plus the German Ambassador with whom I have spoken a lot because he does not know any more English than I do (at least that's what he says). Not many women here – a young girl, Lady X (cannot possibly remember her name), and the wife of the Archbishop who does not give me any desire to make the eminent churchman a cuckold. My host, M. Ferdinand de Rothschild, is a charming man. I greatly prefer him to his guests . . .' [41]

At about the same time Guy sent to his friendly hostess of the Boulevard Haussmann, Mme Straus, some impressions of his stay in England when writing to give her advice on how to prevent her hair from falling out and some other cosmetic matters; as the following letter shows, Maupassant had little chance while at Waddesdon of living up to his reputation as 'Bel Ami':

'I have been in England for a fortnight and have seen a vast number of famous people passing through the Rothschild mansion, beginning with the son of the Prince of Wales. But the men do not interest me very much and the women here have not the charm of ours, I mean of our French women. They say English women are only severe in appearance. However, when one is interested in their appearance, as I am in fact, one has a right to ask them to be more familiar. But I rather fancy that I have been given a terrible reputation before my arrival and so everyone around me is on the defensive for fear of an immediate and aggressive assault by this debauched Frenchman. I am therefore behaving myself like a good little boy who wants to remain so and must seem very timid. No doubt, after my departure, they will speak here of the modesty of the French just as we do, though without believing in it, of that of the English.'

Doubtless Mme Straus was both flattered and amused by Bel Ami's predicament and his preference for the French version of the female species. Maupassant did not, however, remain in his predicament for long. Once in London he met his friend Blanche Roosevelt, a young American from Ohio married to the Italian Marquis d'Alligri whom Guy had often invited to Etretat. She had begun her career as an opera singer but had been encouraged by Longfellow, one of whose poems she had sought to stage, to turn to literature. This she did, writing books on Doré, Sardou, Carmen Silva, and Verdi, as well as several novels, though it was most probably her fine figure, golden-red hair and blue eyes rather than her work that brought her to the notice of Hugo and Browning as well as of Maupassant to whom she had probably been introduced by Count Primoli.

Blanche and Guy dined together at the Café Royal in London's Regent Street and he attended a dinner at her home at 69 Oakley Street, Chelsea, where he met Henry James and Bret Harte. They also went together by train to Oxford to tour the colleges – in the rain alas – and also to Mme Tussaud's waxworks and one of the Savoy operas. It is said, furthermore, that while in London Guy dined out with Henry James in Earls Court and that he kept on asking James about the women sitting at other tables in the restaurant and was surprised to find the American writer so embarrassed and ignorant on the matter! It seems likely, however, that this rumour like so many others derived more from Maupassant's reputation than from reality and was a product of the humour of Oscar Wilde, in one of whose magazines it appeared. Certainly Guy, who had been given a letter of introduction to James from Bourget, was invited by the American writer to take the ferry down the Thames to dine at a fish restaurant at Greenwich with Edmund Gosse, George du Maurier, and Count Primoli, for James still recalled the outing years later. Finally, it is said that it was the cold, wet weather in London which drove Guy back to the sun of the Côte d'Azur; he apparently sent Blanche Roosevelt a telegram as he left saying he was too cold and leaving instantly for France.

Little evidence survives of Guy's stay in England apart, that is, from the following passage from the tale *Sur Les Chats*, published in *Le Figaro* in February 1886, which Maupassant wrote in Ferdinand de Rothschild's distinguished visitors' book in the following April opposite a sketch by Lambert of some cats at play:

'I both love and hate these charming yet perfidious animals. I enjoy touching them, sinking my hand into their silky, swirling coats and feeling the warmth of the fine, exquisite fur they have;

for nothing is softer and gives such a delicate, refined, and quite unique sensation to one's touch as the warm, vibrant coat of a cat. This living fur arouses in my fingers a strange and violent desire to strangle the animal I am caressing. I feel in her the desire she has to bite and scratch me and this feeling, this desire of hers, flows into me like a fluid she is passing into my body; it begins with my fingertips plunged into her warm fur and it goes on rising through my nerves, along my limbs, right up to my heart and into my head; it fills me, runs all over my skin, makes me clench my teeth. And meanwhile I can still feel at my fingertips the sensitive, slight vibrations of the animal's body flowing into and penetrating my own.' [42]

The strange sensation described in this passage on the cats associated with Maupassant's stay in English high society reflects in fact the increasing refinement in his choice of subjects and style as a result of his contact with a sophisticated society that demanded constant and extravagant novelty whether in the ever more unusual originality of its pleasures or the increasingly refined nuances of its art-forms. The exotic fancy-dress parties of Pierre Loti, the equally colourful dandyism of the bejewelled and highly perfumed Robert de Montesquiou and Jean Lorrain, the luxuriantly exotic and erotic paintings of Gustave Moreau and the interest in the perverse and sadistic in the novels of Rachilde, Lorrain, Mirbeau and Huysmans exemplify the first. The neo-mystical, often hermitic and finely nuanced poetry of the 'Symbolists' such as Verlaine, Mallarmé and Ghil, the subtlety of Rodin's sculpture, the popularity of Wagner's music and the works of Debussy represent the second. In the novel there was a gradual swing away from the emphasis placed on physical action and attributes by Zola and the 'Naturalists' in the early 1880s and a greater interest in the analysis of individual feeling and personal sensations, a greater concern for both novelty and subtlety in the depiction of the affairs of the heart and the processes of the mind.

In following this trend, Maupassant was progressing along the path his friend Paul Bourget had chosen for himself and on which he had achieved considerable fame by his novels of emotional and psychological conflict and his critical analysis of the contemporary moral climate as found in literature. So close was Maupassant to come to the type of subject Bourget chose for the psychological conflicts in his novels that critics began to remark on the similarity between Maupassant's later works and Bourget's *André Cornélis, La Duchesse Bleue, Un Cœur de Femme* and *Cosmopolis*.

As well as becoming more interested and subtle in the analysis of his characters' thoughts and feelings, Maupassant sought at the same time to satisfy his reader's desire for novelty. A desire to startle and entertain as well as his own morbid introversion and reading of Sade, Poe and many Romantic writers had always caused Maupassant to dwell in certain stories on the bizarre, the violent and the macabre even at the beginning of his career – *La Femme de Paul, Madame Baptiste, Les Tombales, La Main d'Ecorché*, etc. This element in his work was encouraged both by Maupassant's contact with medical and psychiatric specialists such as Charcot and Potain, whom he consulted for his own and his mother's health, and by Society's dilettante interest in such experimental topics as hypnotism, early forms of psycho-analysis, and the field of the psychopath, which the translation of Gogol's and Dostoevsky's novels had particularly stimulated.

After about 1883 the violent and perverse elements in Maupassant's writing become much more important as his life style and his public become more sophisticated and demanding. Rather sadistic rape such as in *Monsieur Jocaste, La Petite Roque* and *Un Echec*, incestuous relationships as in *Le Port* and *L'Ermite*, sadistic indulgence as in *Les Caresses* and *Un Soir*, perversions – the old man who wears a mask in his pursuit of sex in *Le Masque*, the husband infatuated with orchids in *Un Cas de Divorce*, the elderly actress who gets her servants to re-enact her romances in *Julie Romain* – and cruelty to people – *Chali, Mouron, Mohammed-Fripouille, La Mère aux Monstres* – and to animals – *Sur les Chats, Fou, Amour, Coco, L'Ane* – feature quite prominently in his later work. It is not a gratuitous violence in the context of the stories but it does perhaps reflect to some extent the latent frustration of Maupassant's immense libido as well as his own and his sophisticated readers' greater self-indulgence in the strange and unusual in the human personality.

Another sensation Maupassant increasingly evoked in his stories was that of fear. His own insecurity and uncertainty about life's origins and purpose, his hallucinations of having a double, possibly due to his pathological condition or the effect of his reading of the Romantics and others on his neurotic sensibility, and the public's eternal taste for the mysterious and unusual, encouraged him to write more and more disturbing and chilling tales. Fear caused by hallucinatory visions or terrifying sensations of strange, incomprehensible occurrences features in *La Peur*, *Apparition*, *Lui?*, *Un Lâche*, *Un Fou*, and *La Morte*, while the terror of solitude and a superstitious fear of cats can be found in *L'Auberge* and *Solitude* and in *Misti* and *Sur les Chats*. Madness also occurs fairly often in Maupassant's work, sometimes to convey the impact of unbearable and hence incomprehensible emotion as in *Berthe*, *Madame Hermet*, and *Mlle Cocotte*, or to reflect the character's reaction to mysterious happenings around him, whether apparitions or hallucinations.

One of the more well known of these types of tales was *Le Horla*, which was first published as a short story in *Gil Blas* on 26 October 1886 and enlarged a year later when it appeared separately. The basic plot is that of a man becoming obsessed by an invisible double of himself who gradually, over the few months he lucidly notes down his feelings in his diary, takes control of him. It tries to stifle him when he is asleep and forces him to return home when he is out walking. It also drinks the glasses of milk and water in his bedroom and turns over the pages of his books during the night. Finally, his reading of a German philosopher's work on diabolical manifestations prompts him to burn down his house so as to exterminate the spirit which he calls the 'horla', presumably because it is 'outside of himself' (*hors de lui*).

The account of the character's fears, hallucinations and virtual madness is made all the more gripping by the intimate diary presentation and by the contrast of his feverish madness and his attempts to escape it on the river and at sea. The personal note struck by the narrator's lucidly analysed, feverish struggle to overcome his fears and uncertainties and by his ever more desperate nostalgia for the sanity and peace of the past made the mental conflict of the story so vivid and immediate that many readers at the time and since related it to Maupassant's own condition. There is no doubt some truth in this rumour. As a Norman, Maupassant was superstitious and as an extremely sensitive writer and reader he himself is reported by his valet François, Léon Fontaine, Paul Bourget and Georges de Porto-Riche as having, after about 1884, occasional hallucinatory experiences of a double sitting in his chair or reflected in his mirror when he returned home. It seems probable then that, like the early tale *Le Docteur Héraclius Gloss*, *Le Horla* reflects in its psychological analysis of the narrator's conflict Guy's latent fears and uncertainties about such phenomena and life in general, which were to become more visible in his last years.

Nevertheless, it was essentially a work of fiction derived, like many of his similar tales such as *Lui?* and *Un Fou*, from his reading. Maupassant himself told both Robert Pinchon and Frank Harris that he was quite sane when he wrote *Le Horla*, and is reported by his valet Tassart as calling the story a 'work of imagination' and saying when he sent in the enlarged manuscript in 1887: 'In a week you will see everyone in the press declaring I am mad. Let them, for I am perfectly sound of mind and I knew very well what I was doing when I wrote it.' [43] In sum, *Le Horla* was successful because it derived its analytical forcefulness from within its author and treated a situation that appealed to a public interested in Charcot and Dostoevsky and, like Maupassant himself, enjoyed having its spine chilled and its imagination gripped. The story indicates not Maupassant's insanity but his closer conformity to the taste of his sophisticated readers, who sought new sensations and new pleasures in the increasingly amoral climate of wealth and self-indulgence.

Another indication of Maupassant's greater conformity to his public's taste was his choice of subject and the treatment he gave it in the novel *Mont Oriol*. He had begun to compose it during his stay at Châtel-Guyon in August 1885 and worked at it during the following winter in Antibes. It finally appeared, first in *Gil Blas* and then at Havard's, in early 1887. Maupassant himself realised when writing *Mont Oriol* that he was veering away somewhat from his previous subject-matter and approach; he wrote to Mme Lecomte de Noüy on 2 March 1886:

'I am composing a story about love that is terribly ardent, romantic and poetic. It's causing some changes in me – and is embarrassing me. The chapters analysing the emotions are much more heavily amended than the others. Nevertheless, it's eventually coming along; one can adapt oneself to anything with a little patience; but I cannot help laughing quite often at the frightfully sentimental, tender thoughts that I come up with if I search for long enough! I fear I might be converted to indulging in romance not only in my books but also in real life; when one's mind goes off in a particular direction it keeps on going that way and sometimes when I am out walking at Cap d'Antibes . . . composing a poetic chapter in the moonlight I begin to think that such romantic sensations are not as stupid as one imagines . . .'

No longer was he dealing with prostitutes and low-life or solely with sexual appetites and lustful desires, but with the finer, more sentimental feelings of passionate romance of more refined temperaments; the sentimental, idealistic element that existed in Guy beneath his cynicism and virtual nihilism and very occasionally crept into the pathos of his stories was now to be given fuller rein to please his readers. In *Mont Oriol* this is seen in the passionate love affair between Christiane Andermatt, who has come with her wealthy, Jewish financier husband William to the spa in Auvergne to improve her health so as to bear him a child, and an ardent friend of her brother, Paul Bertigny, who is also visiting the resort and falls in love with both its scenic location and its blonde, blue-eyed female visitor. Christiane, since she does not love her husband, who is more concerned with his speculating than his marriage, quickly falls under the spell of Paul's romantic courtship among the moonlit hills and ruins of the Auvergne countryside; and he is entranced by the natural innocence of his loved one and the idealism of their romance. When, however, Christiane becomes pregnant by him, he, 'who belonged to the race of lovers and not the race of fathers' and believed that 'maternity turned his loved one into a mere animal' – he even compares a woman's breasts to a cow's udders when the child is born! – abandons her and marries Charlotte Oriol, an equally innocent local girl, whose father has uncovered a new source of spa water nearby.

Christiane's abandonment and consequent suffering – made to appear martyr-like by her very name and symbolised in the image of the dead donkey she sees on an excursion in the hills – is paralleled by her husband's exploitation of the new spring he buys from the local farmer Oriol and the ruin this brings on the old spa they were attending. In the case of both the romance and the natural resources, what is ideally innocent and natural is exploited by the opportunist and financier from the city. Both are changed by what happens to them and survive the process; this is symbolised by the old peasant cripple Clovis being cured by the treatment he receives at the new spa. Christiane finds consolation for her broken romance in her love for her baby daughter and the new resort named Mont Oriol after its former owner is highly successful.

In many respects the novel does not differ from earlier works of Maupassant: Andermatt's speculating genius and financial pre-occupations resemble Walter's in *Bel Ami* – indeed, Maupassant's implied criticism of these rather annoyed Rothschild and caused a temporary coolness in their relations; Paul's seduction of Andermatt's wife is similar to, though less violent than, Duroy's of Mme Walter, and his threat to kidnap Charlotte Oriol is also reminiscent of Bel Ami's escape with Mademoiselle Walter; the disgust with maternity and cynical statements on the basic alienation of lovers from each other and the impossibility of real lasting love can be found in many previous stories; and Christiane's suffering can be compared with Jeanne's in *Une Vie*, and her love for her child and, later, her grandson is the same as in the earlier work – but here suffering is not passive but spiritually invigorating as in the recently translated works of Tolstoy, which Maupassant admired so much.

What is impressive in *Mont Oriol* is both the analysis of the lovers' feelings and Christiane's conflict of emotions, mirrored in the simple but highly evocative descriptions of the Auvergne landscape, and also the largely humorous scenes of life in a spa – the squabbles among the doctors, the subjection of patients to all sorts of strange experiments and devices, and the frantic efforts of the resident conductor to arrange a concert and firework display, and the attempts of a young Italian doctor to arrange a wealthy marriage for himself. Thus, apart from some criticism of Andermatt and Bertigny and the city influences they represent in the rural location of the spa and the natural situation of the novel's romance, *Mont Oriol* was intended by its emphasis on romance and the suffering of the heart as well as by its gently mocking humour to appeal to the readers of the more refined society which its author now frequented and which preferred the current trend of the novel under various cosmopolitan influences, such as the Russian novel, away from 'Naturalism's' dissection of Man's instincts towards a Symbolist analysis of his heart and soul.

Unlike other followers of 'Naturalism' Maupassant did not, however, break with Zola or disdain his work. When Zola's novel on country life, *La Terre*, appeared in the summer of 1887 Guy took no part in the *Manifeste des Cinq*, a petition against the pornography of the novel and its author published in *Le Figaro* by five of Zola's younger followers with the encouragement of Goncourt and Daudet. Instead, he wrote to the 'Master of Médan' to declare his preference for the complete volume text of the work rather than for the serialised extracts he had read earlier. He had in any case never been on the best of terms with Goncourt, who disliked his unrefined appearance and was intensely envious of his success, and in fact enjoyed the 'pornographic' element in

Zola's novels and admired his talents. Maupassant remained friends, too, with those of his contemporaries he had met at Médan in earlier years such as Paul Alexis – whose ephemeral newspaper *Trublot* he had supported in 1884 and who had dedicated one of his volumes of stories to Guy – and Hennique and Mirbeau both of whom he still visited and entertained at home despite latent misgivings that were occasionally exposed in temporary disputes. Maupassant's 'Naturalism' had never been like Zola's – systematic, pseudo-scientific, largely concentrating on low-class settings and of epic proportions. Now the stress on instincts and the physical side of life that had played a large part hitherto in his realism had been toned down and had given way to a deeper study of the inner man.

After the publication of *Mont Oriol* in early 1887 Maupassant continued to relax in the South of France until the summer, when he began to plan his next novel *Pierre et Jean*, on which he would work at Etretat for some two or three months prior to his tour of North Africa in the autumn. The beginning of his brother Hervé's illness that was soon to show meningeal symptoms and his mother's continued ill health were the only personal problems to disturb his peace and, together with the decorations to his various homes, make further demands on his purse during the year. Maupassant created something of a stir, however, when he wrote to the paper *Gil Blas* in January to protest at the proposal of the committee set up to obtain funds for the erection of a monument to Flaubert in Rouen, for a charity performance at the Odeon theatre in Paris to raise the 2,000 francs still needed. Guy's letter to *Gil Blas* agreeing with another critic of the proposal and enclosing a donation of a thousand francs at first caused the chairman of the committee, Edmond de Goncourt, to wish to resign, but Guy, who was entrusted with the memorial fund's finances, soon managed to placate him and the committee continued to function under his patronage for the next three years until the monument was finally erected in 1890. Maupassant's generosity on this occasion – which he could ill afford at this time – was itself of course a noble tribute to the great writer who had done so much for him.

Later in the year he also attended a meeting to promote the erection of a statue to the novelist Balzac. He also added his signature to a letter addressed by many writers and musicians, such as the poets Françoise Coppée and Leconte de Lisle and the composer Gounod, to the organiser of the 1889 World Exhibition in Paris to protest at the construction of the Eiffel Tower, the enormous metal skeleton that Guy considered as ugly as a factory chimney. Maupassant never grew accustomed to the profile of the tower on the bank of the Seine and two years later he was still to remark in *La Vie Errante* that he 'fled Paris to flee from the Tower' and compared the art he saw in Italy, which was inspired by aesthetic ideals, with modern architecture such as the Tower which was the product of an age when money, science and popular taste were more important than artistic values. The 'Naturalist' author of *Boule de Suif* and *La Maison Tellier* and the 'industrialist of literature' was clearly still at bottom the artistic idealist who had answered the Commune leader Jules Vallès in *Le Gaulois* on 11 December 1883 that, 'we do not write for the ordinary people ... Art is only for the intellectual aristocracy of a country.' Flaubert would have been proud of him!

Another feat which brought Maupassant's name unintentionally into the newspapers' front pages was his flight in one of Captain Jovis's gas-filled balloons, called *Le Horla* after the novel of the previous year. Guy had met Jovis in Nice in 1886 and then visited the Union Aéronautique de France headquarters in Paris to inquire about the Captain's current projects. It was soon afterwards that the flight, which took place in the late evening of 8 July 1887 from La Villette, north of Paris, was arranged. Several authors such as Paul Bonnetain and Paul Arène and the actress Sarah Bernhardt had already 'flown' in Jovis's balloons and the photographer and journalist Nadar was well known for his balloon flights and his aerial photography, the first ever carried out. Maupassant was thus engaging in a contemporary craze similar to that more popular one in the early days of aeroplane flying.

Many writers – some no doubt envious of Guy's success –

saw the venture as a means of advertising the novel *Le Horla*; the sharp-tongued critic and dramatist Octave Mirbeau wrote to his friend Hervieu: 'Do you know anything more openly vile, disgusting and annoying than the famous author of *Le Horla*? What will we become if every time a work appears we have to invent gimmicky schemes to sell it?' [44] At the time Maupassant claimed, however, that he had not intended to gain publicity from the adventure. Both before and the day after the flight, nevertheless, the papers were full of the news of Maupassant's ascent. Paul Alexis, always a cynical joker, wrote in *Le Cri du Peuple* on 17 June: 'Our friend Guy de Maupassant . . . not satisfied with boating along the river . . . is shortly going to take a ride into the sky.' And Guy himself described in *Le Figaro* of 16 July his experiences in the balloon's basket with Jovis, his engineer Mallet and two other passengers flying ever higher over Paris, the Princess Mathilde's villa at Saint-Gratien, where her guests cheered on its ascent, the suburbs, the fields, and the cities of Lille and Roubaix to a height of 6,000 feet before descending at 3 a.m. the following morning in the middle of a sugar-beet field at Heyst-sur-Mer in Belgium. He clearly enjoyed the exciting experience of gliding over the rooftops – so low at Bruges that they barely skimmed the cathedral spire! – and being able to regulate and estimate the balloon's height just by throwing cigarette papers, grains of sand, chicken bones or drops of water overboard and watching them fall below! Seeing the sun setting and rising from above and gazing at the storm clouds behind them also provided some spectacular moments and Guy sent several telegrams to his closest friends announcing his unusual but safe journey to Heyst before returning by train from Ostend to Paris. Above all, the flight gave Maupassant the sensation of escaping from the earth with all its bustle and anxieties and gliding into a world of silence and forgetfulness:

'I am filled with a strange, penetrating sense of well-being in both body and soul derived from a feeling of nonchalance, of complete relaxation, of forgetfulness, indifference to everything and this new sensation of gliding through space without noise, jolts or jerks or anything that makes movement uncomfortable . . . Every memory has vanished from our minds, every care from our thought, we have no longer any regrets, plans or hopes. We just watch, feel and enjoy to the full the experiences of this fantastic journey. Just us and the moon in the sky! We form a small roving world of our own wandering through space like our relations the planets; and this little globe of ours contains five men who have left the earth behind and have already almost forgotten it . . .'

So delighted was he by the experience that a year later he was to repeat it; but this time, alas, the spectacular journey into space ended somewhat abruptly at Beauvais.

Another journey of escape Maupassant undertook in 1887 was his visit to Algeria and Tunisia, which he began on 3 October at Marseilles. He had almost completed his novel *Pierre et Jean* and was now in need of relaxation and sun. Accompanied by the editor of the periodical *La Revue Britannique* and a close friend of Princess Mathilde, Pierre-Amédée Pichot, and an unnamed lady he first of all stayed in a number of unsatisfactory hotels in Constantine and Algiers while making excursions from there to go walking and hunting in the country. Then he rented some rooms in the Rue Ledru-Rollin in Algiers. He wrote to his mother that he was enjoying and benefiting from the heat of the African sun and dispatched boxes of dates to Princess Mathilde, Mme Straus and others. He also sent a letter to the doctor-writer Henri Cazalis from the spa at Hammam-Rhiza to say he had been visiting 'an absolutely unknown part of Algeria where I still found ravines of fairytale virgin forest' and was going to the cedar woods of Teniet El Haad and the mountains of Ouariensis the next day.

After over a month in Algeria Guy moved on to Tunisia. It was apparently the early setting of the sun and a chill breeze from the sea in Algiers that drove him to the purer, drier air and sunshine of Tunis, where he arrived in early December. As in Algeria he liked wandering here down the winding, narrow streets of the *souks* with their shabby white houses and small domed mosques and enjoyed watching the busy and colourful native life. He also revisited the ruins of Carthage just outside the city and was reminded of Flaubert's journey to them thirty years before for the documentation of his historical novel *Salammbô*.

From Tunis itself he then went on by carriage to the holy city of Kairouan and the walled town of Sousse, passing the remains of Roman cities and miles of cultivated fields on the way. The route was quite a rough one as many of the roads and bridges had been swept away by previous rains and occasionally much of what remained was turned into mud and slime by the rains of the current wet season. They halted for the night at Hammamet, Enfidaville and El Menzel, where they were entertained by the local French or Tunisian dignitaries, before reaching Kairouan on 14 December. Here Maupassant admired the beautiful tiling of the Djama-Kebir and Sidi-Sahab mosques and visited several Islamic seminaries – he had done a large amount of reading on the beliefs and sects of Islam during his stay in Algiers – and took an early morning Moorish bath prior to continuing his journey to Sousse and then going on by boat to Sfax – a section of the trip he most heartily enjoyed. From this southern point he returned to Tunis and some two weeks later arrived back in France on 6 January 1888.

Maupassant has left an account of his travels in his volume *La Vie Errante* of 1890. It is clear from this that it was not only the sun that attracted him during his stay. His sensualist's eye is here, as elsewhere, fixed on the women and girls he sees: he is curious about the veiled, haïk-draped women he sees praying at saints' tombs in Algiers and notes with obvious pleasure that both in their belief and in their life they revere the male whether it is their husbands at home or the saint in the domed *koubas* decorated by them with carpets and lights; he admired the beauty and colourful clothes of the Jewish women of Tunis and watches a display of their belly-dancing. Like Flaubert in Egypt, he is excited by the open prostitution of the streets and the entertainment being given

in a brothel he is taken to – though he confesses that he does not
find Arab women as warm and tender as those in France. It could
be that, as with Flaubert, the sight of the immoral or perverse was
more appealing to his sensual imagination than the urge for actual
involvement and that often his sensuality resulted in little more
than an attempt at shy voyeurism.

Other aspects of Maupassant's impressions of his trip which
deserve attention are his strange and morbid interest in the sick
and death. In Italy, too, Guy had shown a singular attraction to
the grotesque sights of the Palermo catacombs; in Tunisia it is
not only in necropolises and Arab cemeteries that Guy shows an
interest but the mental hospital, where pale, haggard hashish and
kif addicts eye him from their barred cells. In fact, he describes a
number of them with the same artistic detachment and psychological precision that made his readers identify him with the
narrator of *Le Horla*. Although, as with the Goncourt brothers in
their documentary visits to prisons and hospitals for the preparation of their novels, Guy's artistic fascination with such oddities
dominated his attitude towards them, he did nevertheless feel
some pity for their state and also a certain envy of the hallucinatory dreamworld away from reality that they now inhabited.

Such a desire for escapism as this reveals in Maupassant
explains perhaps not only his love of the desert on his visits to
North Africa but also his interest in religion at this time. He
enjoys the bareness and quietness of the mosques he enters and is
clearly entranced by the chanting of prayers he hears inside; and
there is surely a religious sentiment in his documentation on
Islam, particularly when he compares some of its mystics with
Saint Teresa and imagines many of the people he sees in the
countryside as figures from the Bible. Perhaps Maupassant, like
other writers such as Bourget, Loti, Rod, Huysmans and Hennique, had been prompted by the general interest in cosmopolitan cultural imports such as the Russian novel, the Pre-
Raphaelites and Wagner into seeking a spiritual foot-hold at this
time in some form of religious belief to replace the faith they had
earlier lost under the influence of science and 'Naturalism' and

now felt a need for so as to escape from the spiritual impasse these had led them into. Certainly there is a sign of this movement amid the deep pessimism of his volume *Sur l'Eau*, published in 1888. In this he declares his disgust with the limitations and monotony of human life that can only satisfy him by its basic animal pleasures:

'We know nothing, we cannot see anything, we cannot find out anything about our origins nor can we guess or imagine anything about them. We are shut in and imprisoned within ourselves. And to think people marvel at the genius of mankind! . . . I, however, take pride in realising the emptiness of all beliefs and the vanity of hopes that arouse the arrogance of us tiny insects!'

He scorns the idea of Man's progress, the benefits of war, and the purpose of Art, given the limitations of human knowledge and human existence. He mocks at the petty vanity and presumptuous stupidity of aristocratic society on the Côte d'Azur. In his own field he satirises the idolatry with which high society treats its artists and writers; and he complains about the strain on a writer's critical faculty and nervous system that sophisticated society's desire for ever greater refinement puts on his observation and emotional sensitivity:

'No simple feeling exists in him any more. Everything he sees, his joys, his pleasures, his suffering, his despair, become instantly subjects for his closer analysis of them. He analyses the feelings, faces, gestures and intonations around him unceasingly and despite himself and others. As soon as he has seen something, whatever it is, he must discover the why and wherefore of it!'

Like the period's society, literature had become over-refined in its search for originality and nuance and the writer had in turn become over-intellectualised and put under constant nervous stress in his reactions to the world about him; like the society he served, he had abandoned all that was natural and simple for what was complex, unnatural and sophisticated. Countering all these pessimistic observations in *Sur l'Eau* there are, however, a few more positive approaches to life. Always a sentimentalist despite his rather negative realism and cynicism, Maupassant, like the priest in his tale *Clair de Lune*, states how he enjoys musing on love in the moonlight and quotes the Romantic poets in doing so. Like many other writers of these years he also veers away from his scepticism and contempt for humanity by sharing some of the neo-Christian pity for others which had been taught by the recently introduced Russian novels of particularly Dostoevsky and Tolstoy. The episodes where he feels sorry for the ragged old woman he sees in Paris and where he offers help and sympathy for the diphtheria victims he visits in Normany do not imply the end of his scepticism but they do suggest a certain trust in life and concern for humanity which could lead on to some neo-religious belief.

In the meantime, however, Maupassant's response to his pessimistic view of the world, society and the writer is a desire to escape from the opulent and presumptuous people of Europe, and from the mental strains of thinking, analysing and writing for them, to the simplicity, peace and stability of some warm Eastern or North African country. Here, he would forget the anguish of existence and the troubles of the world and just sit and enjoy the simple, natural pleasures of the sunshine and his many wives and of riding over the desert plains on a splendid steed. Some of this he did, of course, experience on his visits to North Africa; what he does not mention in *Sur l'Eau* is his interest in the religion of his escapist's paradise, which clearly played a large part in his appreciation of the peace, stability, and naturalness of the country when he was actually there.

It would seem possible then that, given Guy's greater desire and need for peace, simplicity and escape from the anguish and complexity of his work and family and social matters, he sought not only sunshine and tranquillity in North Africa but also some absorbing religious feeling, however vague, to counter the darkness of his nihilistic pessimism. As in the cases of the poet

Rimbaud and the exoticist Pierre Loti, Maupassant's return in the winter of 1888 to Algeria and Tunisia might in fact confirm his longing for the world of the desert and the mosque as well as for the sun and the heat. This need to escape for the good of both body and soul was, moreover, to remain with him to the end.

The Tragic Face of 'Bel-Ami'

When Maupassant returned bronzed and apparently healthy from his tour of North Africa in the first week of 1888 he little suspected that the next few months would be his last moments of peace and comparatively enjoyable happiness before the stresses of his family, his finances and his work were to accelerate the progress of his fatal illness. Few of his friends could have guessed the agonising fate so soon to overtake him when they saw him, tall, muscular and tanned, sailing with his companions Raymond and Bernard on his new forty-foot yacht *Bel Ami II* along the Côte d'Azur shore, stopping at Cannes, Antibes, Villefranche and La Salis for taking on stores and relaxing on board with his dog and cat and his books or taking his daily swim at 10 a.m. Nor could the distinguished guests whom he invited aboard – Princess de Sagan, the Duke of Chartres, the Duchess of Rivoli, Mme de Galliffet, Countess Potocka and many others from the aristocratic, pleasure- and novelty-seeking society of Cannes as well as Mme Straus, the Kanns, Henri Cazalis, Count Primoli, the journalist Aurélien Scholl, the dramatist of Zola's works William Busnach, and a host of doctors, writers, and artists from the cultural world – be aware of how latently ill their entertaining host was.

He continued to play tricks on them – on one occasion hiding dozens of mice under a table display of prawns, frogs and turtles! And he carried on his flirtation with a number of his female admirers: with his neighbour at Etretat, the intellectual, golden-haired Mme Hermine Lecomte de Noüy – a flirtation that her architect husband's continued absence in Romania and Guy's interest in her small son Pierre merely encouraged, and that even her weak health does not seem to have prevented from being other than platonic at their meetings at Villefranche and along the Seine: with the Kann sisters, whom he visited at Saint-Raphäel where Monsieur Kann was convalescing – in fact, he is said to have written hundreds of letters to Marie, all of which, alas, were later burnt on her instructions: and with Mme Straus, whose maternal friendliness never failed to attract him, and Countess Potocka, whose love of novelty and adventure matched Guy's own – she is said to have teased him on a sailing trip to Paganini's grave on Saint-Honorat Isle near Santa Marguerita by swimming nude in a secluded grotto!

Maupassant's life, like that of the society he now frequented, appeared to contain all he could have wished for – success as a writer whose sales exceeded those of Bourget, Loti and Anatole France, wealth to enable him to live in comfort at Etretat, Paris or with his mother at the Villa Continentale in Antibes, to travel and go sailing, and a host of friends and admirers all over the world. Only a few intimate friends and his family might have bothered to have had doubts about his health, or lent any importance to his visits to North Africa, Châtel-Guyon and Aix-les-Bains for the benefits of sunshine and spa water; after all, so many other people at the time sought these same aids for the most minor of ailments and the habit of going to a health resort was clearly often motivated by a fashionable desire for self-indulgent hypochondria rather than a genuine concern for a medical miracle.

In any case, as he himself wrote in his diary account of his life at sea in *Sur l'Eau*, published in the February to April 1888 issues of Masson's *Les Lettres et les Arts*, his best means of recovering his health and escaping from pessimistic thoughts about the problems of human existence and society and his intellectual sophistication as a writer was going sailing in the natural expanses of the sea; and no one saw more than a hearty sportsmanship in this, though for him it represented a welcome relief from the mental and social pressures of his complex life on the land and an escapist venture in which he could give himself up to the simple sensual pleasures of Nature:

'The waves caressing the sandy shore or sweeping over the granite rocks touches and moves me, and the happiness that fills me when I feel myself driven along by the wind and carried over the waves springs from my sense of giving myself up to the powerful natural forces in life, of returning to Man's primitive state.'

Perhaps, had Fate allowed Maupassant to have benefited for longer from such relief, his health might have survived many more years than it did. Family troubles and the consequent strain on his finances were, however, to force him to return to the land to write and socialise and put unbearable pressures on both his body and mind.

While Maupassant was sunning himself in Algeria and sailing happily along the Côte d'Azur in late 1887 and early 1888 the last work from his pen to be written in trouble-free circumstances appeared in Mme Adam's *Nouvelle Revue* and was published by Ollendorff – Havard, Guy's usual publisher, having fallen from favour because of his delays and poor publicity.

Pierre et Jean tells the story of Pierre Roland's discovery of his brother Jean's illegitimacy when the latter is left a large sum of money in the will of a former frequent visitor to the house, and his consequent persecution of his mother in a frantic attempt to uncover the truth about her relations with Jean's benefactor. As in *Le Horla* and *Mont Oriol*, it is the psychological drama taking place in Pierre's mind that provides the principal interest in the intrigue. It is his progress from a vague envy of his brother's good fortune in contrast to his own frustrations and nagging doubts about his mother's past to a definite jealousy of Jean's wealth and success in romance with Mlle Rosémilly and a disillusioned pursuit of his mother that makes the novel so poignant and harrowing to the point of cruelty. Furthermore, the symbolic reflection of Pierre's psychological state, from curiosity and doubts to shock, envy, disgust and eventually sadism, in the descriptions of the ships and sirens of the mist-enshrouded port of Le Havre provides a claustrophobic, confining backcloth to the protagonist's grappling with the truth, from which he escapes by taking a post as ship's surgeon on a transatlantic liner.

Although the plot itself does not differ greatly from other similar stories concerning illegitimacy and doubtful paternity in Maupassant's works, and although Pierre's views on love and women resemble the pessimistic, misogynistic ones expressed elsewhere, *Pierre et Jean* stands out from his other novels not only by the sheer force of the crisis within Pierre but by the poignancy of the conflict between him and his mother, on whom, unlike elsewhere, so much depends. The scene in which she explains herself to Jean is one of the most moving and dramatic Maupassant wrote; it is, moreover, filled with a pity reminiscent of that often found in Russian novels but rarely in Maupassant's work.

As in *Une Vie* and *Mont Oriol*, the idealism of love is here kept alive and vindicated, despite the ephemerality of the passion itself and the death of the loved-one, by Mme Roland's affection for her illegitimate son Jean. Indeed, just as in *Mont Oriol*, Paul's marriage and Andermatt's return clear all obstacles from Christiane's path and allow her to maintain her passion for Paul in her love for their child, so here in *Pierre et Jean* Pierre's departure and M. Roland's continued ignorance allow the idealistic love that brought Jean into the world to survive unimpaired by the family's criticism or the scandalous gossip of society. Mme Roland's love affair and illegitimate child might show up the hypocrisy and the '*mensonge*' or lie within bourgeois society – hence in part Maupassant's interest in the story – but they also are seen to represent the finer qualities of love and devotion which Mme Roland does not find in her normal married life.

Ever since *Pierre et Jean* appeared there has been a great temptation to read all sorts of biographical connotations into the text. Because of Guy's interest in illegitimacy as a topic with intriguing literary possibilities and because of his affinities with Flaubert, largely on account of his early acquaintance with him, the question of whether Guy was Flaubert's son and was acutely aware of it has always arisen in the context of *Pierre et Jean*; so far, however, not a shred of evidence exists to prove the idea and Guy shows no signs of embarrassment that might suggest that Gustave was not his father.[45] It has also been asserted, though not proved, that Maupassant was interested in the illegitimacy issue because he was the father of three illegitimate children born to Joséphine Litzelmann of Sens;[46] though it is true that Guy did spend some months in Sens in 1883 for military training as a reservist, there is no other evidence to prove that Maupassant was the father of Lucien, born in February 1883, or of Lucienne and Marguerite, born in 1884 and 1887 respectively; the fact that there was an oral tradition in the area that Maupassant was their father, that they kept a photograph of him on the mantelpiece and vague resemblances between the Litzelmanns and the novelist have been noted from photographs cannot be accepted as hard evidence. Moreover, given the busy and varied life Maupassant led, the whole episode – sensational as it may be – seems most unlikely, and its influence on *Pierre et Jean* equally improbable.

In any case, Maupassant himself stated in a letter of 2 February 1888 to the novelist Edouard Estaunié, who had written a novel on the same theme, that he had taken his first ideas for the plot of *Pierre et Jean* from a situation he had read of in a newspaper, and Hermine Lecomte de Noüy records in her diary on 22 June 1887 [47] that Maupassant was basing his novel on an incident which had befallen a friend of his who had inherited a large fortune. It would thus seem likely that Guy amalgamated the news item and his friend's windfall to provide a foundation for his novel and that as elsewhere the biographical element is minimal and limited to some of the sentiments expressed by Jean and his mother.

A short study on the contemporary novel, though written and published separately, was used to preface *Pierre et Jean* because the volume was too short. It echoes Flaubert's attitude to literature in stressing the importance of the writer's individual yet objective interpretation of what he describes both by his style and his discriminating view; literary production is both highly individual and selective; the meaning or purpose of the work produced derives from the slice of life and the language provided by the writer and lies outside the precepts of any literary schools, whether Naturalist or Art for Art. Although merely echoing what Maupassant had long ago stated to Flaubert among his criticisms of Zola and 'Naturalism', the Preface has had, both at the time of publication and since, greater effect than the novel itself. This is partly because many writers such as Goncourt felt under attack in the Preface and protested and because Maupassant's text was mutilated by the editors of the *Figaro*, where it appeared on 7 January 1888, and this caused him to threaten legal action against them – which ended in explanations and not in any prosecution; and partly because it is the most accessible and concise statement of his literary creed. Moreover, as Maupassant realised when writing to his mother in September 1887, *Pierre et Jean* was too cruel to sell well and be popular; furthermore, it appeared at an unfavourable time, when the public was keener to read its newspapers to learn of the latest German diplomatic moves against France than devote its attention to serious literature.

The result of these various circumstances was that, although Zola was later to consider it the best of Maupassant's works,[48] and Henry James was to refer to it in his *Partial Portraits* (1888) as 'a faultless production', Guy did not earn as much from *Pierre et Jean* as he had hoped when he begun it. He had told Laure then that 'I am broke and if I do not want to be obliged to seek a librarian's post I must make the most of my time' and had in fact completed the novel in record time for this reason. Now once more he would have to write in order to survive financially.

He therefore began writing his next novel *Fort comme la Mort* in the spring of 1888, only a couple of months after the publication of *Pierre et Jean*. The effect of this on the morale of the dedicated writer, who in more cynical moments had called himself the 'industrialist of literature' and told someone, when asked why he continued to write, that it was better than stealing for a living,[49] was of course detrimental. Its effect on his health was, however, nothing short of disastrous; by September 1888 he was telling his editor, Havard, that his eyes were so bad and his migraine so painful that he had not written a line for months. Unfortunately, the prolongation of the novel's composition only served to aggravate his medical condition for even longer and he was obliged to seek rest and a cure, first at Aix-les-Bains in July and September and then from October until the following March in North Africa, where, as he wrote to Mme Straus in November, he 'was airing his headaches and neuralgia in the really hot African sun'. This pattern of work, ill health and convalescence was to be that of the few remaining years of Maupassant's life, since temporary escapes to sun and fresh air could not compensate for the strain on his constitution of his increasingly protracted writing.

It might at first seem strange that someone as successful as Maupassant should have been under such financial pressure to continue writing to the detriment of his health. Did an income that rose after 1885 from 40,000 to 120,000 francs (an average worker earned less than 900 francs a year and Guy had earned 1,600 francs as a clerk) on account of the new editions and translations of his works not suffice? Apparently not. It was because of his desire for more money that he constantly demanded higher payments for his works. Octave Mirbeau [50] told his fellow-dramatist and critic Hervieu on 21 July 1886: 'The league at *Gil Blas* against Maupassant increases every day. Castellier told me he was doing all he could to dissuade Ollendorff from taking Maupassant's novel – at 22 sous a line it's too dear, he told me ... and Maupassant keeps on raising the price!' In the end, Maupassant was in fact obliged, after *Le Horla* appeared in *Gil Blas*, to publish his works in other periodicals that would pay what he asked.

This desire for more money arose partly from Maupassant's manner of living and was partly due to circumstances beyond his control. Maupassant enjoyed living luxuriously and there was something of the child imitating the adult and the successful bourgeois aping the wealthy aristocrat – as so many industrialists and financiers of the period did – in his desire to copy the lifestyle of the artists and upper-class personalities he met and be able to impress them when it was his turn to entertain them. To some extent such an attitude was a necessary part of his own publicity but there is also something boastful and egotistic about it, which Laure's pride in her son probably did little to discourage. Both to suit himself and to impress others, Guy thus maintained three main homes – Etretat, Rue Montchanin in Paris and the villa in Antibes – as well as his yachts, his staff and all the various pets he acquired. Moreover, he was constantly having his homes renovated and his yachts repaired. He liked to indulge in buying fine clothes for his socialising and expensive ornaments for his homes and enjoyed giving elaborate parties and dinners for his friends and acquaintances. An idea of his extravagance can be gained from the fact that on his visit to Algeria in 1890 he took along no less than forty-four pieces of luggage including twelve trunks and eight hatboxes! Added to these expenses were the cost of his medical consultations and treatments and the large amounts needed to pay for his ever-longer visits abroad. As if such expenses were not enough, Guy was also obliged to care for his invalid mother and largely contribute to the maintenance of her properties near Etretat, now rented out to tenants, and her various homes at Antibes and to her medical bills. He also helped his father financially when the latter found himself in an awkward situation after having allowed his name to be used in the founding of a review that failed.

A much heavier burden was added to his financial obligations in the mid-1880s when his brother Hervé decided to settle down at last and get married. Brought up without a father's presence at home and with the suffering of his mother constantly before his eyes, Hervé had become an unruly, restless youth who had often run away from home and played truant at school. The character of Paul in *Une Vie* is said to have been based on Hervé's early life. As Laure had told Flaubert, Hervé was unsuited to literary and intellectual matters and for some time after he did his military service in Brittany and Algeria in 1877 it was a problem trying to find him an appropriate job, and he stayed with his father in Paris while Guy sought to obtain him a post in the same Ministry he had worked at in June 1883.[51] When this failed, Guy tried with Louis Le Poittevin's aid to get him a job in the Crédit Lyonnais and also in De Lesseps' construction company in Panama. When this too came to naught, Hervé joined Laure in the south of France, until in early 1886 he married Marie-Thérèse Fanton d'Andon, by whom he had a daughter Simone the following year. The family must have heaved a sigh of relief at last and Guy, possibly believing this would be his last contribution to his brother's welfare, provided him with the cash to set up his own farm near Antibes.

Unfortunately, Hervé's career as an agronomist barely lasted eighteen months, for in the summer of 1887 he fell seriously ill and by the following year had begun to show signs of the madness, presumably syphilitic in origin, that was shortly to lead to his death. Once more it was Guy who had to bear the burden of keeping Hervé's wife and child and of providing medical treatment. It was Guy who took his brother to consult various doctors in Montpellier, Lyon and Paris, but all in vain. By mid-1888 there was no doubt about Hervé's serious condition; Guy wrote to his father at that time: 'Hervé's mind is completely at sea on everything. Yesterday, he began sawing wood in the middle of dinner and only stopped when he was utterly exhausted. . . .' Later in the year Hervé grew even worse and in early 1889 he tried to strangle his wife. Guy knew now that, despite Laure and Marie-Thérèse's reluctance, Hervé would sooner or later have to be interned in an asylum. For the moment, however, he was being looked after in a convalescent home near Paris at Ville-Evrard, where Guy had managed to persuade him to come for treatment.

Apart from the mental stress such an action had on Guy, his caring for his brother and the latter's family as well as for Laure, who was shattered by her younger son's condition, made great demands on his purse. He wrote to his father in 1889: 'It is really terribly hard on me to have to work as I am doing, to exhaust myself for it is impossible for me to do more than I am, to give up

all the pleasures I would have deserved after it, and see all the
money I would have kept by for the future swallowed up like
this.' What makes this plaintive confession all the more tragic is
the fact that these sacrifices of Guy not only did not bring him any
satisfaction but actually imposed such a strain on his resources
and his health as to hasten his own death; for it was indeed both
despite and because of the stresses on him that his next novel *Fort
comme la Mort* appeared as soon as it did in Baschet's *Revue
Illustrée* from February to May 1889.

The fact that Maupassant found it difficult to write the novel
can be seen from his letter to Laure of May 1888, in which he
complained to her how hard he was finding it to instil the
'nuances, things suggested and not stated', of his more refined
psychological analysis of delicate emotions into his text; the
difficulties he encountered in the work's composition are also
obvious from the number of amendments to his original manuscript, particularly in the last sixty pages. This is not, however,
surprising, given the circumstances of its composition and the
psychological complexity of the work itself.

Fort comme la Mort – a title taken from the *Song of Solomon* –
describes the waning of the now ageing society painter Olivier
Bertin's youthful passion for Countess Anne de Guilleroy, whose
portrait he once painted, and at the same time his nostalgic
attraction to and fresh desire for her twenty-year-old daughter
Annette, who, as her identical but diminutive name suggests,
resembles her mother as she was twenty years ago; it is as if his
love for Anne has subsided and then been resuscitated and now
flourishes once more stronger than ever. The situation is similar
to that of the tale *Monsieur Jocaste*, but here the scene is set in
upper-class society and there is no lurid violence or sexual drama.
Instead, there is the psychological drama of the painter's dilemma
when faced with both mother and daughter – how can he hide his
feelings for the young blonde Annette who can tease him and play
tennis with him and so clearly recalls her mother when she first
posed for him, and still show his affection to be as warm as before
for Anne? This dilemma of Bertin's runs parallel with the other

main interest in the novel: Anne's desperate attempt to try with the use of cosmetics and dim lighting to retain her youthful beauty despite the passing of time and its effect on her appearance, aggravated by her grief at her mother's death. The unfavourable contrast between mother and daughter and Bertin's consequent dilemma are poignantly brought out in the scene where Annette, in mourning for her grandmother, stands in front of the portrait of Anne, also in mourning, that Bertin had painted at the height of his passion for her, while Anne, now pale and haggard, looks on full of self-pity and envy at Olivier's obvious admiration of her daughter.

The psychological drama that ensues as Bertin becomes increasingly attracted to Annette and tries to hide it from her mother by buying them both brooches, taking both to the opera and paying equal attention to both, and as Anne becomes more and more desperate and possessive when she realizes the true situation, only ends when the painter is knocked down by a bus while wandering the streets in a highly disturbed state. As Maupassant implied when he told Laure his novel was going to be a view of life that was 'terrible, tender and despairing', *Fort comme la Mort* is pervaded with a sense of despair and death from the very beginning when the deathly stillness of Bertin's studio, now that he is at the end of a lifetime of painting, is described and Anne is seen in mourning in a flashback to when he painted her, right until the novel's close with Bertin's death and Anne's burning of her letters to him.

As if Maupassant's familiar themes of the passing of love, the alienation of the lovers, the fading of beauty and the coming of old age and death were not pessimistic enough, Bertin's rather contemptuous views of the wealthy but shallow and artificial society he has served and frequented over the years, and the emptiness and boredom of his bachelor life in his late middle age, add even further despair. Are these not the views of Maupassant himself in *Sur l'Eau* just published in 1889? After all, Bertin, though older and a painter, does resemble Guy a little in looks, certainly shares his love of recreation, fencing and the countryside, and seems to suffer the same migraine and seek the same cures in hot baths as the author. It seems more than likely then that Bertin's world-weariness, his sense of the futility of more work, his failing inventiveness, and his disdain for the shallowness and monotony of high society, as well as the feeling of imminent old age and a vague longing for the peacefulness of death, were similar to Guy's own in 1888–9, when he was struggling with the novel's composition amid his own and his family's ill health and the financial pressures imposed upon him.

Certainly, if, as Count Primoli reported, Maupassant said he had wanted to describe in *Fort comme la Mort* 'the progress of a feeling at a particular time of life',[52] and had subordinated the portrayal of his characters to the evocation of their thoughts and emotions in order to do so, then the sentiments the novel conveys are those of a desperate idealistic longing for love and an equally desperate awareness of the reality of the passing of all things and the imminence of death. This conflict, though largely derived from the author's personal circumstances, is, however, given a more universal, abstract significance by Maupassant's presentation. The subordination of character to the feeling or outlook appropriate to their role in the plot's psychological and moralistic conflict stresses the symbolic, abstract value that Maupassant's characters were increasingly to assume as representative types. Psychological analysis of characters was thus to give way soon to moral comments on society as a whole.

The clash of the ideal and the real in *Fort comme la Mort* is basically the same as in much of Maupassant's other work and reflects his pessimistic outlook. The difference, however, is that *Fort comme la Mort*'s emphasis on the ageing and death of its main characters and their feelings is so much more cynical and despairing than in *Mont Oriol* and *Pierre et Jean* with their slight amount of neo-Russian pity; and there can be little doubt that this was largely due to the circumstances in which it was written.

Dark clouds continued to gather over Guy's horizon during and after the publication of *Fort comme la Mort*. The state of his brother, who had nowr eturned from his 'convalescence' at Ville-

Evrard near Paris and was at home with his mother and family at Cannes, deteriorated and, as Guy informed his father: 'Hervé is a sick man; he has moments of terrifying violence . . . and puts at risk the lives of those around him.' Guy therefore took upon himself once more the task of trying to find a clinic or home where his brother would be cared for; after numerous inquiries he selected the asylum at Bron near Lyons where conditions were reasonable and Hervé would be in the charge of Professor Pierret, brother-in-law of the noted specialist Bouchard. Before Hervé could be sent there, however, Guy had to wait for Laure and his sister-in-law to give their consent; Hervé's wife was reluctant to see her husband put away for ever and Laure, driven hysterical by her son's condition, feared the scandal and tried to delude herself into believing that her son would recover. Guy wrote to his father at this time: 'The situation is getting worse and worse. But I can do nothing and since I am reproached for what I do and say, I have no wish to give my advice any more.'

Eventually, however, the two women did give way when Hervé became completely unmanageable and a danger to them all. Once more it was Guy who had the unpleasant task of delivering his brother to the asylum. It is said that the journey was arranged under the guise of a visit to a friend's property and that once inside the asylum Hervé was coaxed into a cell by being shown the view from its window and while he was gazing outside Guy withdrew; apparently his brother then realised his situation and angrily clammered at the closed door accusing Guy of being mad and reproaching him for taking such action. Such a horrifying yet pathetic scene must have had an enormous impact on such a sensitive soul and devoted family man as Guy and could not have failed to have left its mark on his declining health. No account survives of this important event in Guy's life as in the case of so many other significant occasions which he felt too deeply to write about, or the evidence of which others destroyed after his death. There are, however, a few letters in which he refers to a visit he later made to Hervé. He wrote in October 1889 to Lucie Le Poittevin:

'I found Hervé absolutely mad, without a glimmer of sanity, leaving us no hope of him ever recovering (something my mother does not yet realise). The two hours I spent with him at the Bron asylum were terrible because he clearly recognised me, he cried, embraced me time and time again and said he wanted to leave, all in his incoherent state . . .'

The effect of this on the already pessimistic Guy can be judged from his letter to Countess Potocka written immediately after the visit:

'I was so upset that I have never suffered like this before. When I had to leave him and he was not allowed to accompany me to the station, he began to whine so pathetically that I could not prevent myself bursting into tears as I gazed at him whom Nature has condemned to death and is slowly killing, who will never leave this prison or see his mother again . . . Moreover, he realises that there is something terrible and incurable taking place inside him but he is not sure what exactly . . . Oh, what a vile thing, what a grotesque creation is this miserable human body and mind of ours! . . .'

Hervé did not, fortunately, survive very long in the asylum. On 13 November 1889 Hervé de Maupassant died there, aged only thirty-three years. Guy, who had witnessed Hervé's last moments, paid for the funeral and simple tomb, which he visited several times in the next few years. He also continued to care for Hervé's wife and little daughter Simone, allowing them to carry on staying with himself and Laure in Cannes or with his father at Sainte-Maxime and setting up a family council to look after his niece's affairs until she was of age. Furthermore, it was to Simone that he later left the greater part of his assets in his will. Hervé's illness and death were not only an emotional and financial strain on Guy, who was already under considerable mental stress as he tried to make progress with the next novel he had begun to undertake in the spring so as to earn some more money; they also had a disastrous effect on Laure. Guy had written to Lucie Le Poittevin in October that 'my mother can no longer walk and hardly says a word'; by the time of Hervé's death he reported to the Princess Mathilde [53] that his mother was living on drugs so as to exist in a numbed state oblivious of her intense grief and that he was renting a villa for her in Grasse where she could remain for a while until she recovered a little.

While his mother was living off sedatives in Grasse, Guy decided he too needed a rest after the ordeal. He therefore planned to sail along the Ligurian coast of Italy on his yacht, stopping to relax and write more of his novel at the small picturesque ports they would call at. During the early summer he had hired a house, Villa Stieldorff, at Triel on the Seine to find some peace and quiet, do some boating and write, but after a few weeks he had found he was being constantly interrupted by friendly callers and the social life of the river-banks and had moved to his home at Etretat. Here, the weather had been too cool for him and in any case he had soon been called to Cannes to deal with his brother's worsening situation. By the late autumn he was thus in need of a break and some peace both to relax and to write.

Life on *Bel Ami* did not turn out to be as restful as he had hoped, however – partly because he could not sleep for his sailor Raymond's snoring! – and he eventually rented an apartment in Santa Margherita for a month so as to complete his novel. From here he took the train down to Pisa, where he stayed overnight before touring the town again and taking a cab out to the place on the Gulf of La Spezia where Byron burnt Shelley's body. From Pisa, Maupassant, accompanied by his valet François, journeyed on to Florence. This time their stay in the city was curtailed, however, by Guy falling ill after six days with a very high temperature and stomach haemorrhages. Clearly, the strains of the past few months had been too much for him and he was rushed back to Cannes with pains in his stomach and his head, put on a strict diet and ordered to rest. It was as if Hervé's shade was already calling to his brother to join him.

CHAPTER 4

Struggling for Survival

When on 23 November 1890, exactly a year after his hasty return from Italy, Maupassant attended the unveiling of Chapu's memorial bust of Flaubert in a square at Rouen, Edmond de Goncourt recorded in his diary his surprise at the sudden change in Guy's appearance; the forty-year-old writer looked thin and haggard with a strange blankness in his stare, and Goncourt was prompted to conclude: 'He is not destined, it would seem, to live to a great age.' At the same time as Goncourt was taking note of his impressions, Guy was himself confiding to the poet José-Maria de Heredia as they stood in the pouring rain in front of the memorial how depressed and ill he felt now that his eyes and his memory were gradually failing him more and more. The man whose book sales were second only to Zola's, whose reputation stood above that of Bourget and Anatole France, and whose name was as well known in the rest of Europe as inside France, was physically and spiritually the most miserable of men.

After his return from Italy in November 1889 Maupassant was hardly ever completely out of pain and suffering, or free of his doctors. As his temporary periods of blindness and his bouts of neuralgia became increasingly unbearable and upset his work schedule, so he sought the advice of more and more doctors and specialists. He had always been one to consult all the medical practitioners available, as Léon Daudet recalls in his memoirs; [54] and when no doctors were available, he would, according to Léon Fontaine, [55] visit the chemist Leroy at Etretat or the Polish druggist at Bezons. Not that he had great trust in the medical profession, but simply because doctors and chemists were the only

people likely to be able to help him or his mother; thus, his attitude towards them varied from an initial reverence and acquies-
cence to visible signs of annoyance and cynicism when their
prescriptions and treatment did not work. Nevertheless, over the
next two years Maupassant took the advice and submitted to the
treatment prescribed by a whole series of doctors – Magitot,
Grancher, Bouchard, Déjerine, Robin, Daremberg, and many
other members of the Paris Academy of Medicine and followers
of Charcot.

Some recommended hot showers and sunshine; others advised
cupping – a procedure Guy's valet was usually obliged to carry
out in the early hours of the morning; another doctor ordered
him to get rid of his slow-combustion stove and not to go out in
the evening air; and still others recommended a variety of spas
and spa waters. Diagnoses varied between influenza, neuralgia,
migraine and neurosis; some doctors such as Bouchard considered Guy's condition a complete mystery. Syphilis, which
Landolt had mentioned back in 1883, was never referred to again.
Guy, groaning with pain, having constant recourse to ether and
morphine for relief, and unable to work, complied, however, with
all their wishes. He rid himself of his fatal stove, he underwent
showers and cuppings, he had a tooth extracted, he avoided the
cold, and he visited a number of spas. In June 1890 he stayed at
the Kann sisters' chalet at Gérardmer high up in the Vosges
mountains, enjoying the damp but fresh air of the forested
valleys and lakes; in July he was back at Aix-les-Bains in the
south; in August it was the turn of Plombières, which had a
sound effect on his stomach but was too cold and did little to cure
his head pains and the failing of his sight; and then in early
September he left Marseilles for three months in Algeria [56] and
enjoyed the extremely hot summer sun of Algiers, Biskra,
Boghar, Constantine and Oran. Travelling by train and landau
from Algiers and Biskra he visited the Chiffa Gorges, the Sidi
Okba oasis, Tolga fortress and the high plateau of Mers-el-kebir
to witness the sunrise over the desert; he was the guest of honour
at a tribal fantasia at Boghar, where he was presented with the

carcass of a gazelle, and also at an Arab wedding at Constantine, to which his hotel manager invited him; and he attended, too, the opening of the Oran to Tiemcen railway as well as the bullfight at Oran – of which he disapproved – before returning home exhausted but bronzed.

None of these attempts were successful in curing him, however; neither cool dampness nor hot sunshine, neither spa water nor Moorish baths prevented the unceasing progress of the disease undermining his whole existence. Moreover, the harder he strove to overcome his difficulties and continue to write when he could, the more intolerable became the symptoms and the more frantic his efforts to cure them.

Signs of the strain Guy was under at this time can be seen in the irritability and indignation behind many of his letters and his irascible and somewhat severe attitude towards those around him. Maupassant had always been a rather harsh, suspicious taskmaster in his business affairs and also sometimes in his romance, as in the case of Marie Bashkirtseff. He had constantly complained to and nagged his editor Victor Havard about the latter's inefficiency. His manner with Quantin and Ollendorff, too, had often been quite blunt and offhand. This was, however, largely owing to his ambition to be both successful and rich; in an occupation where you were paid for each separate word or line and in the days when publicity was your own affair and the competition for readership was extremely high, an author had to be efficient and perceptive if he was to exist as a freelance writer and earn what he wanted. Maupassant's Norman shrewdness as well as his need to find the money for his various obligations and projects therefore dictated his forceful attitude towards his editors since they played such a large part in his gaining his necessary income. This does not, however, fully justify his rough treatment of Havard in late 1890, when he threatened the publisher with legal action if he did not pay up some outstanding royalties. He wrote to another writer Gustave Toudouze on 5 March 1891: 'Has Havard paid you? I am about to ask the law to enquire into his accounts and would like to collect other evidence against him.' [57] Fortunately,

Guy left Paris soon afterwards and the matter was amiably settled by his lawyer.

An equally harsh but more personal dispute arose in December 1889 when Guy moved from rue Montchanin after his cousin Louis Le Poittevin had included in his rent-bill charges for heating when Guy was away from Paris; while it is understandable that Guy was annoyed by such a contravention of their agreement for the upkeep of the building, it is difficult not to see Guy's immediate recourse to his lawyer and the harsh tone of the following letter to Louis, recalling a family dispute with him years before and pointing out the disadvantages of their present association, as exaggeratedly severe:

'I find your claim on me for the heating of the stove during my absence from Paris so surprising . . . that I prefer not to say what I think of it! . . . I am obliged to recall that without my insistent intervention my parents would have broken with you completely over the way you acted to gain an interest in the inheritance of my grandfather . . . With regard to the apartment let me add that you have never laid out any money on it, and that in taking it I not only took on all the expense which was your concern in fact, but I also had water and gas installed, I spent 2500 francs to make the conservatory habitable, and I have embellished it in all sorts of ways. Finally, let me add so as to settle our accounts, that I once lent you 3000 francs, that I have guaranteed your debts against my rent and I am still responsible for them, and that, all in all, my relations with you are too disadvantageous by far.' [58]

Maupassant's lawyer was to be summoned once more, shortly afterwards, when Guy moved from rue Montchanin to an apartment at 14 Avenue Victor Hugo in early December 1889, and was kept awake at night by the noise of the bakery below. Again, Maupassant, all the more irascible because of his lack of sleep, sent a sharply worded letter to his landlord complaining of the lies he had been told about the place and threatening legal action and held a dinner in the apartment for some architects and doctors who could then testify to the disturbing noise below if the need arose! Maupassant had always been a diffident, suspicious person, taciturn and fearing illusion and deceit both in life and in his dealings with others, and it is in a way natural that he should have been so indignant both about the noise from the bakery, particularly after a fortnight of sleeplessness, and at his cousin's rent charges. His readiness to complain, his blunt language full of aggressiveness and cynicism and his swift recourse to the law do, however, seem to indicate in him at this time not only an acute irritability and sensitivity to any inconvenience but also a rather desperate effort by a weak and ill man to give a display of force in order to settle the matter as speedily as possible.

While Maupassant was wrangling with the landlord of 14 Avenue Victor Hugo and, after that had been successfully ended, was making plans for the plush, sophisticated decoration of a new apartment at 24 rue du Boccador off the fashionable street since renamed Avenue Georges V, into which he was going to move in July 1890, yet another example of his acute irascibility and sense of vulnerability occurred. The publisher Georges Charpentier was bringing out a new edition of *Les Soirées de Médan* containing Maupassant's *Boule de Suif* and had decided to decorate the volume with portraits of its six authors by the artist Dumoulin. In late May 1890 the volume appeared and the drawings of the writers were displayed, possibly for additional publicity, in the Exhibition Hall of the Champ de Mars. Guy, who had refused in the past to have his portrait reproduced by the photographer Nadar, his editor Havard, and the periodicals *Le Monde Illustré* and *L'Illustration* and had recently withheld permission from the artist Henri Toussaint to publish a picture of him, was naturally furious when he heard from Huysmans what Charpentier had done. He wrote at once to Charpentier on 30 May pointing out his shock at what had been done without his permission, his refusal in the past to give his permission for the display of his picture, and his intention of having his portrait removed from all copies of the new edition of the *Soirées* still available and from all future ones. Finally, he threatened legal action if this was not carried out and all copies of his portrait were not returned to him or his lawyer Maître Jacob. At the same time as he was telling Charpentier that he found it unacceptable that any artist could come along, make a copy of a photograph of him and display it to the public, and was virtually ordering him to put an end to such action, Maupassant wrote to Dumoulin describing what the latter had done as 'inexplicable and unspeakable' and threatening him too with recourse to the law.

Charpentier did not reply for some time and, as in the case of his dispute with his landlord in Avenue Victor Hugo, Maupassant hastened to acquire prosecuting evidence for a court case. By mid-July, however, the matter was settled out of court by the publisher's complete withdrawal of the offending volume. Moreover, Charpentier wrote to Guy to express his delight at the friendly outcome of what had been but a misunderstanding and even added that: 'I had never supposed that it would displease you so much to have your portrait in the *Soirées de Médan*; indeed, I would go so far as to confess (you see how naïve I am!) that I thought the opposite would be the case.' Had he known Maupassant better, he would have realised that, although *Mademoiselle Fifi* had in fact appeared in 1882 with a portrait of him, the novelist disliked any reproduction of his image in his later years. This was perhaps owing to a desire to avoid being 'made public' or to some more neurotic fear of his own portrait, possibly because of his declining health or dread of his 'double'. Moreover, out of the few photographs that were ever taken of him only those by Thiel at Nice and by the famous Etienne Carjat found favour with him.

Maupassant's increasingly irascible temper and high-handedness were visible once more when the manager of the Gymnase theatre, Victor Koning, asked him in July 1890 to revise Jacques Normand's dramatisation of his tale *L'Enfant*, renamed *Musotte*. Despite his ill health and his doctors' orders not to read or write, Guy, always eager to earn more, did the necessary work on the play and it was performed in March and April 1891 with fair success, though not before his manner had upset Koning and at one time so offended the actors that all rehearsals were broken off. When the play opened, however, he made it up with the theatre manager, but then, not content with his sudden triumph as a dramatist – an ambition he had mentioned to his mother in September 1887 – and the money it brought him in, Maupassant again quarrelled with Koning, this time over his share in the publicity and reviews of the play.

A year or so later, another theatre manager, Jules Claretie of the Théâtre Français, was also to be subjected to Maupassant's angry retorts when the latter came to speak to him about another of his dramatisations, *La Paix du Ménage*, and adamantly refused to have it submitted to a selection committee. Moreover, soon afterwards he was angrily writing to his literary agent Roger and blaming him for not obtaining the famous actress Réjane's services for the play. By 6 March 1891 Maupassant's irritability and sense of vulnerability had become so acute that he was writing a letter to the editor of the *Figaro* complaining about how he had been badly treated by a telegraph-office assistant 'whose duty it is to be polite and behave properly', because the young Spaniard in question had not accepted a telegram from him at midnight. Clearly, as Maupassant's suffering became worse and his awareness of his deterioration became more acute, so his temper became more sensitive to injury and his manner more harsh and offensively demanding.

If this behaviour worsened in this way, it was, however, largely because of the aggravating effects his attempts to work were having on his already disintegrating constitution. During late 1889 and the first half of 1890 he not only published in the *Echo de Paris* the tales such as *Mouche* and *Le Champ d'Oliviers* which were to make up his last volume of short stories *L'Inutile Beauté*, completed his volume *La Vie Errante* and began amending Jacques Normand's play *Musotte*, but also finished his last novel *Notre Cœur*, which appeared in the *Revue des Deux Mondes* in May and June 1890. Although according to Maupassant's valet the circumstances upon which the novel is based date from 1884 to 1885, the actual writing of the work did not begin until the late summer of 1889. It was at that time that Guy wrote to the shrewd, erudite critic and editor of the rather academic and high-class periodical *La Revue des Deux Mondes*, Ferdinand Brunetière, offering him exclusive rights in his work as an incentive and desiring to be paid as much for one novel by the *Revue* as he would normally have received from his various other writings in a number of periodicals:

'Before the short novel *L'Ame Etrangère* that I promised you I intend to complete a short story I was going to submit to *Le Figaro*. The nature of the subject and my enthusiasm for it as I write it cause me to prefer to see it appear in one or two parts in the *Revue* than in fifteen or eighteen sections elsewhere . . . As I mentioned to you and I repeat quite unashamedly, I intend to produce very little very slowly and to give myself fully to each page and each line. I want, however, that this concentrated effort should bring me in as much as the various little pieces for the newspapers. I like to live well, you see . . .' [59]

This was obviously an attempt to overcome the grave impediment of his ill health and yet earn the necessarily high income he wanted. While Brunetière was considering the proposal, Maupassant, though concerned more with his brother than his novel in the autumn of 1889, sent the *Revue*'s editor his article on Kairouan and suggested 1200 francs as a suitable fee for each page of the 'short story' that was to grow into the 'novel' he had intended *L'Ame Etrangère* to be. Despite the size of the sum requested, Brunetière seems to have agreed, for, while in late September Maupassant had written only the first chapter of the short story that he was rapidly turning into a novel, by mid-November he was informing the editor:

'You will have in a short while the novel that my brother's death has interrupted. The title is *Notre Cœur*. What I have written so far pleases me quite a lot. I feel myself on a course towards a supreme truth about life and I am being carried along towards it.

Whenever I have had this impression, the results have never been bad.'[60]

The results were not bad. When the novel appeared in the *Revue* after Maupassant had spent hours revising his manuscript and Brunetière had carefully edited its punctuation, the critics – Anatole France in *Le Temps*, Paul Ginisty in *Gil Blas*, André Hallays in the *Journal des Débats* – were at one in praising the merits of *Notre Cœur*; and although Guy at first feared that the work's publication in the *Revue* would rob him of many of his sophisticated readers when the volume appeared at Ollendorff's in June, this was not so and the sales of the novel – over 30,000 copies in the first few months – were at least as high as most of his other works. Moreover, publication in the *Revue* not only reflected Maupassant's social acceptance by the upper classes who formed the backbone of its readership, but also represented his recognition as a leading writer of serious literary work.

Notre Cœur analyses the relationship between a rich dilettante, André Mariolle, and a charming and attractive high-society hostess, Michèle de Burne, with whom he falls in love after visiting her *salon*. In the unfinished fragment of the 'short novel' *L'Ame Etrangère* published in the *Revue de Paris* on 15 November 1894, Maupassant seems in fact to have intended to deal with a similar character and situation – the meeting in the cosmopolitan, aristocratic casino society of Aix of the wealthy man-about-town Robert Mariolle and the beautiful brunette from Romania, Princess Moska. In *Notre Cœur*, however, the object of Mariolle's desire is not geographically exotic but emotionally distant. While André Mariolle's passion for Mme de Burne is sensual and emotional, her interest in him is more intellectual and derives from her sophisticated curiosity in this new visitor to her social gatherings and her egotistic capriciousness in seducing him as she has already so many others of her male acquaintances. Thus, although she does give herself to him on an excursion to Mont Saint Michel and she does become his mistress when they return to Paris, her fondness for him remains soul-less and impersonal, a product of the refined and artificial society she lives in, and he continues to long for some more passionate satisfaction of his attraction to her. When he realises once and for all the impossibility of this, he leaves Paris and finds consolation and true affection in a simple young girl who serves as his maid in a country cottage near Fontainebleau; but even now he is tortured by his longing for Mme de Burne and he returns to Paris again with his new mistress so as to enjoy both the simple but passionate affections of the one and the cold but seductive charm of the other.

The basic plot is simple, the analysis of thought and feeling even more penetrating and lucidly nuanced than before, and the moralistic symbolism of the characters and action is clearly, possibly too clearly, explained throughout. The over-sophisticated Michèle de Burne's cold, capricious seductiveness is representative of the over-intellectualised, egocentric and hedonistic refinement of contemporary high society produced by its inactive consumption of its own wealth and industry. As a rich widow, Mme de Burne is a typical parasite of such a society and as a seductive woman she epitomises its outlook of refinement and pleasure in her approach to sexuality and love. From the very beginning Maupassant tells us through his character Gaston de Lamarthe, a writer, that Mme de Burne is one of the 'new race of women motivated by a nervous and intellectual hysteria', derived from the disillusioning monotony of the satisfaction of their every desire in the refined world they inhabit and from their continual need for new interests and pleasures to escape their boredom and disenchantment with those they have already experienced. Mme de Burne's involvement with Mariolle is one venture in this direction: she seduces him by her looks and charm and enjoys being worshipped by a new and interesting suitor in her 'weary pleasure-seeking'.

It is not, however, love that she gives Mariolle any more than her own and her society's dabbling in the arts is a genuine interest, as the visit of the authentic artist Prédolé to her *salon* later shows; she simply enjoys having her caprices satisfied and her egotism cosseted. Hence, Maupassant describes her as 'a human goddess ... whom the amorous cult of the men around her ennobled and sanctified like a sort of incense' and refers to her as a puppet and an actress in her impersonal romance. She has the strangeness and preciousness of a bouquet of flowers or a figure in a Watteau painting in her refined artificiality. And such is the inversion of her sophisticated egotism that she is shown to prefer the female admiration of the Princess de Malten to the male pursuit of Mariolle. In short, she has sacrificed her attributes and virtues as a woman to the intellectual demands of the cynical, soul-less sophistication of the society about her; she is the logical outcome of the decision of the Countess Mascaret in the tale *L'Inutile Beauté*, published at the same time as *Notre Cœur*, to abandon her natural role as mother and sexual partner and benefit from the civilising reforms Man has introduced to improve on Nature in the sphere of female emancipation. Mme de Burne can thus be seen as the supreme product of the sophisticated civilisation she has been born into; she has ceased being a woman in the full sense of the word just as Mariolle, representing the cultural aspect of society, fails as an artist and falls into an unproductive dilettantism, the impotence of which reflects the emotional one of Mme de Burne.

Both manage, however, to escape momentarily from their respective impotence when they leave the refined world of Paris for the country; their appreciation of the landscape around Mont Saint Michel and their daring walk along the dangerous 'Chemin des Fous' in the Abbey mark the temporary loss of their sophisticated social veneer and is therefore followed by their first and only authentic love-making; and when Marolle returns to the country after his disillusionment with Michèle de Burne, it is a simple lass, Elisabeth, epitomising the pure and uncomplicated nature of her rural surroundings, who offers him affection and tenderness in his anguish. Moreover, in both rural locations away from the capital, love is seen to bloom from beneath the hardened social veneer of the two characters in the shadow of a church – Mont Saint Michel's ancient abbey and the old Montigny village chapel.

Furthermore, Mariolle's agonised love for Mme de Burne is described as a crucifixion and, later, the enjoyment of the country-side in Montigny is referred to as the happiness of a sinner taking communion. It would seem then that, like his friends Bourget and Rod in their works at this time, Maupassant – similarly influenced by the neo-Christian message of the Russian novelists, though to a lesser extent – was implying in his novel that if André Mariolle and Michèle de Burne were each failures in their own field it was because they and their society lacked not only sufficient heart but also a faith.

When *Notre Cœur* appeared, and virtually ever since, commentators have treated it as a 'roman à clé' and sought to identify the characters. Michèle de Burne was at first thought to be Marie Kann, particularly as she possessed a specially printed and bound copy of the novel, and more recently Hermine Lecomte de Noüy, Countess Potocka, the unknown woman in grey described with some disapproval in François Tassart's memoirs, and even Gisèle d'Estroc; Lamarthe was seen as Bourget; and Prédolé as Rodin. It is of course true that the captivating and wealthy Marie Kann with her dark eyes and her at once pathetic and mocking gaze had, despite her idolising husband's vigilance, become Maupassant's mistress at about the time of the novel's composition after being attached since 1880 to Bourget. Guy had in fact visited her regularly since 1884 in Paris and Saint Raphael, causing her to quarrel and almost break with Bourget in 1886 and 1887, and the two of them had stayed in Rouen together in April 1890 to see the performance there of her brother-in-law Albert Cahen's play *Le Vénitien*.

Nevertheless, it seems more likely that Mme de Burne is a representative amalgam of all Maupassant's society hostesses. Indeed, Mme Julia Daudet states as much in her memoirs [61] when she calls Michèle de Burne a well-known figure in the sense that she was recognisable as typical of her period's *fin de siècle* sophistication. Thus, although Mme de Burne might have the seductive charm and refinement of Marie Kann, the dominating novel hedonism of Countess Potocka, the witty playfulness of Mme

Straus, and the occasional discreet fondness of Hermine Lecomte de Noüy and something of the looks of all of them, particularly the last-named, she is really, like most of the characters in Maupassant's later novels, a symbolisation of the society she represents and that Maupassant used to frequent and wished to comment on in the novel; and the simple country girl Elisabeth is, equally symbolically, her spiritual and social antithesis in the moral and psychological conflict in which André is involved. As Maupassant had already implied in the country scenes in *Le Horla* three years earlier, and was to suggest again by the rather nostalgic tale *Mouche* about his days on the river with his young friends, he longed, while being absorbed into the complex, hothouse society of *Notre Cœur*, to be able to return to the simple, peaceful existence of his youth.

But Maupassant could not go back any more than so many of his contemporaries who similarly longed for a return to their unspoilt, rural origins instead of the ever more intellectually and emotionally sophisticated, feverishly bustling society of the capital, which they compared in its over-refined luxury and hedonism to the last decades of the Roman Empire and therefore diagnosed as 'decadent' in its exhausting and self-destructive affluence and self-indulgence. Maupassant's rise to fame and wealth, his enjoyment of luxury and high society and his refined nervous sensibility and analytical mind – seen in the growing psychological interest and study of finely nuanced, often perverse or morbid emotions in his novels – make him typical of his generation and what has become known as its *fin de siècle* 'decadence'.

Like the hothouse society he frequented he could not now give up his mental and nervous intensity, his love of fine clothes, exquisite perfumes and precious bibelots, his taste for the exotic and cosmopolitan, his toying with the morbid and perverse, or his pleasure in exceptionally beautiful and capricious women whose health had been ruined by over-indulgence and nervous exhaustion, including the one who possessed something of all these elements: Marie Kann, the 'seductive woman whose seductiveness had the unhealthy appeal of one who was dying' as Goncourt described her. Since he could not regain the simplicity of his past, Maupassant could only go on enjoying the fruits of his wealth and the decadent sophistication of his new home and his new mistress. His haggard paleness and blank gaze like the delicate complexion and cadaverous look of Marie Kann predicted, however, that their own and their society's enjoyment of their new luxury was to be all too short.

CHAPTER 5

The Final Agony

The eighteen months of Maupassant's life from autumn 1890 until his internment were like some Manichean battle in which the forces of light were gradually extinguished by the enveloping ones of darkness. Guy's talents, success, and wealth as well as his incisive mind and muscular physique were slowly but surely being sapped by the pain of his fatal disease and the despair that resulted from it when he found his condition was incurable and he would not be able to live properly or write ever again; in a sensitive and talented man of just forty years, a pessimistic one moreover, the awareness of such a doomed existence could only lead to an attempt at suicide. Already on 25 June 1890 Guy, brought to the brink of despair by his brother's death, his mother's illness, and his own problems of earning more money despite his failing health and his increasing difficulty in writing, confided to the Princess Mathilde the personal tragedy behind the success of his recently published novel *Notre Cœur*:

'If I describe, be it well or badly, in the novel the suffering of others, it is because I am so weary myself of living and of not discovering anything to relieve my depression and break the monotony of my life that I have to look at those around me to see if their hearts are more excited and their souls more moved than mine.' [62]

As his volume *Sur l'Eau* made clear, there was little in his personal life or in life in general to cure his despair at his own difficulties or his cynicism concerning the world about him. The success of his play *Musotte* in March 1891, his revision of his domestic drama *La Paix de Ménage*, his plans for making a dramatised version of his short story *Yvette*, and his writing of another novel entitled *L'Angélus* during the last months of his life could do nothing to make him less desperate and less aware of the futility of human existence and of his own imminent doom.

The unfinished manuscript of *L'Angélus*, published in the *Revue de Paris* in 1 April 1895, was in fact to give expression to Maupassant's despair and sense of outrage at the heartlessness of the Creator in its pathetic account of the frustrated love of a young man who has been born a cripple owing to the maltreatment which his mother, the Countess de Brémontal, received at the hands of the Prussians occupying her home in 1870. There can be little doubt that the sufferings of the crippled youth, who cannot use his legs, whose love remains an unfulfilled ideal, and who can only find affectionate consolation in his mother's care of him, reflect Maupassant's own desperate and inconsolable situation at this time; and the final, odd page of the story's manuscript reproaching the Creator for His callousness in creating beings He is going to destroy later must surely be the author's own reaction to the pain and tribulations of his last months. Moreover, the fact that Maupassant mentioned that, like Christ, the cripple was to be born in a stable, where the Prussians had locked up his mother, and that the symbol of the angelus in the title was probably meant to comment sceptically on the failure in love and the suffering of this deformed version of a modern reincarnated Christ reveals both Maupassant's continued interest in religion and at the same time his inability to accept it and his rather perverse, cynical view of an un-Christian, suffering world instead. This negative outlook, which his despair had accentuated, was closer to the pessimism of Schopenhauer, that had appealed to his more cynical nature in earlier years, than to any faith; and deprived of some positive influence which could counter his cynicism and re-awaken the more idealistic side of his nature it was unlikely that he would find either consolation or hope in the religious belief he often thought and wrote about as he approached his end. Only the consciousness of his pain and the knowledge of his despair were to be his companions on his journey to his doom.

In late 1890 Guy had written as follows to his mother on his general condition:

'I have had rheumatic pains but my stomach seemed to improve after four days. My legs became elastic again although I still had cramp in my hands and shoulders. Now that I am back at Etretat I have once more got migraine and am feeling weak and irritable. Work is absolutely impossible. As soon as I have written ten lines, I am no longer in a state to know what I am doing and all my thoughts leave me like water from a skimming-ladle.'

He continued, nevertheless, trying to concentrate on writing *L'Angélus* despite the weakness of his eyes and the blurring of his memory, which constant use of painkilling drugs only increased. By March 1891, however, he was complaining to his mother that he had managed to write very little of the novel and that 'my eyes are so weak that I cannot write a thing; my mind too is terribly exhausted'. Some relaxation was clearly needed and Guy looked forward to going down south to Nice and finishing his novel there in a peaceful apartment he would rent before taking a sailing trip on *Bel Ami II* to Spain and Morocco to get some sun and sea air. The staging of his play *Musotte* and his consultations with various doctors kept him in Paris, however, and the effects of the strain caused by his writing, the severe winter weather, and his lack of a holiday soon began to tell on his health. But Dr Déjerine, whom he consulted, only diagnosed mental strain and neurasthenia from overwork and Guy wrote to reassure his mother on 14 March 1891:

'Do not worry yourself too much about my health. I think it is simply that my eyes and my mind are very tired and that this terrible winter has made me into a frozen plant. I look healthy. I do not have any stomach pains. I just need above all fresh air and a rest.'

He did not, however, look healthy nor indeed was he cured as he tried to convince himself and others; after he had stayed at the Princess Mathilde's at Saint-Gratien and later dined with her in Nice, she wrote to a friend about the change in the appearance and manner of her young guest, whom she had always seen so robust and whose portrait on an enamel miniature she had asked her friend Popelin to paint for her: 'How changed he is! It upsets me very much; he stammers when he talks, he exaggerates the smallest things and he thinks he is cured!' [63] Moreover, a week or so after writing to Laure he was apparently suffering once more all the symptoms of influenza accompanied by losses of vision, pains in his throat and limbs, and a rasping cough. On 18 March he reported to his doctor-writer friend Henri Cazalis: [64] 'I had some very painful experiences yesterday and then a night of anguish, nightmares, and utter delirium.' In April he again writes to Cazalis explaining that he is delaying leaving for Nice because 'my condition has got so bad that I am wondering if I shall be able to leave here' and pointing out that 'my distressing state, the impossibility of my using my eyes and an unbearable physical feebleness, the cause of which is unknown, are making a martyr of me'. At the same time he tells Laure: 'Any eyework makes me ill until nightfall. It is absolutely vital that my eyes are rested.'

Once more he turns to his doctors; this time it is, according to Professor Magitot, a tooth which is affecting his left eye that needs filling. The tooth is soon filled; but this does not prevent Guy suffering in early May from what appears to be another bout of influenza accompanied by further losses of vision and memory and unbearable migraine; nor does it stop the painful divergence of his eyeballs which had occurred on and off in the past but now seemed worse than ever before. Guy was to write to Hermine Lecomte de Noüy later that month that he had not been able to attend to any of his correspondence because he had been 'terribly ill' and his sight was so impaired – 'as soon as I gaze at something, concentrate on it and try to read or write, my pupils become distended, diverge and look extremely odd'.

By late May, however, Guy recovered a little and was able to leave Paris and join Laure in Cannes. He now put his plans for a cruise to Spain into practice; he started out one morning for Marseilles, on his yacht, and after spending the night there set out for Majorca and Valencia; a fierce wind suddenly arose, however, as they reached the open sea and *Bel Ami II* was unfortunately forced to return to harbour. Disappointed and suffering with migraine, Maupassant abandoned his plans for relaxing at sea and seeking the sun.

Instead, he followed his doctors' advice and went to the spa of Divonne-les-Bains, staying first at Vasenex in the home of a doctor's widow and then, when he mistook the sound of rats for ghosts, moving to the more comfortable Hôtel de la Truite in Divonne itself. While there he took some fifty or more ice-cold showers, and cycled to Voltaire's home at Ferney, some seventeen miles away; his body was still fit but it was his nervous system that was worn-out and, as his assertion about the ghosts shows, his mind was beginning to suffer. He had been unable to sleep for four months because of the pains, anguish and nightmares he had had and the antipyrin pills he had taken for his migraine had drugged him so much that his mind became increasingly blurred and vacant – 'they are turning me into an idiot, I cannot write a thing' he told Cazalis in June 1891. Such was his distress and annoyance at his own inability and his lack of success in making his mind as fit as his body that he confided to Cazalis in this same letter how on certain days he felt like putting an end to his misery: 'My body is strong but my head is worse than ever. There are days when I long to stick a bullet in it . . . God, have I had enough of living!' He did not give up so quickly, however, and continued to hope he would be able to complete his writing of *L'Angélus* and realise some of his other plans.

It was with this intention in mind that he took the advice of Cazalis and left Divonne, where Dr Grancher had sent him, for the warmer and drier climate of Champel, near Geneva. Here he settled down in the comfortable warmth of the Hotel Beauséjour and tried to concentrate inbetween more cold showers and walks in the fresh air on finishing his novel; indeed, he is said to have read what he had written so far of *L'Angélus* to the poet Auguste Dorchain, also a friend of Cazalis, and had tears in his eyes as he outlined to him the rest of the novel concerning the cripple's pathetic misery. Were they also perhaps tears of self-pity at his own plight? For despite Maupassant's supposed statement, recorded by Dorchain,[65] that he was so desperately determined to finish *L'Angélus* that he would shoot himself if it were not completed in three months' time, he was unable to work on his manuscript because of his eyes and the effects on them and his mind of the drugs he was taking to give him relief from pain and nervous attacks.

The result of this was, as earlier in Paris, to make him irritable, easily moved to anger and, on this occasion, boastful in an attempt to compensate by impressive or forceful behaviour for the weakness and decline in himself he was becoming so desperately conscious of. He boasted to Dorchain of a love affair he had had in Geneva, of a dispute in a brothel in which he had defended himself against three pimps with his stick, and of a visit he had made to Baron Edmond de Rothschild's villa on Lake Léman; while some of this, particularly the last item, might have been true, much of it was probably mere boasting; moreover, the presumptuous tone in which it was asserted was apparently highly offensive. Further evidence of Maupassant's confusion, irritability and offensive show of vanity is afforded by the fact that he quarrelled with the hotel's restaurant manager and, when the spa's doctor refused to allow him more cold showers, he began a dispute with him too that ended in late September with the novelist's rapid departure for Cannes.

Back on the Côte d'Azur, Guy rented the Chalet de l'Isère, a cottage sheltered from the wind and facing the sun along the Route de Grasse. He had hoped to benefit from the sunshine here and do some, even if only a little, work, as well as go out on *Bel Ami II*. Further trouble with his eyes and some business matters called him to Paris, however. During his fortnight's stay at rue Boccador he contacted his lawyer with regard to his will and, as irascible as ever, instructed Maître Jacob to start proceedings against the New York *Star Magazine* that had brought out without his permission a longer version in English of his story *Le Testament*, and to summons his editor Victor Havard for not having in stock a minimum of five hundred copies of *La Maison Tellier*, for which an English bookseller had applied in vain to the French publisher. He also dispatched a curt, sceptical letter, similar to those earlier sent to Marie Bashkirtseff and Gisèle d'Estroc, as a reply to the enthusiastic inquiries of the young daughter of a Russian family which had settled in Cimiez on the Côte d'Azur; it is noticeable, however, that this time Maupassant showed not the slightest interest in his correspondent and apart from sending her a photograph of himself he merely hastened to stress the secrecy of his private life and close the correspondence; he was clearly too ill and too irritable to care much for female admirers.

Finally, before returning to Cannes in late October, he consulted his doctors Grancher and Daremberg about the treatment he should give himself when he was back on the Côte d'Azur; both told him not to read or write, supplied him with pills, advised him to continue to take cold showers and also to bathe his eyes and face, and recommended morphine and brandy for relieving his pain. The syphilis which had been eating at his nervous system thus progressed largely unchecked and began attacking his spine and undermining his sanity that had already been disturbed by his constant recourse to drugs. It was these that contributed for a while to the strange lucidity with which Guy could watch and comment on his illness and that finally accelerated the unbalancing of his mind. When Maupassant returned to Paris two months later it was to be in a straitjacket.

Back at the Chalet de l'Isère in Cannes Guy attempted some more work and some trips on his yacht; both activities were equally frustrated by the weakness of his eyes, the frequency of his migraine, the cramps he had in his stomach and the stiffening of his limbs. To find relief from his distress he followed Grancher's advice and took doses of morphine; the result was disastrous, as he informed the doctor:

'The morphine I have taken has put me in a state of suffering such as I have never experienced before. My eyes, which I felt had improved a lot, are so drawn and have so contracted that I cannot use them at all and am unable to read or write again. That means that it will be impossible for me to do any work all this winter. My sight has really been ruined this time. As for sleeping, I have just spent the night getting up and going to bed again haunted by nightmares, visions and imaginary noises like after a shot of cocaine . . . Yesterday I spent the entire day in bed . . .' [66]

It was shortly after this that he wrote to his doctor friend Cazalis:

'Now that I am virtually blind I shall be spending this winter like the last alone in some remote place because I cannot bear any light, not even a candle in the evening . . . I am very depressed and annoyed by it all.'

When he then followed Daremberg's advice to take baths and bathe his face with salt solution, things became even worse. Violent headaches, stomach pains, heavy sweating and the flow of a thick slime instead of saliva from his mouth ensued. He wrote to Cazalis on 5 December that 'I am so ill that I fear I will be dead within a few days after this treatment I have been told to follow', and described his feelings as those of a dog plaintively howling in the silence of the night. Both the doses of morphine and the bathing with salt were slowly killing him and yet his mind was still sufficiently lucid, even if slightly unbalanced, to be able to speculate on his decline. He wrote again to Cazalis later in December, using the hallucinatory image of the death's head to express his awareness of his doom:

'I am in a terrible state. I think it is the beginning of my death agony. I did not eat yesterday evening or this morning. I spent a shocking night. I have almost lost the use of speech and my breathing is a sort of horrible, violent rasping sound. My headaches are so agonising that I clasp my head between my hands and it feels like a death's head . . .'

By Christmas Guy's sanity had definitely begun to give way. Instead of spending Christmas Eve as he usually did with his mother, he was with the Kann sisters and on the next day sent Laure a confused telegram saying his two hostesses were extremely annoyed with him and his mother. The same day he told his valet that while he was out walking along the road near the cemetery he came face to face with a ghost of himself. Clearly, Guy wanted to spare his mother further distress and offer Marie Kann some last moments of affection while he still could; the telegram perhaps reflects Guy's awareness of the imminent fatality of his illness – which he possibly blamed on to his mother – and of the impossibility of his affair with Marie now that he was so ill. As for his confrontation with the ghost of himself, this was a more morbid version of the 'Doppelgänger' or double of himself that he claimed to see in his room on and off throughout his life; how far his claims were true and not just effects of the strained imagination of the author of *Dr Héraclius Gloss* or mystifying jokes of the writer of *Le Horla* to impress his friends it is difficult to judge.

Whatever the precise origin of Maupassant's interest in doubles, it is clear that, like the mirrors which fascinated him and which he used in his novel *Bel Ami* to reflect his hero's rise to fame, the contemptuous ghost of himself Guy met during Christmas 1891 represents the abhorrence and annoyance he felt for himself in his semi-sane state. He knew now he could not live much longer. Had he not seen his brother's horrifying decline into insanity and death?

So certain was Guy that the end, or at least insanity, would soon overtake him that he wrote to Maître Jacob to contact his lawyer Colle so as to add a codicil to his will, saying: 'I am dying. I am sure I will be dead in two days' time.' He wrote to Dr Cazalis in a similar mood of imminent insanity and death:

'I am utterly without hope. I am in my death agony. I have a softening of the brain brought on by my bathing my nostrils with salt-water. The salt has fermented in my brain and every night my brains are dripping through my nose and mouth in a sticky paste . . . It means Death is near and I am going mad. My head is all confused. Goodbye, dear friend, you will not be seeing me ever again . . .'

Judging by the diagnosis of his condition Guy makes here, it would indeed seem that his sanity was being destroyed as the syphilis attacked his spinal cord; the softening of his brain was in fact mental and not physical and the idea of the salt having this effect was part of what became more and more an hallucinatory obsession.

At the same time as writing to say farewell to Cazalis, Guy took the opportunity in a sane moment to take leave of Marie Kann; he sent Loulia Cahen the following letter, telling her to pass on an enclosed letter to her sister Marie and to 'wait until all is over with me before saying anything to anyone':

'I will be dead in a few days – that is the opinion of all the doctors here – owing to my having stupidly followed the advice of Dr Daremberg to bathe my nostrils for a week with slightly salty water. I take my leave of you and send you all my heart, all my affection, all my devotion and friendship. Oh, my poor mother . . .' [67]

Having bid farewell to his various friends and correspondents in this way, Guy expected to die; but death did not come so quickly and the idea of suicide, which occurs in many of his novels and seems to have been contemplated by him when he spoke to Dorchain at Champel a few months earlier, began perhaps to take root in his disturbed mind. The fact that it was the beginning of a New Year, as well as the effect on him of a visit to his mother in Nice for lunch, and possibly, if François Tassart's memoirs are to be believed, of a greetings telegram that arrived that night from the mysterious, vampirish 'woman in grey' whom he mentions with regard to *Notre Cœur*, made Guy resolve to do away with himself on 1 January 1892. Despair at his condition, at his inability to write or think properly any more, and at the upset he was causing his mother as well as disgust with himself because he would not be able to write, love or go sailing again must surely have been the major factors in Guy's decision to shoot himself during the night even if, as his publisher Ollendorff told Goncourt on 20 January 1892, his immediate decision to shoot himself had been motivated by his insane desire 'to kill the flies devouring the salt in his brain'. There was, as he wrote to Henri Cazalis and Loulia Cahen, no hope left; he had always viewed life with extreme cynicism and now that he was faced with imminent insanity and the impossibility of a useful existence he had every reason to put an end to his misery.

Unfortunately, his valet had already suspected that his master might be a danger to those around him or tempted into taking such a suicidal course of action and had removed the bullets from his revolver. Instead of passing into the oblivion of death Guy only heard the click of the unloaded trigger. Furious at this frustration of his efforts, he grabbed the paper-knife on his desk and tried killing himself by thrusting it in his throat. When this too was not wholly successful he pounded the window-shutters with his fists in an attempt to smash them and throw himself out. By then, however, his valet had been awakened by the sound of crashing furniture and his master's violent actions and the whole incident ended with Guy, covered in blood and ablaze with anger and frustration, being held down by François and the sailor Raymond while he was attended to by the local Dr de Valcourt.

The next day, January 2, Maupassant's insanity, no doubt increased by the frustration of his suicide attempt, was confirmed when he woke up declaring war had begun and he and François needed to enlist so that they could march together as they had agreed. His continued delirium posed the question of internment in the next few days just as years before he had urged that of his brother. As then, Laure was too upset and too concerned with the scandal of the issue to consent immediately to her famous son's imprisonment in an asylum. Finally, however, she agreed to Guy being sent to the pleasant and comfortable clinic established by the famous psychiatrist Dr Esprit Blanche in the former Louis XV-style mansion of Princess Lamballe at Passy in Paris. On 4 January a male nurse from the clinic arrived in Cannes and two days later Guy, held between his valet and the nurse, was taken by train to Paris. Before leaving, however, he was shown for the last time his yacht *Bel-Ami II* lying in the harbour at Cannes; it was thought that perhaps the sight of the yacht would startle Guy out of his madness; it did not and Guy, vaguely aware of his plight as his brother had been at the Bron asylum in Lyons, is said to have stared blankly at the boat for a while before shedding a few pitiful tears of tragic farewell.

Met at the station in Paris by Dr Cazalis and his publisher Ollendorff, Guy was taken in a straitjacket to the clinic at Passy to be placed in the care of Dr Meuriot and Dr Franklin-Grout. Despite reports in the press both before and after his internment that he was mad, Maupassant did not become completely insane until some six months before he died; his long periods of confused thinking and madness were interrupted by shorter ones of normal behaviour and sanity when he would read the newspapers and stroll in the clinic's park with François, who still looked after him, and his doctor or a nurse. He also received visitors such as Cazalis, Henry Céard, Léon Fontaine and Albert Cahen.

It was only towards the end of 1892 and the beginning of 1893 that, as Goncourt unsympathetically remarks in his diary on 30 January, 'Maupassant begins to turn into an animal' and that his mind disintegrated completely. He accused François of embezzling his money and plagiarising his work, insulted God and said he was God's son by his mother, referred to his urine as diamonds and was obsessed by the idea of piles of eggs, and constantly mentioned his train journey to Purgatory and his dialogue with Lucifer about taking over the world. Such outbursts are of great interest, no doubt, to the psycho-analyst but for the reader of Maupassant they merely show the tragic collapse of a fine mind and sensibility into the megalomania and sense of victimisation that often characterise his form of madness from tertiary syphilis.[68] Although he recovered a little at Easter 1893 and, unsteady and unshaven, was able to go out into the clinic's park to admire the coming of spring to the trees and flowers, he was soon suffering again from his madness and epileptic-type fits, during which he hurled a billiard ball at another patient and shouted and screamed for hours. These noisy, violent outbursts were followed by periods of atony and utter debility in which his eyes were blank, his body hung limp and he could hardly stand. During late June 1893 Guy suffered an even more violent series of convulsions but his heart sustained these attacks and he fell into a coma after them. It was not until 11.45 a.m. on 6 July, barely a month before his forty-third birthday, that death eventually released him from the torment of his ordeal.

CONCLUSION

Conclusion

Maupassant's funeral took place with all the usual ceremony and pomp, first at the church of St Pierre de Chaillot and then at the cemetery of Montparnasse, on 8 July 1893. Although he had been a sceptic all his life, Guy was laid to rest with full religious ritual; despite his request in his will to be buried without a coffin so that his remains might mingle with the soil and Nature which he revelled in, he was placed in a triple casket of oak, pine and zinc; and though he had long since veered away in his literary approach from 'Naturalism', it was Zola who gave the main speech at the graveside, declaring that Guy had been one of the happiest and also one of the unhappiest of men. The crowd was large and composed of many famous names: Edmond de Goncourt, Mme Pasca, Catulle Mendès, Jean Lorrain, Henry Céard, Paul Alexis, José-Maria de Heredia, Paul Bourget, Rodin, Marcel Prévost, Alexandre Dumas *fils*, Albert Cahen and Flaubert's niece Mme Commanville; and the pall-bearers were Zola himself, Ollendorff, Maître Jacob, and the brother-in-law of Hervé de Maupassant, Dr Fanton d'Andon. The last of these was the only member of Guy's own family present; neither Laure, who had not seen her son since his internment, nor Gustave de Maupassant attended the funeral; Laure's maid and François the valet were the only real representatives of Guy's private life present. Was it illness or embarrassment that kept his parents away?

Clearly, their state of health might have dictated their absence – Laure was now seriously addicted to narcotics and Gustave had suffered a stroke in January 1893 – but it seems likely that what also deterred both parents from attending was the desire to prevent any aspect of their son's private life from impinging on the formal glorification at the funeral of the famous writer he became. They wanted for him and for their own pride glory rather than scandal. Laure had sought this for her child ever since he was born in the Château at Tourville and been tutored by Flaubert; she did not want anything to harm his reputation and wound her pride now. Gustave de Maupassant, too, wanted to keep his own, his son's and the family's reputation out of the mire.

Thus, while Guy was still alive in Dr Blanche's clinic, Laure had sold his yacht, sent many of his belongings for auction – most were sold at the Hôtel Drouot salerooms in December 1893 – and written to his friends to say her son was progressing well; and Gustave had similarly tried to delude himself and others when he refuted charges in the press that Guy was mad and had been the victim of heredity, by asserting that his son was merely suffering from over-work, Hervé had sat too long in the sun, and there was no insanity in the family. Laure too was to confirm later that Guy died from nervous strain and Hervé from sun-stroke; this was in an interview she gave Paul Alexis for an article he wrote on Maupassant republished in *Le Figaro* on 24 October 1897 to mark the unveiling of Verlet's bronze bust of the writer in the Parc Monceau in Paris. Nothing was to stain their son's glory as a great writer; the painful realities were therefore to be hidden under an illusory and Romantic notion of his immortal fame. The myth of her son's greatness which Laure had begun to delude herself with during his contact with Flaubert was to be maintained after his insanity and death. Anything connected with the realities of his fate such as his vacant yacht or his empty homes was to be got rid of both to fill her purse and above all to satisfy her illusions.

This attitude can also be seen in the letter,[69] quoted earlier, which she sent to Henri Gadeau de Kerville in 1894 describing Guy's spectacular birth in the Château de Miromesnil, as well as in the letters both parents sent in 1892 to Alexandre Dumas *fils* when he sought their permission to revise and stage Guy's play *La Paix du Ménage*. While Gustave gave Dumas *carte blanche* to do whatever he required with the play 'in the best interests of Guy's reputation', Laure was more concerned with the public's acclaim of her son's name:

'Under your illustrious patronage the little play will go ahead and the family of the poor sick man will be obliged to you for hearing his name acclaimed once again . . .' [70]

If Laure's illusory ambitions for her son had been exaggerated solely by his decline and death, it might have been possible to find sympathy for this ageing mother, bereft of a husband and of both her sons, who lived as an invalid and was addicted to ether and laudanum as cures for her physical and emotional suffering. But she had shown her vanity and ambition throughout her life, whether it was marrying the aristocratic, dandyfied Gustave or promoting Guy's career. It was, moreover, to become clear in the cult she devoted to her son [71] as well as in her selfish, violent quarrels with her daughter-in-law after Guy's death and her disputes with any critics or friends of her son who wrote about him, that she remained the same, if not worse, until her death in December 1904 at the age of eighty-three. Although it could be said in her defence that by her promotion of her son's literary efforts she provided the world with a first-rate writer, it must be said too that she started him off on the road of ambition and sophistication that contributed, with the nervous temperament he inherited from her, to his undoing.

These same motives, ambition and sophistication, were in fact those of the society of the period and were related to the changes taking place in it. The commercial world Balzac had described in the 1830s and 1840s had developed into the industrialised one portrayed by Zola. As in the latter's series of novels, the *Rougon-Macquart*, tracing the history of a family in the Second Empire, the city had assumed far greater importance than the village or town with the coming of industrial expansion; and with the advent of railways people had drifted to the cities to make money from the new developments. Men like Zola's character Saccard did make their fortune in the evolving industrial society and, as Zola's novels *La Curée* and *La Débâcle* show, they then applied the financial fruits of their ambitious activities to their private lives. Sophistication and luxury were the order of the day; they gave a civilised veneer to one's participation and success in the competitive dealings of bank, stock exchange and industry, and transformed provincial bourgeois into virtual aristocrats and foreign investors and speculators into respectable Frenchmen. In the arts, while many writers followed Zola in depicting the new society around them, many others such as the Impressionist painters, Goncourt, and Loti began to evoke in their work the freshness and simplicity of the country in contrast to the urban areas of industry. In the sphere of belief, too, industrial affluence and scientific advances had with other factors produced a pessimistic scepticism, against which many thinkers and writers began to revolt in the late 1880s and 1890s in their search for the faith of their unspoilt youth prior to coming to the city. Despite these efforts to return to the past's comparative simplicity and traditional ways of life and the promotion of recreation and holidays to allow people to do so temporarily in the last decades of the nineteenth century, the industrialisation and sophistication of bourgeois society continued, shielded from the realities of the world about it by its luxury at home and its colonial dominance overseas. Only the Russian Revolution and the First World War were to shake it out of its egotism and reveal its inadequacies and fatal weakness.

Maupassant's career follows a pattern similar to that of the evolving society of the second half of the nineteenth century. Like most of the writers and painters of the age, he had come from the provinces to Paris to work and to write and used the ever larger circulation of the capital's press as the instrument of his popular success. Like them too, he had been attracted to certain features of Zola's 'Naturalism' and began to portray in his short stories scenes from urban bourgeois life; and, tutored by the cynical Flaubert, he had also been receptive to the current of scepticism and pessimism that had spread among thinkers and writers particularly after France's defeat in 1870. When, moreover, he gained success and wealth, he, like other provincial bourgeois, provided himself with luxurious homes and entered upper-class society, enjoying its refined pleasures and largely concerning himself with it in his novels. Like the society he frequented, he needed more and more money to indulge in his sophisticated tastes as well as to pay for other personal expenses at home and he turned himself into a 'literary industrialist', writing story after story to earn more cash and often forgetting the effect this was having on his constitution in the discipline of his labours and the benefits and comforts he gained from them.

Having become accustomed to the sophisticated society of the capital, Maupassant still looked back over his shoulder at the life in the countryside and on the river, which he had never completely abandoned; like the Impressionists, he drew scenes from the countryside in his stories and novels for his bourgeois readers in the cities, who found in them a similar exoticism to that they enjoyed in Loti's works on the sea and overseas; and like many other writers of the age, he enjoyed escaping from the bustling society, sophistication and scepticism he found in the capital by living in the provinces, going sailing and travelling abroad; here at least he found some of the peace and simplicity of his youth. His final choice of a home on the Côte d'Azur represents a compromise between the sophisticated world of the capital's upperclass society, which also relaxed in sunshine and comfort at Nice and Cannes, and the fresh air and simplicity of the provinces, which existed along France's southern seaboard.

Unfortunately, his escapism was not sufficient to halt the progress of the fatal disease which his ambitious industry and self-indulgent sophistication had aggravated. Rather like the closed pre-1914 world of wealth and leisure that last-minute reforms conceded by its monarchs and the various treaties and alliances of its governments could not save from revolution and war, Maupassant's constitution eventually collapsed despite all the consultations and treatment he had submitted to in his last years.

Guy de Maupassant's life was thus highly representative of the changes in France in the latter half of the last century and of the greatness and the weakness of the society he lived in; both became too self-indulgent and introverted to pay attention to the corrosive force undermining them. If his life is representative of his age, his work has a universal value; his characters, though belonging by their dress, habits and way of life to their age, live on by the timeless features of their behaviour and by the fact that it is on these that Maupassant concentrates for the motive of his stories. It is, moreover, his detached, discriminating concision in presenting so succinctly and yet so convincingly what is essential for the reader's interest in and understanding of a story, and for the comments on human behaviour to be inferred from it, that have given him the great reputation and constant appeal he has. In these qualities lies the originality of his talents as a *conteur*. In addition, in adapting a literary expertise, not seen in the short story since Mérimée, to his journalistic needs, Maupassant succeeded in bringing the genre to a much wider modern public. Readers today still appreciate his succinctness and the lucid and rapid flow of narrative it provides just as Tolstoy, Chekhov, Henry James and Somerset Maugham did in the past. It was indeed largely because of the brevity and brisk pace of his work that Maupassant was so easily translated and became so popular outside France. Only those more concerned with the academic criticism of his style rather than the clear presentation and readability of his work complain of his allegiance to what is partly a journalistic technique rather than an exercise in literary preciosity. As a freelance writer Maupassant could not afford to write for just a literary élite and needed to exploit his talents to live; he wrote in the manner and form he did for the newspapers and periodicals who paid him and their readers. In so doing, he virtually resuscitated the short story and gave it both a worthy literary form and a new popularity. The fact that his stories and novels are today as exciting, provoking or amusing as they were when they first appeared shows that, while his life is representative of his age, his work belongs to the timeless realm of classic literature.

NOTES

Unless listed in the notes that follow, the letters of Maupassant and his mother quoted in the text derive from the volumes of published correspondence shown in the *Bibliography*. References to or quotations from letters of Flaubert are based on the thirteen-volume correspondence of the novelist published by Conard, Paris, between 1930 and 1954 and all extracts from or references to the Goncourt *Journal* are from the four-volume edition of it published by Flammarion in Monaco in 1956. The translations given below are by the author of this book. The obscene poems of Maupassant quoted in the text have not been translated because of the crudeness of the language used and the difficulty of rendering this in English with the same effect as the original.

1   Letter of 5 July 1894, Bibliothèque Municipale de Rouen, p. 54, f.2.
2   G. Dubosc, *Trois Normands* (Rouen, Defontaine, 1917), p. 224.
3   But in the lonely cloister
    Where we lie buried
    We only know of cassocks and surplices,
    Wretched exiles that we are.
    We must just sing of the nice things of life
    And other men's happiness
    Without ever appearing envious.
    (G. Dubosc, op. cit., p. 228).
4   Life is like the wake of a departing ship,
    It is the flower that blooms for a short time on the mountain-slope,
    The shadow of a bird sweeping through the sky,
    The cry of a sailor swallowed up by the deep . . .
    Life is like a mist that is dispelled in the light of day,
    A unique moment allowed us for prayer.
    (A. Lanoux, *Maupassant le Bel-Ami* (Paris, Fayard, 1967), p. 31).
5   Maupassant, 'Louis Bouilhet', *Le Gaulois*, 21 August 1882.
6   Maupassant, 'Souvenirs sur Louis Bouilhet', *Le Gaulois*, 4 December 1884.
7   Man realised his power and shaking off his chains
    Uttered a joyous cry of humanity's freedom,
    Crushed the sacred emblems beneath the temple's ruins,
    And, holding in his own hand the crown of kings,
    He wrote out his rights with the tip of his sword
    In the dust of the soil soaked with his blood,
    And to defend his cause evoked without remorse,

As if before some great senate, the wretched memory of past centuries.
Now he was free and his own master. O what misery, what madness it
    was!
Life was but a mysterious cycle that never ceased!
Now, alas, like some pale old man
Bent under the weight of his six thousand years of existence,
Who had accomplished all his labours well,
He stops anxiously on the threshold of his destiny . . .
His thoughts terrify him and his belief has gone!
Left to himself, he continues on his way in the setting sun
And his uncertain soul from which hope has gone
Drifts like some lost ship in the wind propelling it.
    (L. Bouilhet, *Œuvres* (Paris, Lemerre 1871), p. 137).

8   God, that mysterious being whose face no one has seen,
King of all kings who reigns out in space,
Whose boundless infinity fills the immensity of the universe,
Is weary of being always alone and occupying by Himself alone
His sombre isolated position in time and space,
Of being the same as He has always been,
Solitary and all-powerful for all eternity,
Bearing the indelible mark of His greatness,
And of being the only one for whom Time never changed,
The whole of the past was without any memories
And the whole vast future could hold nothing new
Since He alone could penetrate the dense nocturnal darkness of the
    years;
He was weary of being the only one for whom all was indifferent, all
    was fused
Into the infinite boredom of an infinite present,
Lonely and powerful and yet powerless
To change a destiny over which he had no control,
The great God who could do all could not stop Himself existing!
And the sovereign Lord, tired of His fate,
Had in fact in the midst of His greatness desired to die! . . .
Finally, weary of being alone with His boredom,
He populated space with gold-faced stars
And from the impure matter floating in space
Like some foul mass He created the world . . .
Then suddenly, one day, the whole earth shook
And its surface found itself no longer empty and unspoilt;
The great forests trembled, for an unknown being
Had suddenly stretched his naked arm over the submissive earth;

The whole world bowed allegiance to this new creature.
Looking at Nature, he said: you are mine.
Looking up at the sun, he cried: you too are mine . . .
Alone, lost in space, he created a world of his own making.
Everything submitted to his laws – fire, earth and water.
And he has been continuing thus for six thousand years;
Nothing has been able to reduce his insolent progress,
And often when he talks it might be thought
That life was created from the void just for him . . .
Is Man, however, not just like an incomplete work,
The sketch and model for a more perfect being? . . .
Lord God omnipotent, when I want to understand You,
Your greatness dazzles and prevents me doing so.
When I stretch my reason to grasp Your infinity
I am lost in doubt and uncertainty
And I can only glimpse in the surrounding darkness
A passing flash of light that shines and then fades.
But I continue to hope because You are smiling up there!
Often when day breaks sombre and grey
And only gloomy shadows can be seen everywhere,
A ray of sunlight shines from between two clouds
And reveals to us a small patch of blue up there.
When Man doubts and all seems dark
He has always a ray of hope in his soul;
For there remains always, even in times of suffering,
In moments of the deepest despair and darkness,
A little blue in the sky and a little hope in one's heart.
(*Le Lycée de Rouen* (Rouen, E. Augé and Ch. Borel, 1892), pp. 239–44).

9 See the swallow leaving:
It flies away so fast
But always returns faithfully
To its nest
Once winter's harsh cold is over.

Man according to his fancy
Moves about in life
With the memory
Of those places
Where he enjoyed his childhood and his family now lie.

And when he feels
Age cooling his great ardour,

He regrets them and, wiser,
He returns
To find peace and happiness in his native village.
(A. Lanoux, op. cit., p. 46).

10 Day breaks. The sun gilds
The fine mist that still drifts
Like a veil over the water's surface.
Standing at the front of his boat
The fisherman watches, waits and bends
Towards the net he holds and casts;
And the net opens out in the water
In a large circle before going down
To the depths below to find its prey.

The cocks' joyful crowing rings out.
Flies hum away in the breeze.

Suddenly, one after the other,
A flock of ducks arrives
In procession on the river-bank,
Tottering like a group of drunks,
And with green wings and blue heads,
They move along wagging their tails!

A male jumps in the water. His mate follows.
The drakes swim about and the ducks flee them,
Stirring the water with their feathers
In front of the large drakes
That the joyous sun lights up on the flowing water.

Then altogether they dive down,
Their heads plunging in front of the drake ahead
And one sees floating on the water
The tufts of their pointed tails
Like islets bobbing up in the light waves.
(Unpublished poem, Bibliothèque Nationale, Nouv. ac. franç., ms.
14480, f. 199).

11 Maupassant, 'Souvenirs sur Louis Bouilhet', *Le Gaulois*, 4 December
1884.

12 He is dead, my master: he is dead, but why?
He who was so good, so great, so kind to me . . .

Oh God, why do you want such people to die? . . .
There now remains nothing but a mere body,
Nothing of his personality. Not even that kind smile
Which attracted me so much and seemed to say:
'I am fond of you'. And that charming gaze,
Those big, clear, soft eyes so full of understanding.
One feels they must be suffering terribly
To have to remain so still in their tomb . . .
Since nothing dies completely in the universe
And all is a progression and a transformation,
He has only left behind his mortal remains.
But, dear God, what is happening to his soul? . . .
Oh, if you had seen him under the blossoming pear-trees,
When, with his arm in mine, chattering away in his poet's manner,
He opened his fine soul during our long talks
That left me dreaming for so long afterwards,
For he was such a frank, straightforward, natural person.
Poor Bouilhet! Alas, he is dead, who was so good and fatherly,
Who appeared to me like another Messiah
Bearing the key of the heavens where Poetry lay!
And now he is dead and has vanished forever
To that eternal world to which all genius aspires.
No doubt he is looking down on us from up there
And can read what I feel inside and know how I loved him.
(A. Guérinot, 'Maupassant et Louis Bouilhet', *Mercure de France*, 1922,
   Vol. 156, pp. 373–95).

13   P. Bourget, *Etudes et Portraits* (Paris, Plon, 1906), II, pp. 307–8.

14   R. Dumesnil, 'La Jeunesse de Maupassant', *Les Œuvres Libres*, 1933,
     No. 142, p. 210.

15   Letter of 16 May 1872, Bibliothèque Municipale de Rouen, ms. 273, f.1.

16   Letter of 20 January 1878, Bibliothèque de l'Arsenal, ms. 15072, f. 631.

17   Letter of March 1879, Bibliothèque Spoelberch de Lovenjoul, ms. BIV,
     f. 357.

18   *Dr Héraclius Gloss*, trans. J. E. Jeffery (London, Brentano, 1923),
     pp. 71–3.

19   Joanna Richardson, *Princess Mathilde* (London, Weidenfeld and
     Nicolson, 1969), p. 234. Maupassant's letter to the Princess's suitor and
     close friend, Claudius Popelin, asking him to be his 'guide' on this first
     visit to Saint-Gratien is also quoted here.

20   G. Flaubert, *Lettres à Tourguéneff* (Monaco, Ed. Rocher, 1946), p. 90.

21   Maupassant, *A La Feuille de Rose, Maison Turque* (Paris, 1945), p. 11.

22   Ibid., pp. 29–31.

23   I would not want any girl to remain prudent on my account,
I would like to choose one girl today and take another on the morrow;
I would like to pick them up as I went along
Just as one picks fruit by stretching out one's hand.

Then, not having anguish in my heart or pangs of regret,
I would without a care leave one such fantasy of love for another.
– One should only sink one's teeth into the outside of such fruits
For one would find a bitter taste deeper within.

24   But a body suddenly fell on her body;
Burning lips closed upon her mouth;
And in the thick grass as soft as a couch
The firm hold of a man's arms restrained her efforts to free herself.
Another man held her down under him . . .
Then suddenly a blow flattened this man too
Upon the ground just as one would stun an ox . . .
But this new man also soon reeled back,
His face struck by the fist of another.
Then throughout the forest there was the sound of many more footsteps
And in the shadows there was an obscure mass:
A crowd of men in heat struggling like rutting stags
Whom the fair doe has made bellow with desire.

25   Notes of H. Céard, Bibliothèque de l'Arsenal, ms. 13421, f. 34.

26   L. Edel, *Henry James, The Middle Years* (London, Hart-Davis, 1963), p. 114.

27   Flaubert, *Lettres à Tourguéneff*, p. 220.

28   Notes of 10 June 1880, Archives de France, F. 17. 1198.

29   See E. Halperine, *Ivan Tourguéneff et ses amis français d'après sa correspondance* (Paris, Fasquelle, 1901), p. 269.

30   F. Tassart, *Souvenirs sur Guy de Maupassant* (Paris, Plon, 1911), and *Nouveaux Souvenirs intimes sur Guy de Maupassant* (Paris, Nizet, 1962)

31   Letter of 22 July 1884, Bibliothèque Nationale, Nouv. ac. franç., ms. 24277, f. 693.

32   P. Borel, 'Une Adoratrice de Maupassant', *Les Œuvres Libres,* June 1939, No. 216, op. 71–100.

33   P. Borel, 'Guy de Maupassant et Gisèle d'Estoc', *Les Œuvres Libres,* 1962, No. 195, pp. 137–80.

34   Papers of Robert de Montesquiou, Bibliothèque Nationale, Nouv. ac. franç., ms. 15041, f. 101, and ms. 15115, f. 68.

35   Letter of 22 July 1884, Bibliothèque Nationale, Nouv. ac. franç., ms. 24277, f. 694.

36   Undated letter, Bibliothèque Municipale de Rouen, ms. 273, f. 47.

37 Undated letter, Bibliothèque Municipale de Rouen, ms. 274, f. 32.
38 Undated letter, Bibliothèque Municipale de Rouen, ms. 273, f. 47.
39 *J. N. Primoli – Pages Inédites*, edit. M. Spaziani (Rome, Edizioni di Storia e Letteratura, 1959), p. xxxiii.
40 A. Lumbroso, *Souvenirs sur Maupassant* (Rome, Bocca, 1905), pp. 566–568.
41 *Studi in onore di Vittorio Lugli e Diego Valeri* (Venice, Pozza, 1961), II, p. 931.
42 F. de Rothschild, *Livre d'Or* (1957), p. 180.
43 F. Tassart, *Souvenirs*, p. 93. See also A. Lanoux, op. cit., pp. 247–8.
44 Letter of July 1887, Bibliothèque de l'Arsenal, ms. 15060, f. 54.
45 René Dumesnil dismisses the idea by referring to the infrequency and formality of Laure and Flaubert's meetings and relations in his *Guy de Maupassant* (Paris, Colin, 1933), pp. 66–8.
46 *See* L. Dx, 'A propos des enfants de Guy de Maupassant', *Mercure de France*, 1927, Vol. CXCIII, pp. 249–51.
47 A. Lanoux, op. cit., p. 276.
48 Zola, *Œuvres Complètes* (Paris, Cercle du Livre Précieux, 1969), Vol. 12, p. 684.
49 Hermine Lecomte de Noüy, *Amitié Amoureuse* (Paris, C. Lévy, 1896), p. 122.
50 Letter of 21 July 1886, Bibliothèque de l'Arsenal, ms. 15060, f. 52.
51 Letter of 6 June 1883, Archives de France, F. 17. 2634.
52 *J. N. Primoli – Pages Inédites*, p. 24.
53 M. Spaziani, *Gli Amici della Principessa Matilde* (Rome, Edizioni di Storia e Letteratura, 1960), pp. 227–8.
54 L. Daudet, *Fantômes et Vivants* (Paris, Grasset, 1931), p. 47.
55 P. Voivenel & L. Lagriffe, *Sous le Signe de la P. G.* (Paris, Renaissance du Livre, 1929), p. 193.
56 F. Tassart, 'Maupassant en Algérie', *Les Œuvres Libres*, 1961, No. 188, pp. 99–134.
57 Letter of 5 March 1891, Bibliothèque de l'Arsenal, ms. 15072, f. 637.
58 Undated letter, Bibliothèque Municipale de Rouen, ms. P 54, f. 5.
59 Letter of 17 August 1889, Bibliothèque Nationale, Nouv. ac. franç., ms. 25044, f. 346.
60 Ibid., f. 358.
61 J. Daudet, *Souvenirs autour d'un Groupe Littéraire* (Paris, Charpentier, 1910), p. 165.
62 M. Spaziani, *Gli Amici della Principessa Matilde*, p. 229.
63 J. Richardson, op. cit., p. 288.
64 *See* 'Lettres à son Médecin' (ed. P. Borel) in *Les Œuvres Libres*, 1960, No. 165, pp. 13–14.

65 G. Normandy, *La Fin de Maupassant* (Paris, Albin Michel, 1927), pp. 114–19.

66 Telegram, undated, Bibliothèque Municipale de Rouen, ms. P 54, f. 6.

67 Letter of 2 December 1891, Bibliothèque Nationale, Nouv. ac. franç., ms. 15892, f. 54.

68 P. Voivenel, op. cit., pp. 227–35.

69 *See* note 1 above.

70 Letter of 5 November 1892, Bibliothèque Nationale, Nouv. ac. franç., ms. 24638, f. 510.

71 *See* A. Albalat, *Souvenirs de la Vie Littéraire* (Paris, Fayard, 1920), pp. 261–2; *also* A. Lumbroso, op. cit., p. 111.

BIBLIOGRAPHY

I MAUPASSANT'S WORKS

a. Maupassant's complete works were published by Louis Conard, with an introduction by Pol Neveux, in 29 volumes in the years 1908 to 1910. Another edition of them, in 15 parts, edited by René Dumesnil and published by the Librairie de France, appeared in 1934–8. More recently, A.-M. Schmidt edited a three-volume compilation of Maupassant's novels and tales published by Albin Michel in 1956–9 and G. Sigaux has provided a fuller selection of Maupassant's literary output produced by Editions Rencontre in 1961–2. All these editions were published in Paris in French. A new edition of Maupassant's works is currently being produced in Gallimard's 'Bibliothèque de la Pléiade'.

b. Some translations of Maupassant's works appeared during his lifetime and a ten-volume edition of his novels and stories was produced in English by Werner Laurie, London, in 1923–9. A large number of his tales were published collectively as *88 Short Stories* by Knopf and Cassell of London in 1928 and 1933 respectively and, more recently, his *Complete Short Stories* were brought out by Cassell of London in 1970 and by Hanover House, New York, in 1955.

c. Numerous single volumes of his novels and smaller editions of his tales have appeared in both French and English and are presently available in the French paperback lists of Livre de Poche, Folio and Garnier-Flammarion and in English in Penguin Classics, Dent's Everyman Series, the New American Library and Elek's Bestseller Library as well as in Arrow, Bantam, Digit and Pan Books. Many school editions with short introductions and notes such as those by F. C. Green (Cambridge University Press, 1945), J. H. Matthews (University of London Press, 1959), and H. F. Collins (London, Macmillan/New York, St Martin's, 1967) are also available. Maupassant features, too, in Harrap's and Bordas' lists of advanced French school-texts.

II CORRESPONDENCE

Many series of Maupassant's letters have appeared in separate articles; the following editions of them have, however, over the years succeeded in reproducing an increasingly comprehensive collection of his correspondence, although many documents are still unpublished and lie in archives or private hands:

a. Chroniques, études, correspondance de Guy de Maupassant, prés. René Dumesnil, Paris (Grund), 1948, 526 pp.
b. Correspondance inédite, prés. A. Artinian & E. Maynial, Paris (Wapler), 1951, 343 pp.
c. Correspondance de Guy de Maupassant, ed. J. Suffel, Paris (Cercle du Livre), 1973, 3 vols.

III STUDIES OF MAUPASSANT

Borel, Pierre, *Le Destin Tragique de Guy de Maupassant* (Paris, Ed. de France, 1927).
Borel, Pierre, *Maupassant et l'Androgyne* (Paris, Ed. du Livre Moderne, 1944).
Borel, Pierre, *Le Vrai Maupassant* (Geneva, Cailler, 1951).
Boyd, Ernest, *Guy de Maupassant* (London/New York, Knopf, 1926).
Cogny, Pierre, *Maupassant, l'homme sans Dieu* (Brussels, Renaissance du Livre, 1968).
Coulter, Stephen, *Damned shall be Desire, The Passionate Life of Guy de Maupassant* (London, Cape, 1958; Pan, 1961; World Distributors, 1966).
Dubosc, Georges, *Trois Normands* (Rouen, Defontaine, 1917).
Dumesnil, René, *Guy de Maupassant* (Paris, A. Colin, 1933, Taillandier, 1947).
Ignotus, Pol, *The Paradox of Maupassant* (London, University of London Press, 1967).
Jackson, Stanley, *Guy de Maupassant* (London, Duckworth, 1938).
Kirkbridge, R. de L. *The Private Life of Guy de Maupassant* (London, Hamilton, 1961).
Lanoux, Armand, *Maupassant le Bel-Ami* (Paris, Fayard, 1967),
Lumbroso, A. E., *Souvenirs sur Maupassant* (Rome, Bocca, 1905).
Maynial, Edouard, *La Vie et l'Œuvre de Guy de Maupassant* (Paris, Mercure de France, 1906).
Morand, Pierre, *Vie de Maupassant* (Paris, Flammarion, 1942–3).
Normandy, Georges, *La Fin de Maupassant* (Paris, A. Michel, 1927).
Schmidt, A.-M., *Maupassant par lui-même* (Paris, Ed. du Seuil, 1962).
Sherard, Robert, *The Life, Work and Evil Fate of Guy de Maupassant* (London, W. Laurie, 1926).
Steegmuller, Francis, *Maupassant* (London, Collins, 1950).
Steegmuller, Francis, *Maupassant, A Lion in the Path* (London, Macmillan, 1972).
Sullivan, Edward, *Maupassant the Novelist* (Princeton University Press, 1954 and 1972).
Sullivan, Edward, *Maupassant – the short stories* (London, Edward Arnold, 1962).

Vial, André, *Guy de Maupassant et l'art du roman* (Paris, Nizet, 1954).
Wallace, Albert H., *Maupassant* (New York, Twayne, 1974).

The above bibliographical list is necessarily a selection of the large amount of material available on Maupassant. Further information can be found in many of the above-mentioned studies. Details of the vast number of articles and minor studies concerning Maupassant's life and work can be found in the October–December 1949 issue of the *Revue d'Histoire Littéraire de la France* and the June 1969 edition of *Europe* as well as in copies of 'Bel Ami', the journal of the Société des Amis de Maupassant, the 'Cahiers Naturalistes', and such annual publications as the British *Year's Work in Modern Language Studies* and the similar American P.M.L.A. report.

INDEX